Radicals & Realists

Political Parties in Ireland
– A Concise History –

Radicals & Realists

Political Parties in Ireland
– A Concise History –

Lila Haines

welsh academic press

Cardiff

Published in Wales by Welsh Academic Press, an imprint of

Ashley Drake Publishing Ltd
PO Box 733
Cardiff
CF14 7ZY

www.welsh-academic-press.wales

First Impression – 2022

ISBN
Paperback: 978-1-86057-158-9
Ebook: 978-1-86057-159-6

British Library Cataloguing-in-Publication Data.
A CIP catalogue for this book is available from the British Library.

Typeset by Prepress Plus, India (www.prepressplus.in)
Cover design by Welsh Books Council, Aberystwyth, Wales

Contents

For Dominic, Martin, Sofia, Gwilym and Esme

Acknowledgements

The Covid-19 pandemic was sweeping the globe when I began work on this book. I am therefore more than normally indebted to the many fine historians whose writings sustained as well as informed me throughout what was, in a very real sense, my lockdown project. Without their scholarship, works such as this would not be possible. Publications by some of Ireland's excellent journalists and public servants also provided invaluable details and insights, as did political memoirs, biographies and commentators.

I am deeply grateful to my good friend Karen Manahan Thomas, who read my drafts. Without her support, insightful suggestions and eagle eye for detail I might not have persevered. Prof M Wynn Thomas' suggestions and kind comments were hugely helpful and encouraging; as was the support of Prof John Lovering (1947-2022) even during his terminal illness.

I'd also like to thank Ashley Drake of Welsh Academic Press who suggested that I write an introductory history of political parties on the island of Ireland, an idea that developed until it became this book.

I am grateful to my daughters Mirén and Rhianon for encouragement and practical support, my sister Jo Walker who kept me grounded and in touch with the real Ireland, my brother Frank Heraughty for astute comments and Gaspar Herrera for helping me edge towards some understanding of the psychology of violence.

I could go on, but hope that all the friends who shared their expertise, responded to questions, or in any way encouraged or rejuvenated me will take this as an expression of my genuine appreciation. Heartfelt thanks to all of you - *gurbh maith agaibh – diolch – gracias – teşekkür ederim!*

Any errors or misinterpretations are, of course, my own.

Lila Haines
Cardiff, Wales
May 2022

Introduction

This book began as an attempt to compile a short history of political parties in Ireland, concise enough to act as a useful reference for readers in a hurry. Each chapter tells the story of a single party in relevant but not overwhelming detail, with a little light futurology as a bonus for aficionados of contemporary politics. In my more ambitious moments I thought that, together, they could offer a history of modern Ireland in 12 parties.

Which parties? The foundational parties of the main traditions – nationalism, unionism and labour – had to be included, dead or alive (even if barely breathing). After that I was spoilt for choice.

The official registers north and south listed more than 50 parties across the two jurisdictions: eight had representatives in the Northern Ireland Legislative Assembly while nine, plus a four-party alliance, sat in Dáil Éireann, the Republic's lower house. Other small parties, some unregistered, maintained a degree of activity. Over the decades others had emerged, usually from the main traditions, while sections of society such as farmers, housewives and local taxpayers formed their own parties, but few lasted long.

Impact had to be the key to inclusion, and each of the chosen 12 passes that test, though I'm aware that another author might have made different choices, of parties or of topics to discuss or highlight. I'm also conscious that Ireland's political history often appears complex – even party names can look mysterious – therefore I hope that the following notes will help to provide context.

The parties

Ireland's first modern political party emerged as a parliamentary force in the 1874 UK general election. It aimed to regain a national parliament, which had been abolished when the Acts of Union of 1800 absorbed Ireland into the Union of Great Britain and Ireland, the culmination of the conquest of Ireland. The Irish Parliamentary Party, known as Home Rulers, became a formidable political machine whose parliamentary activity, alongside popular agitation, shook up the constitutional relationship with Britain and helped to revolutionise the land ownership system.

In reaction to the push for Home Rule, another formidable force emerged to support continued union with Britain. Morphing into Ulster unionism, this movement also mobilised mass protest and forced the British government to reverse course on all-Ireland devolution, which had been agreed in 1914. The Ulster Unionist Party (UUP) won control of post-partition Northern Ireland in 1921 and held power for more than 50 years.

The Labour Party stood aside in the 1918 general election to let it become a plebiscite on independence and thus, it claims, brought constitutional politics to Ireland. Having repeatedly participated as junior partner in coalition governments, it was reduced to minor party status by 2016. The Northern Ireland Labour Party (1924-1987), stymied by sectarian measures and divisions, never achieved political significance.

Sinn Féin's very brief dominance in Dublin after the 1918 election ended with a split between supporters and opponents of the 1921 Anglo-Irish Treaty. Over time, and after a civil war, the Fine Gael and Fianna Fáil parties developed from the opposing sides. One or other formed or led all subsequent Dublin governments, until entering coalition with one another and the Green Party in 2020.

The remnants of Sinn Féin re-emerged in the 1960s as a campaigning party of the left and spawned other left parties, one of which merged with Labour. In 1970 a breakaway group claimed the Sinn Féin name and supported the Provisional IRA throughout the 30-year Northern Ireland conflict. The party benefitted electorally from the hunger strikes by republican prisoners in the early 1980s. After the 1998 peace agreement it joined a power-sharing NI Executive and in 2020 its southern division became the official opposition in Dáil Éireann.

The parties that formed the Dáil's first coalition government came together to oust Fianna Fáil from power in 1948. A newcomer, Clann na Poblachta (1946-65), injected an acknowledged passion and focus into the experiment and was the main source of its radical policies. It was also associated with the change of constitutional status from Free State to Republic, a move it didn't propose formally but certainly influenced.

Two new parties were established in 1970 in response to the danger of a descent into chaos in Northern Ireland. Both were dedicated to peaceful democratic politics and committed to countering sectarianism. The Social Democratic and Labour Party (SDLP) brought Labourites and moderate nationalists together in unprecedented unity, and the Alliance Party of Northern Ireland offered a liberal and non-sectarian alternative to middle-ground voters.

A radical loyalist newcomer, with origins in opposition not only to Irish nationalism but also to Catholic civil rights, burst onto the northern political scene in 1971. The Democratic Unionist Party opposed the 1998 peace accord but assumed office in the new Northern Ireland Executive, surprisingly sharing power with Sinn Féin from 2007.

Meanwhile, new kinds of parties were emerging in the Republic. The Progressive Democrats (1985-2009) helped to sway government policy towards neo-liberalism; this intensified the permissiveness of the financial and economic operating environment and contributed to the severity in Ireland of the 2008 global financial crash.

The Green Party was also making its way towards the centre of political power in the Republic, bringing with it a new policy benchmark – environmentalism. Its first entry to Cabinet (2007-11) won some small green gains but ended in parliamentary wipeout for the party. During their second term in office, from 2020, and helped by greater public awareness of climate change, the Greens made rapid progress with environmental legislation.

Complications

My original, comparatively straightforward plan was often in danger of becoming more complex as research proceeded. The urge to expand backstories or share anecdotes was often overwhelming. I resisted, mostly, but omit Máire Butler, a nationalist who coined the title 'Sinn Féin' yet who happened to be a cousin of the preeminent unionist leader Edward Carson? No, that was too tempting, if only because it offered a chance to mention one of the women often omitted from political histories.

Other temptations stalked me. I was haunted by the phrase 'In dreams begins responsibility', with which WB Yeats opened

Responsibilities, a collection published in 1914.[1] Enigmatic, yes, as was most of Yeats' writing, but its timing and the poet's involvement in Ireland's pre-1914 cultural and political scene seemed to suggest that he might be hinting at challenges revolutionaries would face if they ever won power.

This brought me back, time and again, to a theme running through Ireland's political story, the path from dreams to reality, from rebellion or reaction to the day-to-day pragmatism of government. Another theme also intruded too often: the conflict between democracy and the traditions of authoritarianism and militarism.

A poet and a politician

In 1921-22 the dreamers took over the Cabinet – or didn't. Northern Ireland's unionists had a plan and they didn't hesitate to implement it to win control of government. In Dublin, the faction of Sinn Féin that accepted the Anglo-Irish Treaty took on the challenge of establishing an independent state, but they didn't hesitate to use military repression against the rebel faction opposed to the treaty that had ended war between Ireland and Britain. After the Irish civil war, the anti-treaty rebels entered parliament and went on to win power via the ballot box.

The poet Yeats became Senator Yeats, when he joined the upper house of the Irish Free State parliament. There, in 1925, he opposed a proposal to ban divorce, a move that, he declared, 'a minority of this nation considers to be grossly oppressive'. Proclaiming himself a proud member of the Protestant minority, he added: '... your victory will be brief, and your defeat final, and when it comes this nation may be transformed'.

It took 70 years for Yeats' prophecy to begin to come true, when citizens of the (by then) Republic voted in a referendum to liberalise access to divorce. Later referendums would highlight the extent of the Republic's transformation – the first country in the world to legalise same-sex marriage via a popular vote, for example. By then, economic transformation was well advanced too but had also suffered serious setbacks.

---

1   W.B. Yeats, *Responsibilities and other poems*, Macmillan, New York, 1916.

Emigration and economic policy

Deserted villages, mass emigration and the loss of the Irish language were amongst the effects of the 1845-49 famine, in which an estimated one million people died. A century later Ireland was still haemorrhaging people.

It was the sheer scale of ongoing emigration that led Fianna Fáil leader Seán Lemass to abandon the 'Sinn Féin' policy of self-sufficiency in favour of free trade and inward investment.

The path to a modern economy was far from smooth and emigration fluctuated in line with economic swings. By the late 20th century, the population of the Republic was growing but there was a new problem: a shortage of workers to fill vacancies in the Celtic Tiger economy. In an extraordinary role reversal Ireland became a destination for immigrants from other countries, often dubbed the 'New Irish'. who accounted for one in eight of the population by 2021.

At the time of partition in 1921, northeast Ulster had by far the strongest economy on the island. The economic base turned out to be less solid than it appeared, however, and UK Treasury subsidies became central to maintaining living standards in Northern Ireland.

In the 1960s a new NI prime minister, Terence O'Neill (1963-69), launched a drive for inward investment similar to that in the Republic, to replace declining industries. His meetings with Taoiseach Seán Lemass suggested the dawn of a new era in north-south relations, but O'Neill and his initiatives were amongst the casualties of the crisis that erupted at the end of the 1960s. The 30-years conflict known as 'the Troubles' damaged the NI economy, which did not gain an economic peace dividend on the hoped-for scale after the 1998 peace accord, despite European Union support and US investment.

In contrast, while Northern Ireland was suffering from bombs and bullets and their repercussions, the Republic was beginning to reap the benefits of a development strategy based on attracting foreign direct investment, upgrading education and training, and making the most of European Union membership.

The southern economy, long characterised by agriculture and micro businesses, became a major exporter of modern manufactured goods and a base for global service companies. The transformation was a long time in the making, however, and the economy's openness and global integration carried their own risks.

Death of the Tiger

While the north was inching towards a peace deal in the 1990s, the south was enjoying its Celtic Tiger phase. Productivity and manufacturing exports rose sharply, though growth eased as Ireland reached average European levels around 2000.

The Celtic Tiger died definitively in 2008, in a crash few could have imagined during the boom years. The immediate trigger was a global financial crisis but this was exacerbated by domestic policy errors and, it is argued, an environment in which cronyism and greed flourished.

The Republic had to be saved from bankruptcy by loans from a Troika of the International Monetary Fund (IMF), European Central Bank (ECB) and the European Union (EU), with stringent conditions attached. However, it exited special measures in 2013, the first EU member state to do so. This swift recovery suggested economic resilience but it came at the price of a very tough period for most of the population.

An associated result was a deepening distrust of political parties. In the 2011 general election voters punished Fianna Fáil and the Greens, the parties in government when the economy crashed. In the 2016 general election they did the same to Labour and Fine Gael, the parties that picked up the baton in 2011 and had to continue implementing the recovery conditions attached to the Troika's loans.

There were also questions about the reality of the so-called economic miracle. How accurate were the GDP data? To what extent did they reflect multinational corporations moving intellectual property assets to gain tax advantages? Was Ireland ever one of the world's richest countries?

Patrick Honohan, a former Governor of Ireland's Central Bank, concluded that the data placed the state somewhere between 8th and 12th on the EU 'rich list' - prosperous, yes; 'but not as prosperous as is often thought because of the inappropriate use of misleading, albeit conventional statistics'.[2]

For some political parties this was an acceptable place to be if, as it did, it guaranteed good employment and taxation flows. For others it was a rich source of anti-government attack points.

---

2   P. Honohan, *Is Ireland really the most prosperous country in Europe?*, *Economic Letter*, Dublin, Central Bank of Ireland, February 2021

Party faces

The face of party politics in Ireland remained white and predominantly male throughout the 20th century. Minorities were rarely seen in politics, north or south, and few women got anywhere near the political glass ceiling – until Mary Robinson broke it in 1990.

Robinson's election as President of Ireland shocked the political establishment. Parties concluded that having an occasional female candidate might be good politics. In 1997, proposed by Fianna Fáil, Mary McAleese won the presidency and Mary Harney became the Republic's first female tánaiste (deputy prime minister), having led the Progressive Democrats since 1993. It took another decade, however, for the idea that women could lead parties or governments to gain momentum.

A century after partition almost a quarter of Dáil deputies and one third of NI Assembly members were female. The male dominance of parties and politics had certainly eased, but not yet profoundly changed.

For people of colour the journey had barely begun. The peak of inclusiveness to date was the moment in 2017 when Leo Varadkar, a gay man of mixed Indian and Irish parentage, became Fine Gael leader and taoiseach (prime minister).

Although research has suggested that a large majority of people on the island were welcoming to incomers, there was also ample evidence of open racism. Hazel Chu (Green Party) suffered racist abuse when she became Lord Mayor of Dublin, the first person of colour to hold that historic post; so too did Anna Lo, also of Asian heritage and an Alliance Party member of the NI Assembly.

Ideology and religion

Pinning down a party's precise ideology can be challenging in Ireland, but that's not to say there have been no ideologically motivated parties. The neoliberal Progressive Democrats never achieved significant size, but they were influential in steering the Republic's fiscal and economic policy to the right. On the left, Labour and others adopted a responsible approach, joining centre-right coalition governments to achieve social progress.

Government by coalition has been routine in Dublin since the early 1980s. Coalitions would normally be expected to form between parties that are adjacent on a policy scale, but that wasn't necessarily so in Ireland. The right-of-centre Fine Gael and left-of-centre Labour have been the most frequent coalition partners, echoing the population's centre-right to centre-left views as expressed through elections.

After courageous politicians successfully negotiated a peace deal with paramilitaries in 1998, political parties in Northern Ireland were legally required to cooperate. Devolved government didn't always work well, however, and not at all for the best part of eight years. Intended to promote cross-community consensus, power sharing kept the peace but concentrated control in the hands of the dominant parties on either side of the historic divide while marginalising moderates on both sides as well as non-aligned 'Others'.

For most of the period under consideration religion was a better indicator of political affiliation than class, but not always. Charles Stuart Parnell, the outstanding leader of the 19th century Irish Parliamentary Party (IPP) who also helped overturn the colonial land ownership system, was a Protestant and a landowner. Others in the early IPP shared similar characteristics although the party later became more middle class and heavily Catholic.

Although there were no overt religious barriers to political participation in the Irish Free State (1922-49) or the Republic of Ireland (1949-), and non-Catholics won high office including the Presidency, a strong Catholic ethos permeated life and politics. Powerful bishops were able to block policies they considered 'communistic', exemplified in the failure of a 1951 proposal to give free medical care to children and pregnant women. However, with time and prosperity the southern state became more open and secular, and the Catholic hierarchy much less powerful.

Northern Ireland's very formation in 1921 involved a headcount of religious affiliation, aimed at ensuring a Protestant majority that would, it was assumed, vote unionist. Together with sectarian measures, that strategy succeeded in keeping the UUP in power for half a century and limited both labour and nationalist opposition. Later, working class unionists' votes – and fears – helped the right-wing DUP reach the top of NI politics.

Religion declined in importance in Northern Ireland, however, especially amongst younger people and middle-class voters. In contrast to earlier decades, by the 21st century NI's political marketplace offered liberal, environmentalist and radical left parties, as well as varieties of unionism and nationalism.

Democracy vs militarism

Despite the dominance of rebellion as an image of Ireland's history, and the indisputable impact of armed conflict, modern Ireland is primarily a product of democratic decisions, by elected representatives or directly by voters.

Some elections were pivotal, such as the 1918 general election in which women and poorer men were allowed to vote for the first time, and a majority of the Irish MPs elected backed independence. Likewise referendums, particularly those in 1998 in which very substantial majorities, north and south, backed the terms of the peace agreement negotiated by the Irish and British governments and NI political parties.

That's not to downplay the history of civil war and political violence, or to overlook lingering militarism – or to suggest there cannot be a resurgence of violence – but both electorates have shown a preference for parliamentary democracy, blaming political parties rather than democracy for policy failures.

Although small republican groups occasionally launched armed attacks against the British presence in Northern Ireland following partition and the 1922-23 civil war, none was truly major until the Provisional IRA's late 20th century armed campaign. With the actions of loyalist (extreme unionist) paramilitaries and the British armed forces added to the mix, that conflict was on a much more serious scale and duration, but that too ended in a negotiated return to parliamentary democracy.

With power sharing mandatory since 1998, consensual politics could have posed interesting challenges to the distinctiveness and viability of Northern Ireland's political parties. Then in 2016 a seismic event distorted the apparent direction of political travel. The United Kingdom of Great Britain and Northern Ireland voted to end its membership of the European Union, following a campaign to 'take back control' from Europe, although Northern Ireland, like Scotland, voted to remain in the EU.

The border between Northern Ireland and the Republic, effectively open since 1998, became an international border and the focus of years-long negotiations. Brexit and the border also refocused attention on divisions, though those did not necessarily reflect either monolithic party positions or the simple sectarian lines of earlier times.

Radicals and realists

From whichever tradition they evolved, whether they aimed to maintain or to overturn the constitutional status quo, bring about social or economic change, achieve peace and reconciliation, or save the planet from environmental collapse, each of the parties highlighted here was radical by some definitions.

Whatever methods they originally adopted to pursue their aims, sooner or later each party participated in the democratic process, even if some were only 'slightly constitutional' at first, as a Fianna Fáil leader said of his own party in its early days.

Some would not have considered themselves rebels, though an outside observer could be forgiven for thinking otherwise. Unionists like Edward Carson or James Craig fought against Home Rule, seeking to keep Ireland united with Britain, but at times their methods resembled rebellion. Then, in 1921, they accepted a new reality, Home Rule for part of Ulster. Or at least Craig did; Carson claimed that he, Ulster and Ireland had been pawns 'in the political game that was to get the Conservative Party into office'.

Early nationalists could hardly object to being labelled rebels or radicals, but look closer and you'll find nuances. Arthur Griffith, founder of the original Sinn Féin and a revolutionary nationalist, was also a self-proclaimed realist who was willing to retain the English monarchy if that would lead Ireland a step closer to independence. Michael Collins saw the Irish Free State as a stage on the road to a republic, a stance Éamon de Valera and Fianna Fáil adopted a few years later, but only after a civil war. Those in the rump Sinn Féin may have been slow learners, but they weren't the last.

A century after the partition of Ireland into two jurisdictions (one constitutionally independent, the other a region of the UK) the island has been transformed in many ways. Some of the parties included here made positive contributions to that transformation, others less so, while some could be said to have been dragged by circumstances into accepting democracy.

Readers may draw their own conclusions about which parties belong in each category or to what extent each of the contemporary crop is fully signed up to parliamentary democracy. Or why they all, sooner or later, became political pragmatists. Or what the future may hold for parties if more inclusive forms of decision-making flourish.

Hopefully, these short histories will also help readers to assess how Ireland's contemporary political parties handle the many challenges facing them – social, environmental, economic or constitutional, global or local – during the next phase of the island's intricate political history.

Notes on Terminology

I have opted to use the official names of jurisdictions as far as possible: Northern Ireland rather than the North, the Six Counties or Ulster; Ireland, the Free State (pre-1949) or the Republic (post-1949) rather than the South or Éire. I use the terms southern or northern (lower case) if geographically appropriate.

The word 'jurisdiction' is preferred to 'state' because of the major differences between the two territories, i.e. one is an independent state, the other a devolved region of the UK.

Terms such as 'unionist' or 'republican' are capitalised in party names or other titles, but otherwise are in lower case. Similarly, whatever the language, a title is capitalised when it precedes an office holder's name (e.g. First Minister Arlene Foster) and in lower case as a description (e.g. Enda Kenny, the taoiseach).

Irish language terms for political offices or institutions (e.g. Tánaiste, Dáil) are used in line with everyday norms in the Republic.

The many treaties and agreements are named in full when clarity requires that, but are otherwise in lower case (e.g. the Anglo-Irish Treaty, the treaty). In the case of the 1998 Belfast or Good Friday Agreement, most commonly called the Good Friday Agreement but also the Belfast/Good Friday Agreement or the GFA, I have opted for Belfast Agreement, personally preferring the geographic rather than the religious allusion.

Glossary

Ard Fheis	Annual conference of many Irish political parties
Consociationalism	A system of cross-community power sharing of the kind mandated for Northern Ireland
Dáil Éireann	The Lower House of the Oireachtas or Irish Parliament
Éire	Ireland
Irish Free State	Previous name (1921-48) of the territory now called Éire or Ireland and described as the Republic of Ireland
Legislative Assembly	The Northern Ireland Assembly is also known as the Legislative Assembly
Leinster House	The Republic's parliament building, home of both Houses of the Oireachtas
Loyalist	Radical supporter of NI union with Britain
MLA	Member of the Legislative Assembly (in Northern Ireland)
New Irish	A term for recent immigrants into Ireland
Oireachtas	Ireland's legislature, consisting of an elected president, a lower house (Dáil Éireann) and a senate or upper House (Seanad Éireann).
Orange Order	An ethno-religious association for the protection and promotion of the interests and culture of Protestants
Republic of Ireland	Description of the territory officially entitled Ireland or Éire
Seanad Éireann	The Upper House of the Oireachtas, referred to as Seanad or Senate
Six Counties	A colloquial term for Northern Ireland, which encompasses six counties of Ulster
Stormont	Northern Ireland's parliament building, often used as a synonym for the NI Legislative Assembly and previously for the NI Parliament
Tánaiste	Deputy Prime Minister of Ireland. Plural: Tánaistí

Taoiseach	Prime Minister of Ireland. Plural: Taoisigh
TD	Teachta Dála = a member of Dáil Éireann
Teachta Dála	Member of Dáil Éireann. Translation: Deputy or delegate to Dáil
Ulster	Name of the historic nine-county northern province; used inaccurately as a synonym for the six-county NI jurisdiction
Unionist	Supporter of continued Northern Ireland membership of the UK
Uachtarán	President. Uachtarán na hÉireann = The President of Ireland (elected head of state)

1

The Irish Parliamentary Party

Ireland's first modern political party

Overview

19 May 1870, Dublin: The story of Ireland's modern political parties begins when a disparate group of people – Protestants and Catholics, Conservatives and Liberals, Fenians and moderate nationalists – launch the Home Government Association. Its aim: to seek the establishment of an Irish parliament with full control over domestic affairs.

Its re-launch three years later as the Home Rule League led to the election in 1874 of 59 Irish MPs pledged to secure an Irish parliament. This embryonic new party was led by the conservatively inclined Isaac Butt, who had become disillusioned with the impact on Ireland of the 1800 Act of Union which created The United Kingdom of Great Britain and Ireland.

Under the more dynamic leadership from 1880 of Charles Stewart Parnell, a Protestant landowner, the Home Rule MPs became a formidable parliamentary presence. Renamed the Irish Parliamentary Party (IPP) in 1882, it developed a forceful style of politics that combined parliamentary and extra-parliamentary action.

It had the numbers – 86 MPs at its height – to negotiate deals with prime ministers in return for constitutional reform. Prime Minister William Gladstone introduced a Home Rule Bill in 1886 and again in 1893, but both were defeated and split the Liberal Party.

Through an alliance with the Land League, a radical tenants' rights organisation, the IPP helped achieve reforms that eventually revolutionised Irish land ownership. The land agitation also cleared a path for 'physical force' nationalists to take their first footsteps into constitutional politics.

Crucially, the IPP's success in putting Home Rule high on the political agenda sparked a powerful fight-back by those who favoured continuation of the Union between Ireland and Britain, and were as prepared as the IPP to take extra-parliamentary action.

However, in 1890, Parnell fell victim to a very Victorian sex scandal when the estranged husband of Katharine O'Shea sued for divorce, naming Parnell as co-respondent. This offended the prevailing morality and alienated many in both the IPP and the Liberal Party, including Prime Minister Gladstone. Ousted as IPP leader, Parnell was dead within a year and his party bitterly divided.

Reunited in 1900 under John Redmond, the IPP looked set to finally win a parliament for Ireland when the Commons passed the Home Rule Bill in 1912. Though it received royal assent in 1914, the Act's implementation was delayed by the First World War.

By the time hostilities ceased in November 1918 the Irish political arena was a vastly different place. Unionism had become a very powerful force and a more radical form of nationalism was on the rise.

The extent to which separatism was displacing Home Rule became abundantly clear when Sinn Féin swept up the bulk of IPP seats in the 1918 general election, thanks to the widening of the franchise to women and poorer men, and helped by IPP activists transferring their allegiance to the new party.

The vanguard party in the movement to establish an Irish parliament wound itself up in 1922 after Ireland was partitioned and two new parliaments were established on the island, but its influence didn't die.

Getting the party started

Those who attended the meeting convened by Isaac Butt in May 1870 had one thing in common: the belief that Ireland needed a parliament with 'full control over our domestic affairs'.[1]

Their motivations and aims varied and not all stayed the course with many of the 'Ascendancy' Protestant landowners in particular changing direction. Yet the launch of the Home Government Association (HGA) was a critical step in the direction of a new era in constitutional politics.

---

1   F.S.L. Lyons, *Ireland Since the Famine*, London, Fontana Press, 1985, p.149

Isaac Butt himself was a conservative by inclination who nevertheless, as a lawyer, had defended Fenian rebels and campaigned for an amnesty for separatist political prisoners. Shocked by the 1845-49 famine, Butt had become increasingly convinced that the Union was not in Ireland's interest. The country's problems could only be solved by a national parliament, he concluded, and he envisioned Ireland forming a federation with England, Scotland and Wales within the British Empire.

Isaac Butt, founder of the Home Rule League, which became the Irish Parliamentary Party in 1882.

When the HGA became the Home Rule League in November 1873, the launch event drew undercover Fenians and 50 Catholic priests as well as 25 MPs[2] – an early sign of significant alliances to come. Like its predecessor, the League's aim was self-government 'by means of a national parliament' while remaining part of the United Kingdom. This echoed Daniel O'Connell's Repeal movement of the 1840s that had stressed loyalty to the Queen while campaigning to repeal the Act of Union.

The 59 Irish MPs elected in 1874 were not a party in any recognisable modern sense, as Lyons notes. They had little in common other than aiming to achieve some form of self-government. In social composition they were mainly upper or middle class – landowners or sons of landowners, 'rentiers', merchants, bankers, newspaper proprietors, plus lawyers and other professionals – but there were fewer landlords in 1874 than in the previous parliament and, most strikingly, for the first time two tenant farmers were elected.[3]

The 1874 Home Rule group signalled the rise of a politically active middle class, but its social composition militated against its ability to act as a cohesive party. Remedying that initial paralysis would come

---

2 R. Kee, *The Green Flag*, London, Penguin, 2000, p.360

3 F.S.L. Lyons, *Ireland Since the Famine*, op.cit., p.153

later, under a very different type of leadership from that offered by Isaac Butt.

Meanwhile a tactical divide emerged between those who, like Butt, adhered to Westminster's polite debating conventions and the less orthodox members of the new intake. The stand-out figure was Joseph Biggar, a Belfast provisions merchant, who is credited with introducing what became a renowned IPP tactic: obstructionism – blocking normal parliamentary business by talking interminably in any and every debate to draw attention to Ireland's demands.

Biggar's background, appearance and abrasive character militated against him ever being able to supplant Butt as party leader but a more likely candidate emerged in 1875 when Charles Stuart Parnell won a by-election and quickly made his mark. In 1877 the new MP replaced Butt as president of the Home Rule Confederation of Great Britain (formed by Butt to spread his ideas amongst the Irish in Britain but infiltrated by Fenians).[4] Though suffering from ill health, Butt struggled on as party leader and on his death in 1879 William Shaw took his place but only for a year. Then it was Parnell's turn.

Judging the Union

What Isaac Butt and his MPs were looking for was the re-establishment of an Irish parliament. The Act of Union between Britain and Ireland had abolished the 300-member Dublin parliament and transferred Irish affairs to Westminster, with 100 Irish seats in the House of Commons and 32 in the House of Lords.

Did the Act of Union deliver any of its promised benefits to Ireland? Possibly in parts of the northern province of Ulster where existing industry was able to share in the wealth created by Britain's industrial revolution.[5] Elsewhere, the daily lives of ordinary people on most of the island showed little if any sign of improvement.

Early opposition to the Union came from those in the republican United Irishmen tradition: Robert Emmet staged a rising in 1803; the Young Ireland nationalists rebelled in 1848 in a desperate gesture as famine ravaged the land; and the Fenians tried and failed to overturn the Union by force in 1867.

---

4   F.S.L. Lyons, *Ireland Since the Famine*, op.cit., p.150
5   R. Kee, *The Green Flag: A History of Irish Nationalism*, London, Penguin, 2000, p.189

Scepticism increased after the Great Famine, when a new and fatal fungal disease ravaged Ireland's potato crop. The loss of their main source of food from 1845 until 1849 was 'a sentence of death for those trapped in the subsistence economy of the west and south-west, and great suffering elsewhere'.[6]

The death toll is reliably estimated at about one million, with about as many again emigrating to escape death by starvation. After the famine, emigration continued at a very high rate: in 1841 Ireland had a population of 8,175,124 but only 4,456,546 by 1901.[7]

The rural landscape was more and more characterised by 'deserted villages, the bachelor farm, and the late marriage', says Foster. Another casualty was the Irish language, as he notes. Overall, the British government 'had conspicuously failed to solve the problems of Ireland'.[8] That was the view of a growing number of 19th century non-radicals like Isaac Butt.

Land rights

The structure of land ownership, concentrated in the hands of a minority of large owners while most tenant farmers lacked security, was central to the political events that unfolded in the later 19th century.

Given the agricultural basis of most of the island's economy, the failure to change relations between landlords and tenants in any meaningful way left the root causes of rural poverty undisturbed. This failure was unsurprising, according to Kee, because it would have meant 'striking, in a way that seemed inconceivable, at the whole system of land ownership'.[9]

Yet by 1870, the year in which Isaac Butt launched his campaign for an Irish parliament, 'Ireland had assumed an appearance of economic, social, and political stability unknown since the 18th century' according to Fitzpatrick.[10] However, this stability

---

6   R.F. Foster, *The Oxford History of Ireland*, Oxford University Press, 1992. p.166

7   D. Ferriter, *The Transformation of Ireland 1900-2000*, London, Profile Books, 2005, p.28 [census.nationalarchives.ie]

8   R.F. Foster, *The Oxford History of Ireland*, op.cit., pp.166-9

9   R. Kee, *The Green Flag: A History of Irish Nationalism*, op.cit., p.191

10   D. Fitzpatrick, *Ireland Since 1870*, in R.F. Foster (Ed.), *The Oxford History of Ireland*, p.174

was 'dangerously dependent upon population drainage through emigration'.[11]

The question of land rights, though very far from resolved, appeared to have become less contentious as a result of Gladstone's Land Act of 1870, which introduced some land purchase rights and gave some legal standing to tenant rights where they already existed. But as F.S.L. Lyons notes, 'in practice the Land Act of 1870 was a disappointment'[12] and by the end of the 1870s Ireland was in the throes of an agricultural depression.

As Irish MPs were pressing the cause of self-government by parliamentary means, another force emerged to fight for land rights. The National Land League of Ireland, founded in October 1879 by Michael Davitt, organised tenant farmers to protect those threatened with eviction, win rent reductions and seek ownership of the land they tilled.

This campaign would eventually lead to transformation of the land system, bringing the dominant position of the landlord class to an end and transferring land into the ownership of those who worked it. *En route* to that revolution, it also transformed the Irish Parliamentary Party.

Agitators and politicians

There had been sporadic opposition to the Union from its very beginning in the form of minor rebellions. More significantly, agitation for repeal of the Union won immense support in the 1840s. The 1829 Catholic Relief Bill, which followed a mass movement led by Daniel O'Connell, had allowed Catholics to sit as MPs and a group of 39 pro-repeal MPs, led by O'Connell, formed 'the nucleus of a distinctively Irish party'.[13]

O'Connell's 1834 Bill to repeal the Act of Union failed miserably in the Commons, but his repeal movement attracted mass support. Aided by a group of middle-class young men known as Young Ireland, half of them Protestants, his campaign to repeal the Union became

11   D. Fitzpatrick, *Ireland Since 1870*, op.cit., p.175
12   F.S.L. Lyons, *Ireland Since the Famine*, op.cit., p.146
13   R. Dudley Edwards, *An Atlas of Irish History*, London, Methuen, 1973, p.101

'by far the most comprehensive national movement in Irish history'.[14]

'Monster meetings' for repeal each attracted crowds of 100,000 or more, at a time when travel was far from easy or cheap. In spite of the size of the crowds, says Kee, 'the meetings were conducted with a disciplined order which frightened the government'.[15] When the authorities banned a rally at Clontarf, in north Dublin, called for 8 October 1843, O'Connell cancelled it rather than risk bloodshed. That was the beginning of the end of the mass campaign for repeal of the Union. Then came the famine.

The power of extra-parliamentary agitation was not

Monument in central Dublin to Charles Stuart Parnell, leader of the Irish Parliamentary Party. (© S. de Gunst)

forgotten. When Parnell and Land League founder Michael Davitt resurrected the strategy, 'a startled world learned for the first time how explosive a combination of a mass agrarian movement and a tightly disciplined party under leadership of genius could prove to be'.[16]

A modern political machine

Elected leader of the parliamentary party in 1880, Charles Stuart Parnell began to transform the amorphous troupe of Irish MPs into a modern political machine. The Irish Party, as it was commonly called, became a disciplined phalanx that disrupted Westminster's decorous parliamentary conventions and used its strength to win the support of the Liberal prime minister, William Gladstone, for Home Rule, though that came at the cost of a rift in the Liberal Party.

---

14   R. Kee, *The Green Flag: A History of Irish Nationalism*, op.cit., p.207
15   Ibid., p.202
16   F.S.L. Lyons, *Ireland Since the Famine*, op.cit., p.122

The Irish Parliamentary Party at its greatest strength (86 MPs) in the UK House of Commons, led by Charles Stewart Parnell (standing, centre). (© US Library of Congress)

Parnell made two significant moves in 1882: he renamed his group the Irish Parliamentary Party (IPP) and founded the Irish National League to give the party its own nationwide structure at constituency level for the first time. The IPP became more tightly disciplined and effective, developing into what Kee termed 'the first British democratic political machine of modern times'.[17]

The general election of 1885 was the first fought in Ireland mainly on the issue of Home Rule. It gave the IPP its best result, a total of 86 MPs, one of them in Liverpool where journalist T.P. O'Connor won a seat and kept it for 50 years. Parnell held the balance of power in a hung parliament and developed the party's most significant parliamentary relationship, that with Liberal Party leader William Gladstone, who introduced his first Home Rule Bill in 1886.

Significant alliances

The Irish Party also developed significant alliances beyond parliament, an approach embraced by Butt but perfected by Parnell,

---

17   R. Kee, *The Green Flag: A History of Irish Nationalism,* op.cit., p.384

who forged mutually beneficial relationships with Ireland's Catholic bishops on education, and with the Land League in the fight for the rights of tenant farmers.

Parnell also appealed to 'the men of the hillsides', the physical force nationalists of the Irish Republican Brotherhood (IRB), known as Fenians. Fenianism was, in many ways, the non-constitutional enabler of the IPP. The Land League and the IRB, which were already closely interconnected, provided activists on the ground for the party, although the IRB's aim went far beyond Home Rule to full independence.

The Land League's early branches were mainly organised by Fenians, says Fitzpatrick, and the League in turn 'acted as a bridge for Fenian pragmatists weary of awaiting the call to arms'.

Parnell, Fitzpatrick claims, packed his party with ex-Fenians and made it easy to achieve the transition from gunman to parliamentarian. In this he pioneered a route that would be followed by future generations of those who had initially favoured the bullet over the ballot box.

In strictly parliamentary terms the First Home Rule Bill was the peak of Parnell's achievement, despite its failure. Gladstone introduced the Bill in 1886 but he couldn't rely on his own party and unionist Liberals joined with Conservatives to defeat the Bill in the Commons. Gladstone's second Bill passed the Commons in 1893 but was defeated in the Lords, although Parnell didn't live to see that.

Sex scandal

On Christmas Eve 1889, Captain William O'Shea, a former nationalist MP, filed for divorce from his wife, citing Parnell as co-respondent. It was true that Mrs Katharine O'Shea and Parnell were in a relationship, had been for several years, and had children together. The case was undefended because Parnell and Katharine wanted to marry (and did so).

However, once in the public domain the long relationship became political dynamite. The morals of the time militated against the couple and Liberal nonconformists such as Gladstone, as well as a majority of the IPP, turned against Parnell. He rejected the party's call to stand down as leader, but his health was failing and he died in October 1891.

The party initially split into the pro-Parnell Irish National League led by John Redmond, and the anti-Parnell Irish National Federation under John Dillon but, in 1900, the two wings of the party were reunited under Redmond's leadership.

The last hurdle

As with the Home Rule Bills of 1886 and 1893, a third Home Rule Bill – introduced in 1912 – resulted from a minority Liberal government's need for the support of Irish MPs. The IPP's demands also included an end to the House of Lords' veto on legislation. Supported by 40 Labour MPs, the Parliament Act of 1911 removed the Lords' veto and replaced it with the power of delay.

The 1912 Home Rule Bill has been justifiably described as an ungenerous measure, offering Ireland a parliament with an elected lower house and a nominated senate but only a limited range of responsibilities. Final control would remain in London, giving Westminster the power to nullify or amend any Act of the Irish parliament.

The proposed power to vary standard UK taxation but not to introduce new taxes was contentious, both to nationalists and unionists.[18] Attacking the lack of financial autonomy, IPP leader John Redmond described the Bill as a provisional settlement. 'When the time for revision does come', he declared, 'we will be entitled to complete power for Ireland over the whole of our financial system'.[19] Unionist leader Edward Carson retorted that coupling legislative autonomy with financial independence was an argument against a separate government in Dublin.

Despite the Bill's weakness nationalist reaction was mainly positive. Even 'advanced' nationalists such as Pádraig Pearse, who would later lead (and be executed for his part in) the 1916 rebellion, welcomed it as a step in the right direction.

Unionists, on the other hand, were fiercely opposed and organised mass opposition, convening mass meetings and raising an armed militia. Almost half a million people, from all classes, signed the Ulster Covenant, an oath to resist Home Rule.[20]

---

18   Hansard, 11 April 1912
19   F.S.L. Lyons, *Ireland Since the Famine*, op.cit., p.302
20   nidirect.gov.uk

The Bill was carried in January 1913 and received royal assent in 1914 but the outbreak of the First World War postponed implementation. About 35,000 Irish died in the war, of the 210,000 who volunteered. During the war, Redmond's decision to call on members of the Irish Volunteers[21] to join the British forces sparked deep divisions. It split the Volunteers and underlined the gulf between the party and other strands within the nationalist movement.

By the 1918 Armistice the political dynamic had changed. The manner in which the British government had crushed the 1916 rebellion helped to shift sentiment in Ireland. The unionist opposition to Home Rule, led by Edward Carson, had gained in influence due in part to Carson's inclusion in the War Cabinet, an opportunity also offered to but rejected by IPP leader Redmond.

Twisting the knife

After the war had ended and the 1918 election had shown that the IPP's days might be numbered, there was yet another constitutional twist that fatally wounded the notion of Home Rule, and the IPP itself.

Yielding to immense pressure from unionists – whose strength the IPP had underestimated – Lloyd George's government abandoned the Home Rule Act and replaced it with the 1920 Government of Ireland Act. This legislated for partition of the country and the creation of two devolved parliaments, one in Dublin and another in Belfast.

Sinn Féin, now the dominant political party, had abstained from Westminster and set up a parliament in Dublin. A guerrilla war for independence ended in a truce in July 1921 and the Anglo-Irish Treaty was signed in December 1921. The Irish Free State was established but a bitter civil war ravaged the country from June 1922 until May 1923.

Unionists, who had marshalled mass protest and an armed militia against Home Rule, settled for a strategic geographical retreat into northeast Ireland and control of the Belfast parliament.

---

21   The Irish Volunteers were formed in 1913 in response to the rise of the unionist Ulster Volunteers but also as an armed front for the IRB

Diverging realities

In early 20th century Ireland, as Roy Foster comments: '... what was evident was the energy, imagination, diversity of talent and powerful sense of history in the making represented by those active in the politics and cultural initiatives of the day.'[22]

While the IPP focused on its core aim of achieving Home Rule legislation in London, in Ireland a ferment of cultural, feminist and trade union activity was shaking up society, alongside a more radical form of nationalism. The party appeared to be out of touch with this vibrancy and the new political environment. Some of its leading figures even alienated future voters. IPP leader John Redmond opposed votes for women and his successor James Dillon, once a radical reformer, declared: 'Women's suffrage will be the ruin of our western civilisation'.[23]

The votes of newly enfranchised women would prove significant in the 1918 general election, which didn't go well for the IPP. Sinn Féin swept up the bulk of IPP seats, thanks to the widening of the electorate and to IPP activists transferring their allegiance to the new party.

The times had caught up with the Irish Parliamentary Party. It dissolved itself in 1922, but many of its members refused to fade away.

Judging the party

When the prize of Home Rule was in sight, events conspired to cheat the Irish Parliamentary Party of its primary aim of a single national parliament, which John Redmond made clear would be only the first step to greater autonomy. However, the party left other legacies.

By putting Home Rule on the political agenda, it had changed the terms of debate about how Ireland should be governed, a debate that evolved in other directions, for and against independence. Inevitably, one repercussion was a powerful unionist fight-back in favour of remaining united with Great Britain, the effects of which are still being played out.

---

22   R.F. Foster, in *Revolutionary States: Home Rule & Modern Ireland*, Dublin, Dublin City Gallery The Hugh Lane, 2012, p.35

23   G. Moriarty, 'De Valera, Dillon's 'jaundiced' view of women's suffrage', *Irish Times*, 27 April 2012

John Redmond, leader of the Irish Parliamentary Party (1900-18), addressing a public meeting in 1917.

The IPP, under Parnell in particular, contributed significantly to progress on land reform (which would lead to a revolution in land ownership). Parnell attributed this to the determination and tenacity of tenants themselves, acting through the Land League, but Lyons argues it would hardly have been achieved without Parnell's 'superb ability to combine the explosive force of agrarianism with a mastery of parliamentary pressure at Westminster'.[24]

Later political parties learned from Parnell's creation of what Lyons summarises as 'a disciplined, efficient and pledge-bound parliamentary party' and others have called the first modern democratic political party. The party, Lyons adds, 'offered a living proof that Ireland was ripe for self-government [and] provided the country with essential experience in the democratic process'.[25]

24   F.S.L. Lyons, *Ireland Since the Famine*, op.cit., pp.200-201
25   Ibid., pp.200-201

Many of its members integrated into the new political landscape after the party was dissolved. In Northern Ireland, they regrouped as the Nationalist Party and, for the first election to the NI House of Commons, agreed an electoral pact with Sinn Féin that led to each winning six seats to the Ulster Unionist Party's 40.

In the Free State many former IPP politicians and activists joined other parties, stood as independents or formed new parties. Some had switched to Sinn Féin before 1918 but tended to gravitate to the pro-treaty side after the civil war.

Martin O'Donoghue argues that their ongoing presence in politics demonstrated 'the shadow of the [Irish Parliamentary] party over Irish political life'.[26] The IPP's methods also persisted, informing the political culture and 'highlighting continuities between pre- and post-independence Ireland'.[27]

Irish Parliamentary Party	
Founded:	1873 as the Home Rule League; known as the Home Rule Party or Irish Party from 1874; renamed Irish Parliamentary Party 1882.
Dissolved:	1922
Leaders:	Isaac Butt 1874-1879; William Shaw 1879-80; Charles Stuart Parnell 1880-91; John Redmond 1891-1918; John Dillon 1918; Joseph Devlin 1918-1921

---

26 M. O'Donoghue, 'Independence and the shadow of Home Rule: the legacy of the Irish Parliamentary Party', *Irish Times*, 17 February 2020

27 T.O.M. O'Donoghue, *The Legacy of the Irish Parliamentary Party in Independent Ireland, 1922-49*, National University of Ireland Galway, PhD. Thesis, 2016

2

The Ulster Unionist Party

Former Protestant supremacists seeking moderate role

Overview

Could a party that deliberately constructed a 'Protestant supremacist state'[1] re-invent itself for a more pluralist society? That was the challenge facing the Ulster Unionist Party (UUP) following its fall to minor party status despite having co-brokered a peace agreement that ended 30 years of violent conflict in Northern Ireland.

Founded in 1905 from a pre-existing unionist movement, the Ulster Unionist Party spent its early years fiercely opposing Irish Home Rule. Accepting partition as a compromise, its political weight secured an opt-out from devolution for six Ulster counties[2] selected to ensure a safe majority of Protestants (presumed unionist) over Catholics (presumed nationalist).

After partition in 1921 the sectarian delineation of the border delivered control of the devolved parliament to the UUP. James Craig, Northern Ireland's first prime minister, set about engineering ongoing dominance for his party with measures that included anti-Catholic discrimination in employment, housing and public appointments, the gerrymandering of constituencies, and the abolition of proportional representation. All while developing dependence on UK Treasury subsidies as the economy proved to be less robust than expected.

---

1   R.F. Foster, *Modern Ireland 1600-1972*, London, Penguin Books, 1989, p.592
2   Antrim, Armagh, Down, Derry, Tyrone and Fermanagh; the other three, Donegal, Cavan and Monaghan, were allocated to the southern state.

Half a century after NI's foundation a series of events shook the system the UUP had constructed. In 1968 a peaceful campaign for Catholic civil rights met a violent backlash from extreme loyalist Protestants. After the police also attacked marchers, sectarian conflict and political violence were unleashed and peaceful protest receded.

The UK government conceded most of the civil rights movement's objectives and NI Prime Minister Terence O'Neill introduced a programme of reforms, but the UUP leadership was divided, its judgement poor and responses often inappropriate. Instead of peaceful reforms, Northern Ireland suffered 30 years of conflict in which more than 3,500 people, mostly civilians, were killed.

The UK government closed down the Belfast parliament in 1972 and introduced direct rule. Attempts to re-establish a legislature failed in face of opposition from unionism, most dramatically a loyalist workers' strike in 1974 that paralysed the region. The UUP lost support to more extreme parties, while loyalist paramilitaries and the Provisional IRA waged violent campaigns involving assassinations and bombings.

After tortuous negotiations, the British and Irish governments and main Northern Ireland parties (but not the DUP) signed the Belfast Agreement on 10 April 1998. The peace brokers included UUP leader David Trimble (1995-2005) who received a Nobel Peace Prize for his efforts, jointly with the SDLP leader John Hume (1979-2001).

The UUP emerged as the largest party in the 1998 Legislative Assembly but not with the absolute control it had exercised previously. The peace agreement required power sharing between unionists and nationalists, which the UUP initially exercised alongside the moderate nationalist SDLP. Outstripped by the Democratic Unionist Party in 2003, the traditional party of unionism found itself on a downward path that saw it fall to fourth place in the 2022 Assembly election.

The Ulster Unionist Party had helped to achieve peace but lost its political dominance and direction post-conflict. Having been one of the most hegemonic parties in Europe for half of the 20th century the UUP became just another small party in the 21st, one that was struggling to find a relevant role in a more pluralist society.

Defending the Union

'It was 8 April 1886. On that afternoon Mr Gladstone went down to the House to introduce his Government of Ireland Bill, known to history as the First Home Rule Bill'.[3]

This was the exact moment of unionism's creation, according to Geoffrey Lewis, biographer of Edward Carson, the Dublin barrister and Ulster Unionist Party leader (1910-1921) who led the revolt against a later Home Rule proposal, resulting in partition.

It was certainly a historic moment, both for the Irish Parliamentary Party's crusade for a devolved all-Ireland parliament and for its unionist opponents who engineered the Bill's defeat in the House of Commons. The unionist movement had complex roots, however, and the Ulster Unionist Party *per se* was not established until 1905.

Defeating the 1886 Bill involved intensive campaigning by freshly energised supporters of the union between Ireland and Britain (in force since 1 January 1801). These included a well-funded 'think tank' based in Dublin (the Irish Loyal and Patriotic Union) that produced pro-union propaganda, and a mass resistance movement in Ulster, the province with the highest concentration of unionists. The result was inevitable when unionists from Gladstone's own Liberal Party joined with the Conservatives to vote against the Bill.

The same *modus operandi* thwarted another Irish Home Rule Bill in 1893. While unionists failed to prevent a third Bill becoming law in 1914, intensified opposition led to the establishment of two devolved legislatures, one in Northern Ireland that the UUP controlled for the next half century, and the Irish Free State (later the Republic of Ireland) covering the rest of the island.

In anticipation of the 1886 Irish Home Rule Bill, its opponents organised on three main fronts: parliamentary opposition, propaganda and mass agitation. They didn't need to look far for inspiration on how to leverage such methods – the Irish Parliamentary Party's fusion of legislative and extra-parliamentary action offered the prototype.

Initial attempts at fashioning a 'rudimentary model' of a parliamentary party were amateurish, according to Lyons, until

---

3   G. Lewis, *Carson: The Man Who Divided Ireland*, London and New York, Hambledon & London, 2005, p.ix

Colonel E. J. Saunderson, a wealthy Anglo-Irish landlord, took on leadership of the Irish Unionist Association (IUA).[4]

The IUA, also referred to as the Irish Unionist Party, had evolved from the Irish Loyal and Patriotic Union (ILPU), founded in May 1885 by a group of 'wealthy, close knit and influential' southern Irish landowners, businessmen and academics.[5]

A different but highly influential group, the Ulster Loyalist Anti-Repeal Union, was founded in January 1886 to whip up popular opposition to Home Rule. It grew rapidly and, says Lyons, was 'quite openly directed towards arousing religious passion'. An early highlight was a stage-managed visit to Belfast by Randolph Churchill who claimed that the future of the British Empire, not just of Ireland's union with Britain, was at stake.

While Churchill may not have declared on that occasion that 'Ulster will fight and Ulster will be right' – a phrase he used elsewhere – his words crystallised the commitment to block Home Rule by any means necessary.

During that visit Churchill also chose to whip up Protestant fear of the Catholic 'other' in Belfast, a tactic that became known as 'playing the Orange card' – a risky move in a city with a long history of rioting. Soon after his visit, sectarian violence broke out in Belfast, leading to 32 deaths (although many were the result of police firing on rioters[6]), and continued sporadically throughout the summer despite the Bill being defeated in June.

Another campaign group, the Ulster Defence Union (UDU), was founded to oppose the 1893 Home Rule Bill and following the defeat of that legislation in the Lords the UDU faded. The prospect of devolution also receded, largely because the Irish Parliamentary Party was in disarray following Parnell's death and the preceding divorce scandal (see chapter 1).

It also proved difficult to maintain a cohesive movement without its only unifying factor, the threat of Home Rule legislation. Social class or denominations within Protestantism normally divided the potential support base. The landlord class was synonymous with the Church of Ireland and overwhelmingly voted Conservative.

---

4   F.S.L. Lyons, *Ireland Since the Famine*, op.cit., p.292
5   Ibid., p.291
6   M. Radford, 'Closely Akin to Actual Warfare', *History Ireland*, Winter 1999, Vol.7

Presbyterians and Methodists were more likely to be tenant farmers or middle or working class and to vote Liberal. A shared fear of Home Rule blurred such divisions.

Origins, identities, politics

Home Rule aroused fears of Catholic supremacy, a prospect that chilled radical and liberal Presbyterians as much as it did staunch conservatives, according to Graham Walker, and, as Walker notes, resulted in the bulk of Presbyterian Liberals joining with Conservatives to oppose Gladstone's Bill in 1886.

Those fighting to keep the Union of Great Britain and Ireland intact were protecting their religious identity and economic interests which they believed were inherently connected with British citizenship. Both were rooted in the 17th century plantations of Ulster, when land confiscated from its indigenous occupants passed into the possession of planters (colonisers) from England and Scotland.[7]

The Battle of the Boyne in 1690, when the forces of the Protestant William of Orange defeated the Catholic James II of England and Ireland (James VII of Scotland) during one of many post-Reformation religious wars in Europe, is still celebrated as a central event in Ulster Protestant culture.

After 1886, an Ulster Scots identity was nurtured in what Walker calls 'a conscious effort to sharpen an Ulster Protestant ethnic profile'. He notes a steady stream of literature extolling the Ulster-Scots, who were presented as a 'pioneering people who had endured a history of sacrifice and struggle in Ulster'. Such texts 'helped to embroider the stereotype, in some ways racial, of a uniquely self-willed, self-reliant and indomitable people steeled by a covenanting Calvinist heritage, and not to be bent to the political designs of Catholic Ireland'.

The identity being nurtured both opposed and paralleled nationalism: 'To the civic strain of argument against any change to their British citizenship was added the decidedly ethnic one of an Ulster Protestant distinctiveness with its own right of self-determination, albeit to be held in reserve'.[8]

---

7   For discussion of plantations in Ireland see R.F. Foster, *Modern Ireland 1600-1972*, London, Penguin, 1989, pp.59-78

8   G. Walker, *A History of the Ulster Unionist Party: Protest, Pragmatism and Pessimism*, Manchester, Manchester University Press, 2004, pp.6-7

Unionist Clubs and Orangemen marching to Belfast City Hall to sign the Ulster Covenant, on Ulster Day, 28 September 1912. (© R. Welch)

Ulster unionism's case was later presented as a matter of democracy: the majority must prevail, but which majority? The 1918 general election had shown that an Ireland-wide majority favoured breaking the link with Britain, Ronald McNeill[9] admitted, while also stressing that a majority in Ulster did not. On the basis of his 'two nations' theory of Ulster's right to independence from an Irish state, 'if one of the two had a right to "self-determination", the other had it equally.'

Becoming an Ulster phenomenon

Initially an all-Ireland movement that aimed to keep the entire island united with Britain, unionism became a specifically Ulster phenomenon when faced with the inevitability of Home Rule. Attention focused first on keeping the entire province in the UK but later shifted to identifying the optimum territorial arrangement to ensure unionist control of a smaller entity.

9   R. McNeill, *Ulster's Stand for Union*, London, John Murray, 1922

Edward Carson signing the Ulster Covenant in Belfast City Hall on Ulster Day, 28 September 1912.

During 1904-05, largely in reaction to new proposals for limited devolution, younger middle-class politicians set about transforming Ulster unionism. The outcome, in March 1905, was the formation of the Ulster Unionist Council (UUC) as a coordinating body for unionism. Half of the 200-member Council represented local unionist associations, while the Orange Order[10] had 50 places, with MPs and peers filling the rest.

As part of this process the Ulster Unionist Party was formalised, with policy oversight by the UUC that limited the party's autonomy. The Council's composition made it hard at times for party leaders to win its support, as David Trimble found at pivotal points during the 1998 peace negotiations.

Killing the Bill

When Liberal Prime Minister Herbert Asquith introduced a third Home Rule Bill in April 1912, unionism reacted with radical, multi-faceted resistance.

---

10   The Orange Order, or Loyal Orange Institution (LOI), was founded in 1796 to further the aims of Protestantism and protect the link with Britain; it was contemporaneous with the United Irishmen, who sought to unite 'Protestant, Catholic and Dissenter' to establish a republic.

In September 1912 the UUC made preparations for a provisional government to assume control of Ulster after Home Rule came into force. In January 1913 it sanctioned the raising of an armed militia, the Ulster Volunteer Force (UVF), incorporating the many who were already secretly drilling.

In a PR triumph masterminded by UUP deputy leader James Craig, nearly half a million men and women were mobilised to sign a solemn oath of resistance. Over ten days in September 1912 a series of meetings took place, beginning in the west and sweeping towards Belfast for Ulster Day, Saturday 28 September.

Belfast was hushed, its workplaces closed, as Edward Carson led a parade to City Hall. Inside, the Ulster Covenant sat on a table draped with the Union flag. Carson signed first, followed by political and religious notables. Then men lined up in batches to sign: 'Four at a time the men stooped and fixed their signatures and were quickly replaced by the next batch. Down the street in a market house the women were signing ... '.[11]

One faith leader caught the spirit driving the unionist revolt against a decision of the Union they were campaigning to keep: 'We hold that no power, not even the British Parliament, has the right to deprive us of our heritage of British citizenship'.[12]

The propaganda value of the Ulster Covenant campaign was heightened by the drama and military precision with which it was organised. The UVF militia, having acquired 25,000 rifles from Germany in 1914, offered persuasion of a different kind.

Dividing Ireland

Implementation of the 1914 Home Rule Act was postponed following the outbreak of the First World War. By the end of the conflict, however, the political context had changed utterly: Irish nationalism had taken a new direction following the 1916 rebellion; Sinn Féin won a majority in the 1918 general election, though not in Ulster; the Irish Parliamentary Party was sidelined; and the Unionist Party was poised to exert maximum political pressure.

---

11   Contemporary description, in PRONI: Public Record Office of Northern Ireland, nidirect.gov.uk

12   Ibid.

David Lloyd George, the Liberal leader, had formed a coalition government in December 1916 and, with UUP leader Edward Carson in the Cabinet, unionist influence was stronger than that of the nationalist IPP, that had declined to participate. Lloyd George gained nationalist agreement to a temporary exclusion of six Ulster counties from the Home Rule settlement, while simultaneously offering permanent exclusion to the unionists.[13]

In October 1919 Lloyd George set up a Cabinet committee to advise on Irish policy, chaired by former UUP leader Walter Long (1906-10). The committee proposed the establishment of two devolved administrations in Ireland, and this became the central provision of the Government of Ireland Act 1920.[14]

Partition wasn't what UUP leader Edward Carson wanted. A highflying barrister whose career included a courtroom cross-examination that destroyed Oscar Wilde, Carson was a Dubliner and an Irish unionist. As a charismatic orator and public face of the revolt against Home Rule he is credited with dividing Ireland – but he was more than ably assisted by his deputy James Craig, a stockbroker and whiskey millionaire who succeeded him as UUP leader in 1921.

Liberal Prime Minister Herbert Asquith conceded partition in principle on 9 March 1914, when he suggested excluding Ulster for six years. Edward Carson dismissed this concession, wrung by Asquith from Irish Parliamentary Party leader John Redmond. As early as autumn 1911, however, at a meeting with the Ulster Unionist Council, Carson had agreed to 'frame and submit a Constitution for a Provisional Government for Ulster, having due regard to the interests of loyalists in other parts of Ireland' – evidence, says Lewis, that Carson was already seriously considering partition.[15]

In July 1914, at a cross-party conference on Ireland, Carson proposed that all of Ulster be excluded from the Home Rule Bill. Andrew Bonar Law, then leader of the opposition Conservatives, recorded Carson's view that if this were 'done generously' a united Ireland would be likely 'within a reasonable time'. However, if Ulster

---

13   I. Gibbons, *Partition: How and Why Ireland was Divided*, London, Haus, 2020, p.40

14   A proposed Council of Ireland, with a view to 'the eventual establishment of a Parliament for the whole of Ireland, and to bringing about harmonious action between the parliaments and governments...', was not activated.

15   G. Lewis, *Carson: The Man Who Divided Ireland*, op.cit., p.80

*Statue of Edward Carson at Stormont, seat of the Northern Ireland parliament.
(© Shutterstock)*

were to be coerced, 'a united Ireland within the lifetime of any one
now living would be out of the question'.[16]

When Ireland was partitioned, Carson lamented in the House of
Lords: 'What a fool I was! I was only a puppet and so was Ulster and
so was Ireland in the political game that was to get the Conservative
Party into office.'

Home Rule by any other name

In June 1921 the party that had campaigned so hard to block Irish
devolution won control of a devolved legislature in Northern Ireland,
with a very comfortable majority of 40 to 12. The Ulster Unionist
Party retained control of that legislature until the UK government
dissolved it in 1972, and the region reverted to direct rule from
London.

UUP hegemony was due to several factors, one of which was its
nature as an umbrella party for all unionists – although some were

---

16   Ibid., p.164

The Northern Ireland Cabinet, July 1921: (left to right) Dawson Bates, the Marquess of Londonderry, James Craig (prime minister), H.M. Pollock, E.M. Archdale, J.M. Andrews.

more equal than others and it was led by men from the landed and mercantile classes.

Stormont, as the institution became known after its imposing new building, was a parliament of men in suits, with added Orange Order sashes. Only nine women were elected to it in half a century, six of them UUP members. Although that was not unusual for the times, the Orange Order influence was very much an Ulster phenomenon.

Orangeism 'saturated the official unionist party', according to Kaufman.[17] The numbers suggest he was right: 138 of the UUP's 149 MPs between 1921 and 1969 were Orangemen. Northern Ireland's first prime minister, James Craig, declared himself to be an Orange Order member first and foremost, perhaps wisely given the importance of the Order to his party's hold on power.

---

17   E.P. Kaufman, *The Orange Order: A Contemporary Northern Irish History*, Oxford
      University Press, 2007, p.15

Was Northern Ireland a sectarian state created to serve the aims of unionist politicians? The historian Roy Foster called it a 'Protestant supremacist state'[18] and Craig himself boasted that it was a Protestant state: 'All I boast is that we are a Protestant Parliament and Protestant State'.[19]

Craig had calculated that settling for just six of historic Ulster's nine counties, a unit in which Protestants would comfortably outnumber Catholics, would ensure unionist control. He successfully lobbied for the 1920 Government of Ireland Act to be amended accordingly and the May 1921 election confirmed his expectation when the UUP won more than three-quarters of parliamentary seats.

Copper-fastening control

Winning control was one thing – Craig's sectarian headcount ensured that – but how did the UUP hold it for so long? Brendan O'Leary[20] lists the ways, including electoral engineering, anti-Catholic discrimination in employment, housing and public appointments, and a repressive police force.

The constitutional settlement was key: achieving the optimal territorial division in the partition deal laid the foundation stone. Electoral engineering was fundamental: redrawing electoral boundaries and changing the voting system, but retaining a class bias in local elections after Britain had moved away from this also disadvantaged poorer Protestants.

O'Leary and others point to the Derry/Londonderry local authority area as a striking example of how effective the redrawing of ward boundaries could be: approximately two and a half times as many non-unionist votes were required to elect a non-unionist councillor compared with the number of unionist votes required to elect a unionist.[21]

Replacing proportional representation (PR) with first-past-the-post voting also upped the UUP's advantage. O'Leary quotes the case

---

18 R.F. Foster, *Modern Ireland 1600-1972*, op.cit., p.572
19 Parliamentary Debates, Northern Ireland House of Commons, Vol. XVI, Cols 1091-95
20 B. O'Leary, *A Treatise on Northern Ireland: Vol. 2 | Control*, Oxford, Oxford University Press, 2020 edition, pp.17-59
21 Ibid., p.44

of Belfast where the party held 62% of council seats in 1920; its share rose to 83% in 1923 after PR was abolished for local elections, the main loser being the Northern Ireland Labour Party.

Beyond any anti-Catholic gerrymandering – and there is little reason to doubt that intent – the class bias in the local franchise's property qualification and additional business votes also disadvantaged poorer Protestants, and stored up trouble for the UUP in the longer run.

Some analyses of social housing allocation policies, a major focus of the NI civil rights movement in the late 1960s, are more nuanced than O'Leary's.[22] In particular the Housing Trust, set up in 1945, used a points system to allocate homes. Henry Patterson notes: 'The main criticism of unionist councils made by Lord Cameron in his 1969 report was not that they did not build sufficient houses for Catholics but that they used housing allocation to maintain electoral advantage.'[23]

Nevertheless, when the totality of control measures is considered, the overall impression is one of sectarian practices that were meant to produce election results that favoured unionists and, in practice, disadvantaged Catholics who were presumed (with reason) to be nationalists.

The control system erected by the UUP effectively marginalised Catholics, but nationalist parties posed no real threat to the UUP as they abstained from parliament in the early years and were notoriously divided.

The Northern Ireland Labour Party (NILP) (1924-87) was a greater potential risk. Bew *et al* note losses of Protestant working class votes to the NILP, as well as the UUP's solution: 'to weld ever more tightly the links between the unionist elite and the Protestant working class'.[24]

Ongoing dominance depended on keeping various elements in equilibrium under the UUP umbrella. It was a strategy they mostly

---

22   See e.g. R. Rose, *Governing Without Consensus: An Irish Perspective*, Faber & Faber, 1971; G. Gudgin, *Discrimination in Housing and Employment under the Stormont Administration*, in P.J. Roche and B. Barton (eds.), *The Northern Ireland Question: Nationalism, Unionism and Partition*, London, Ashgate Publishing Ltd, 1999

23   H. Patterson, 'Defending the Union', *Dublin Review of Books*, October 2020

24   P. Bew, P. Gibbon, H. Patterson, *Northern Ireland 1921-1994 – Political Forces and Social Classes*, London, Serif, 1995, p.68

managed – but not always: notably and uniquely in 1932, instead of fighting one another, Catholic and Protestant workers rioted side-by-side in protest against a paltry rate of outdoor relief (a form of unemployment benefit).

Facing realities

Northeast Ulster was the most industrialised area in Ireland by far and correspondingly prosperous compared with the mainly agricultural economy elsewhere on the island. Belfast was a city of job opportunities for women as well as men, in linen mills, shipyards and engineering workshops. The city had a dark side too, with 'a notorious reputation for sectarian violence'.[25] Additionally, behind the prosperous façade lay weaknesses in the pillars of the economy, as the new government would discover.

On 12 July 1920, addressing a 25,000-strong rally in Belfast, UUP leader Carson called for action not words to stop Irish Home Rule, warning the British government: 'these are not mere words; I am sick of words without action.' This was widely interpreted as a threat to deploy the Ulster Volunteer Force, an armed loyalist militia. What happened next may not have been Carson's intention but few doubted the power of his words.

A week later the expulsion of thousands of workers, mainly but not exclusively Catholic, from Belfast's shipyards began. A fight between a Catholic and a Protestant may have been what sparked the pogrom, but what it unleashed was large-scale sectarianism.

Historian David Fitzpatrick estimates that some 5,500 Catholics and 1,900 Protestants were driven out of the Belfast shipyards during July; of these about a quarter were women and some 700 were Catholic ex-servicemen. Some sources put the total at 10,000 Catholics and about 1,000 'rotten Prods' (Protestants suspected of nationalist or socialist sympathies).

A year after those riots, allegedly supported by the UUP-backed Ulster Unionist Labour Association (UULA), the Ulster Unionist Party was in government in Belfast and about to discover some economic facts.

---

25   E. O'Connor, 'A Concise History of the Labour movement and the Birth of Northern Ireland', sluggerotoole.com, 29 September 2019

In April 1922 an official memorandum informed Prime Minister Craig that the unemployment rate had been 'consistently in excess' of that in Britain by as much as 50%. In 1923 another memorandum warned of limited prospects in the 'quasi luxury' linen industry or the 'notoriously unstable' shipbuilding sector.[26]

What was to be done? Prime Minister Craig secured UK Treasury subsidies, but hid the extent of growing financial dependence on London. Subsidies remained central to the NI budget under Craig's successors, John M Andrews (1940-46) and Basil Brooke/

ULSTER IS OURS

WHAT WE HAVE WE HOLD

Poster featuring James Craig, Northern Ireland's first prime minister, c. 1940.

Lord Brookeborough (1946-63). Andrews made 'incautious promises of social expenditure' which helped to end his premiership, while Brooke pushed through the welfare state against the opposition of his more conservative colleagues.[27]

By 1950 populists and their opponents differed only regarding the degree to which Northern Ireland could secure the benefits of the welfare state 'whilst resisting the erosion of its autonomy by other aspects of Westminster legislation'.[28]

The political high point of Brooke's 18-year tenure was the Ireland Act 1949 enacted by the UK government in response to Dublin's declaration of a republic in 1948.[29] The 1949 Act guaranteed Northern Ireland's status as part of the UK unless the parliament of Northern Ireland should decide otherwise. This strengthened NI's

---

26   D. Ferriter, *A Nation and not a Rabble: The Irish Revolution 1913-1923*, London, Profile Books, 2015, pp.311-12 [Memos dated 27 April 1922 and 28 August 1923]

27   Bew et al, *Northern Ireland 1921-1994 – Political Forces and Social Classes*, op.cit., p.17

28   Ibid., p.95

29   www.legislation.gov.uk/ukpga/Geo6/12-13-14/41/

Terence O'Neill, prime minister of Northern Ireland 1963-69.

de facto constitution – the 1920 Government of Ireland Act – until the 1998 peace treaty superseded both Acts.

Refreshing the project

Northern Ireland experienced little change until Terence O'Neill became prime minister in 1963. The Eton-educated, ex-Irish Guards officer set an upbeat tone and raised expectations of economic improvement. O'Neill reputedly revelled in being described as 'Ulster's JFK' – but was often accused of gesture politics.

O'Neill's approach to modernisation echoed that of Taoiseach Seán Lemass in the Republic with its focus on attracting inward investment by multi-national companies. The two held a historic meeting in Belfast in January 1965, followed by another in Dublin a month later. However, as Walker notes, while Lemass had prepared his party, Fianna Fáil, for the political changes entailed, O'Neill had not.[30]

While his parliamentary colleagues acquiesced in O'Neill's plans, grudgingly in some cases, on the more extreme end of the unionist spectrum unrest was brewing. In the most loyalist working class districts of Belfast a group called Ulster Protestant Action (UPA) was attracting not just locals but also the support of some UUP politicians.[31] At the same time, hard-line preacher Ian Paisley was shaping the UPA into a political force.

Beyond unionism another force was emerging, at first cautiously, seeking equal rights for Catholics and an end to sectarianism. The active period of the Northern Ireland Civil Rights Association (NICRA) would be short but its impact far-reaching.

---

30   G. Walker, *A History of the Ulster Unionist Party*, op.cit., p.156

31   Ibid., p.157 [As reported to Sam Napier, secretary of the NILP]

In its official history, NICRA judged Terence O'Neill harshly: 'He seemed to successfully bring Northern Ireland from the crude sectarianism of the Brookeborough era into the more fashionable sectarianism of the sixties. But his success was nothing more than a media illusion...'[32] O'Neill, they claimed, 'changed the façade' but left the reality untouched. Nobody could say that NICRA left the reality untouched, but it's unlikely they could have foreseen what followed.

The Northern Ireland Civil Rights Association, founded in 1967, held its first protest march on 24 August 1968. Less than four years later, on 30 March 1972, the UUP-dominated Stormont parliament ceased to exist.

NICRA did not set out to topple Stormont, but achieving equality for Catholics required an end to the sectarian practices underpinning much of the UUP's control. It also became clear that the Unionist Party remained too enmeshed in the system it had constructed to respond promptly or appropriately, even under pressure from the UK government.

Some 2,000 people took part in the first civil rights march, from Coalisland in central Ulster to nearby Dungannon, where young mothers had previously protested against discrimination in house building and allocations.[33] Police stopped the marchers from entering Dungannon where counter-demonstrators were lined up under the banner of the Protestant Volunteers, a group 'politically inspired by Ian Paisley and para-militarily groomed by Major Ronald Bunting'.[34] The marchers' defiance mainly took the form of singing and a sit-down but some were injured. Gerry Fitt MP sent a report to the UK prime minister, in which he complained about the role of the police.

The next march was planned for 5 October in Derry, in association with Derry Housing Action Committee. The loyalist Apprentice Boys countered with notice of an event on the same day along the same route. Both were banned but the civil rights march went ahead. Police baton-charged the crowd that they had 'kettled' in the narrow streets, injuring many, and television broadcast the dramatic images,

---

32   Northern Ireland Civil Rights Association (NICRA), *We shall overcome: The History of the Struggle for Civil Rights in Northern Ireland 1968-1978*, Belfast, NICRA, 1978. https://cain.ulster.ac.uk/events/crights/nicra/nicra78. htm#contents

33   www.irishtimes.com/news/politics/the-lost-story-ofnorthern-ireland-s-first-civil-rights-march-1.3605463

34   NICRA 1978

including of Gerry Fitt MP bleeding from his head as a result of police baton blows. Rioting in the city continued for several days.

'Ulster at the Crossroads'

The NI premier, Terence O'Neill, grasped the implications of the RUC attacking unarmed civilians.[35] He warned his ministers that London would insist on reforms and could impose financial penalties, but his warning had little impact. O'Neill was right: UK Prime Minister Harold Wilson and Home Secretary James Callaghan insisted that Stormont introduce reforms or face the consequences.

After a few fractious weeks, on 22 November O'Neill presented a programme of reforms but they didn't include 'one man, one vote' – which would have been a bridge too far for much of the party. Nevertheless, the proposed reforms and his 'Ulster at the Crossroads' speech broadcast to the public on 9 December bought O'Neill some time.

Then, on 4 January 1969, a 'long march' from Belfast to Derry organised by a radical new student group, People's Democracy, came under attack at Burntollet Bridge. Some 200 loyalists attacked the 40 marchers with sticks, iron bars, bottles and stones. The 80 Royal Ulster Constabulary (RUC) officers who had accompanied the march failed to provide protection from the attackers,[36] who were said to include off-duty members of the B-Specials, an all-Protestant auxiliary police force.

Some identify the events in Derry as the moment when Northern Ireland turned inexorably towards the Troubles. Historian Paul Bew, who was a member of People's Democracy and later an adviser to UUP leader David Trimble, takes a different view: 'No one did as much damage to the unionist cause as the people who attacked the marchers at Burntollet.'[37]

Both Derry and Burntollet were flashpoints, badly handled. Northern Ireland really was at a crossroads and the UUP Cabinet was divided over how to respond.

---

35   G. Walker, *A History of the Ulster Unionist Party*, op.cit., p.165

36   Cameron Report, *Disturbances in Northern Ireland*, September 1969. (Cmd 532) (Summary of Conclusions; paragraph 15)

37   S. O'Hagan, 'Northern Ireland's lost moment: how the peaceful protests of '68 escalated into years of bloody conflict', *The Observer*, 22 April 2018

Discrimination confirmed

O'Neill set up an independent Commission of Inquiry into the events 'on and since 5ᵗʰ October 1968'[38] believing it would undermine moderate support for the civil rights movement. However, the commission, chaired by the Scottish judge Lord Cameron, found evidence of discrimination and was critical of the NI government.[39] It listed unionist-controlled councils that 'used and use their power to make appointments in a way which benefited Protestants'; mentioned one that 'showed no clear cut pattern of discrimination' and another controlled by non-unionists that employed very few Protestants, but noted that it was in an area with 'relatively few Protestants' whereas 'in the other towns Catholics make up a substantial part of the population'.

On 3 February 1969 O'Neill dissolved parliament. The election on 24 February saw the highest turnout since 1921 and the highest UUP vote, although almost one third of that vote went to anti-O'Neill candidates. The election failed to resolve the internal party divisions or calm the wider mood. O'Neill resigned on 28 April 1969 in the wake of a spate of loyalist bombings.

Also in April, a People's Democracy activist, Bernadette Devlin, won a by-election in Mid-Ulster as a 'unity' candidate, but unity was in short supply in unionism or on the streets, and violence, frequently sectarian, became increasingly commonplace.

O'Neill's successor, James Chichester-Clark (1969-71), tried to proceed with the reforms, but he was too late. In August, fighting between police and residents of a Catholic area of Derry known as the Bogside raged for days. In Belfast, loyalist mobs attacked Catholic districts, burning businesses and driving thousands (mainly Catholics) from their homes.

On 14 August 1969 Britain deployed troops to Northern Ireland with a peacekeeping remit.[40] Catholics initially welcomed the British troops, but not for long. The military quickly became 'the perfect target for traditional physical force nationalists, under the cover of

---

38   https://cain.ulster.ac.uk/hmso/cameron.htm#warrant

39   Northern Ireland Parliament, *Disturbances in Northern Ireland*, (Cmd. 532), Belfast, HMSO, September 1969, Paragraph 138; cain.ulster.ac.uk/issues/discrimination/quotes.htm

40   https://cain.ulster.ac.uk/othelem/chron/ch69.htm

protecting the Catholic community from the very real attacks by militant unionists'.[41]

In the June 1970 UK general election Labour lost power to the Tories and the UUP lost two seats, leaving them with eight MPs in Westminster. The new Tory government continued its predecessor's Northern Ireland policy, while Chichester-Clark confirmed that reforms in housing and local government would go ahead and, in what was probably a futile gesture, spoke of welcoming 'loyal Roman Catholics' into the Unionist Party.

When he resigned on 20 March 1971, Chichester-Clark said it was because he could see 'no other way of bringing home to all concerned the realities of the present constitutional, political and security situation'.

Brian Faulkner (1971-74) was next at the helm of the UUP. His greatest political misjudgement was the introduction of internment without trial in August 1971. An intelligence and security disaster, by arresting many who had no paramilitary connections, internment acted as a recruiting agent for the Provisional IRA.

Faulkner admitted in his memoirs that it was a desperate measure, a straw he grasped 'more in hope than confidence' according to historian Joe Lee. To reduce tensions he wanted to ban an Apprentice Boys march, scheduled for 12 August, but feared the loyalist reaction unless he offered an irresistible palliative. 'Faulkner felt himself prisoner of the tribal imperative', says Lee, and chose internment as his palliative.[42]

'An utter disaster'

By 1972, in historian Roy Foster's words, 'half a century of the Protestant supremacist state had come to a bloody and chaotic end'.[43]

UUP leader Brian Faulkner (1971-74) unsurprisingly saw his party's role differently. On his election he declared that direct rule from London would be an utter disaster: 'Our problems can only be satisfactorily solved by Ulster's own people'.[44]

---

41   P. Yeates, 'A Revolutionary Janus', in *Dublin Review of Books*, www.drb.ie/essays/a-revolutionary-janus

42   J.J. Lee, *Ireland 1912-1985: Politics and Society*, Cambridge, Cambridge University Press, 2010, p.437

43   R.F. Foster, *Modern Ireland 1600-1972*, op.cit., p.592

44   H. Kelly, *How Stormont Fell*, Dublin, Gill and MacMillan, 1972, p.19

However, neither 'Ulster's own people' nor any combination of governments and parties succeeded in solving Northern Ireland's biggest problem. Violent conflict continued to be the norm for many years until the 1998 peace agreement mandated ways of working across sectarian political divisions.

A grassroots Women's Peace movement, founded by Mairéad Corrigan and Betty Williams in 1976 in an attempt to shame politicians and the paramilitaries into a solution, found more sympathy abroad than at home.

An attempt to restore devolution, in the form of a 78-seat Belfast legislature elected by proportional representation, saw the UUP top the poll in June 1973, taking 31 seats. That total was deceptive, however, as only 24 seats were 'official' UUP representatives, while the remainder were UUP members opposed to the terms of the UK government White Paper that set up the new Assembly.

An Executive failed to take office until after the Sunningdale Conference, which British Prime Minister Ted Heath and Irish Taoiseach Liam Cosgrave agreed to convene.[45] On 9 December 1973 the Irish and British governments and the Northern Ireland Executive (designate) signed an agreement ratifying a power-sharing executive as well as a Council of Ireland. The latter concept had figured in the Government of Ireland Act 1920 but was never activated – now it was about to spark a crisis.

The Assembly Executive took office on 1 January 1974 with the UUP's Brian Faulkner as leader and the SDLP's Gerry Fitt as deputy leader, but it was short-lived, brought down by two events: the Ulster Unionist Council's rejection of a Council of Ireland and a strike against the Sunningdale Agreement called by the Ulster Workers' Council (UWC).

Modern rebellions

The UWC's 'modern rebellion'[46] against the Sunningdale Agreement paralysed Northern Ireland for 14 days (15-28 May 1974). It drew support from workers in key industries including power generation

---

45 S. Collins & C. Meehan, *Saving the State: Fine Gael from Collins to Varadkar*, Dublin, Gill Books, 2020, p.151

46 M. Dillon, in D. Anderson, *Fourteen May Days: The Inside Story of the Loyalist Strike of 1974*, Dublin, Gill & Macmillan, 1994

and gas and petrol distribution, sectors that were also racked by unrest in Britain. It succeeded in its aim of sabotaging Sunningdale because it was able to harness a 'deep sense of alienation that had grown in the Protestant community during the previous five years'.[47]

On 28 May 1974 Brian Faulkner resigned, the Assembly collapsed and control of Northern Ireland again reverted fully to London.

The other rebellions continued, with little let-up, for another quarter century. The Provisional IRA waged its 'Long War' against British rule, and a plethora of loyalist terror gangs carried out bombings and assassinations. The British Army, having quickly lost its initial popularity with the Catholic civilians it had been deployed to defend, was both a target and a perpetrator in this complex conflict euphemistically known as the Troubles.

There were more than 50,000 quantifiable crimes of extreme violence during the Troubles, including more than 16,200 bombings and almost 37,000 shootings. Known deaths surpassed 3,500, according to research by Malcolm Sutton.[48] Republican paramilitary groups were responsible for 2,058 of those deaths, loyalist paramilitaries for 1,027 and British security forces for 365.

Civilians bore the brunt of the violence and its many associated effects. Of the dead, 1,840 were civilians, while 1,114 were members of British security forces, 397 were republican paramilitaries and 170 loyalist paramilitaries.

A titan crumbles

The UUP, meanwhile, got new leaders – Harry West (1974-79) followed by James Molyneaux (1979-95) – but continued to disintegrate. However, Joe Lee argues, 'it remained true to form even in its disintegration'.[49]

Breakaway parties – Brian Faulkner's Unionist Party of Northern Ireland and the Vanguard Unionist Progressive Party founded by ex-

47   https://cain.ulster.ac.uk/events/uwc/sum.htm
48   M. Sutton, *Bear in Mind These Dead: An Index of Deaths from the Conflict in Northern Ireland*, Belfast, Beyond the Pale Publications, 1994; the database was expanded as new information emerged and is hosted by The Ulster University CAIN project at cain.ulster.ac.uk
49   J.J. Lee, *Ireland 1912-1985: Politics and Society*, op.cit., p.449

minister William Craig – may have appeared ideologically distinct but, says Lee, while Faulkner's party may have been slightly more middle class than Craig's, their real differences were about constitutional/ideological issues, not social or economic policies.

Hunger strikes during 1980-81 by IRA prisoners demanding political status shifted public sympathy considerably and threatened even greater instability, with repercussions in the Republic. The impact on NI politics was epitomised by the victory in a by-election of hunger striker Bobby Sands, who narrowly defeated former UUP leader Harry West, and died shortly afterwards.

In October 1982 Sinn Féin won 10% of the popular vote in elections to an ultimately ineffectual Constitutional Assembly. The UUP won 26 seats and the DUP, with 21, were not far behind.

Prime Minister Margaret Thatcher and Taoiseach Garret FitzGerald signed the landmark Anglo-Irish Agreement in November 1985. This granted the Republic a voice in NI affairs via an intergovernmental conference, a proposal that had emerged from the New Ireland Forum convened by FitzGerald's government. Unionists, including the UUP, had refused to participate in the Forum and were duly traumatised when Prime Minister Thatcher signed the Agreement. UUP leader James Molyneaux and DUP leader Ian Paisley ran a joint anti-Agreement campaign that not only failed, but also reinforced the image of unionists as 'an obdurate people' in the eyes of the public in Britain and beyond.[50]

Peace negotiations

When Molyneaux resigned in 1995 the Unionist Party found a new kind of leader in David Trimble (1995-2005). From a more humble background than any of his predecessors, he became a law lecturer in Queen's University Belfast. His political journey included membership of the Vanguard Progressive Unionist Party. A policies person and devolutionist, he was pleased that Wales and Scotland voted for Tony Blair's devolution project because that strengthened Northern Ireland's case.

Described as 'a Protestant and a seeker of compromise' by the Nobel Institute when it awarded him its Peace Prize, he was willing to compromise for peace but was a tough negotiator, whether

---

50   G. Walker, *A History of the Ulster Unionist Party*, op.cit., pp.234-6

David Trimble, UUP leader 1995-2005, first minister of Northern Ireland 1998-2002 and Nobel Laureate 1998 for his contribution to peace in Northern Ireland. (© Shutterstock)

with British or Irish heads of government or his own complex party and its controllers in the Ulster Unionist Council.

In the peace negotiations Trimble pushed for the Republic to abandon its claim of jurisdiction over Northern Ireland and redefine its national territory. Taoiseach Bertie Ahern responded positively, and Trimble claimed: 'Bertie's given me this opportunity to negotiate the Irish Constitution and to separate nation from state'.[51] Voters in the Republic approved that separation in the 1998 Constitutional referendum.

He knew he had gone a good deal further than many unionists wanted him to, for example in accepting North-South structures. Negotiations almost ran off the rails near the end but, with the intensive last-minute involvement of Prime Minister Blair and Taoiseach Ahern, an agreement was signed on 10 April 1998.[52]

Voters in NI and the Irish Republic gave their approval in simultaneous referendums on 22 May 1998, the UK and Irish parliaments passed enabling legislation and the agreement was deposited with the United Nations as an international treaty.[53]

Full-scale direct rule from London came to an end at midnight on 1/2 December 1999. The UUP was back in government, but this was a different form of power to that the party had enjoyed for half a century. The rules required cross-community power sharing, with leadership shared between unionist and nationalist parties.

---

51   Trimble, in D. Godson, *Himself Alone: David Trimble and the Ordeal of Unionism*, Harper Collins, 2013, chapter 22

52   For an account of the final talks from Trimble's perspective see D. Godson, chapter 24

53   https://peacemaker.un.org/uk-ireland-good-friday98

After the peace

Though the UUP helped to end the conflict it lost out electorally in the new democracy, as did the SDLP (see chapter 9). As the largest party in the new Legislative Assembly the UUP took the first minister role in June 1998, with the SDLP providing the deputy first minister,[54] but in November 2003 the Democratic Unionist Party and Sinn Féin became the largest parties. Furthermore, Trimble lost his own Westminster seat in 2005 and resigned as party leader. By 2022 the UUP had fallen to fourth place in the Assembly, retaining just nine seats and losing its only female MLA.

A succession of men – Reg Empey (2005-10), Tom Elliott (2010-12), Mike Nesbitt (2012-17) and Robin Swann (2017-19) – led the UUP through years of declining popularity. The party's Assembly presence had fallen to 10 seats by 2017, while the DUP had soared to a clear first place. The UUP, once the only party of Ulster unionism at Westminster, found itself without even a single representative in the UK parliament.

More recent leaders – Robin Swann (2017-19), Steve Aiken (2019-21) and Doug Beattie since 2021 – have shown varying degrees of political realism. While still majoring on its core policy of political union with Britain, the Ulster Unionist Party appeared to be trying to find a role in a more pluralist and less religious Northern Ireland, positioning itself as a moderate option to its rivals in the DUP.

The Ulster Unionist Party has come a long way since it constructed a sectarian state. A long way from when Prime Minister James Craig declared: 'All I boast is that we are a Protestant Parliament and Protestant State.'[55] Although not as far as David Trimble expected when he said in 1998: 'I believe we can provide a pluralist parliament for a pluralist people.'[56]

Northern Ireland has certainly become a more pluralist society, in which traditional religious and political affiliations have weakened. It's also one in which the UUP is struggling, both to win elections – having tumbled from 30% of Assembly seats in 1998 to 10% in 2022 – and to clarify its place in a changing society.

---

54 The Assembly and Executive did not function continuously

55 Parliamentary Debates, Northern Ireland House of Commons, Vol. XVI, Cols 1091-95

56 Address by David Trimble, first minister designate, at the Waterfront Hall, Belfast, 3 September 1998, cain.ulster.ac.uk/events/peace/docs/dt3998.htm

A more moderate UUP – dramatically more moderate than the founders of the sectarian 1921 state – was struggling to find a convincing political position in a society in which many who would once have been its natural supporters had deserted it. Liberal unionists were shifting to the political centre, mainly to the Alliance Party, while loyalists mostly backed the DUP or the more hard-line Traditional Unionist Voice.

The constitutional question appeared to be of waning interest to the public. A survey conducted by University of Liverpool in January 2020, for example, found that a mere 5% of respondents chose constitutional issues when asked what mattered most to them, compared with over 80% who cited education, health, jobs or the economy.

Such priorities, echoed in other research, put a more positive gloss on the UUP's seemingly bland approach to doing politics,[57] but if the same themes dominated the everyday activity of most NI politicians, what could differentiate the UUP? The 2022 Assembly election should have concentrated the thoughts of its leadership on that question.

Becoming a pan-unionist party once more, regaining support as broad as in the days of Trimble, never mind in Craig's heyday, might be the stuff of UUP dreams, but its leaders knew it was impossible to recreate the old UUP. The party understandably remained committed to its foundational aim of union with Britain, but there was little public evidence of fresh thinking about how to define and communicate the benefits of that union to the Northern Ireland public.

Recognising the limits of full-blown traditional unionism, how could the UUP re-define what it stands for in a way that might energise its members and supporters? Could it dare to attempt a wide-ranging consultation on possible futures and new relationships, perhaps with the nations of Great Britain? Or would appearing to question the union's solidity inflict too much damage on the UUP's *raison d'etre* and remaining support?

If unification with the Republic was off the agenda – as could be reasonably assumed – what other options could be explored? Professor Peter Shirlow has suggested interdependence, a middle way reflecting 'the reality of lives as lived on the island'. This, Shirlow suggests, could build on the structures of the Belfast Agreement,

---

57   See UUP archives, http://archive.uup.org

the Northern Ireland Protocol and the Dublin government's Shared Island initiative.[58]

Meanwhile, in the short-to-medium term, the UUP may have to accept a role as better representatives of the significant middle-of-the-road cohort of British-identifying citizens – with an eye on representing their interests in the event of a future constitutional shake-up.

Ulster Unionist Party (UUP)	
Founded:	1905
Leaders:	Edward Saunderson 1905-06; Walter H Long 1906-10; Edward Carson 1910-21; James Craig 1921-40; John M Andrews 1940-46; Basil Brooke 1946-63; Terence O'Neill 1963-69; James Chichester-Clark 1969-71; Brian Faulkner 1971-74; Harry West 1974-79; James Molyneaux 1979-95; David Trimble 1995-2005; Reg Empey 2005-10; Tom Elliott 2010-12; Mike Nesbitt 2012-17; Robin Swann 2017-19; Steve Aiken 2019-21; Doug Beattie 2021-
In office:	NI Parliament: 1921-1972. First Minister 1998-2002; in NI Executive 1998-2002, 2007-11, 2007-16, 2016-17, 2020- 22
Affiliations:	European Conservatives and Reformists Party
Elected representatives:	2022: 9 MLAs (9M)

58   P. Shirlow, 'Interdependence is the antidote to Northern Irish politics', *Irish Times*, 1 January 2021

3

Sinn Féin

Political parties, secret armies and a double power push

Overview

Parties operating as Sinn Féin have existed in Ireland since the early 20th century, occasionally of strategic significance, dormant at times, sometimes re-orienting, splitting or competing for the right to the brand, and often associated closely with practitioners of 'armed struggle'.

Few of the several iterations of Sinn Féin could be described as a normal political party, largely because the power behind the party has often been a secretive paramilitary organisation.

An early Sinn Féin benefitted fortuitously from the 1916 rebellion, in which it did not participate. A suddenly expanded party won a landslide victory across Ireland in the 1918 UK general election and took that as a mandate to convene a breakaway parliament in Dublin. This peaceful secession, a revolution via the ballot box, was short-lived. During the following frenzied few years Ireland experienced a war of independence, the partitioning of the country into two states, a civil war, and rifts in Sinn Féin that led to the emergence of new political parties.

The first open divorce was between supporters and opponents of the 1921 Anglo-Irish Treaty. The pro-treaty faction focused on making the new state work and relinquished the Sinn Féin name. In 1926 Éamon de Valera led a major breakaway from the anti-treaty Sinn Féin; his new party, Fianna Fáil, became the most successful in the state for most of the following eight decades.

The remains of Sinn Féin and its offshoots played minor roles at various times, even though there was not always a fully functioning party. Whether active or not there was one constant: the symbiotic relationship with the Irish Republican Army (IRA) that distorted the distinction between political and paramilitary activities.

The party currently known as Sinn Féin claims direct descent from the original party but their most significant ancestor is the breakaway group that established Provisional Sinn Féin in January 1970, mirroring the split on the paramilitary side that produced the Provisional IRA (PIRA). Provisional Sinn Féin was the political face of the PIRA throughout 30 years of bloody conflict in Northern Ireland, known as 'the Troubles', during which the PIRA was responsible for the largest share of killings.

Sinn Féin signed the 1998 Belfast Agreement, having negotiated the ending of hostilities on behalf of the republican paramilitaries. It was a major beneficiary of the peace accord, becoming the main nationalist party in the NI Assembly and, in 2007, ascending to the deputy first minister role in the Executive alongside the largest loyalist party, the DUP. It thus recognised the legitimacy of the Northern Ireland state and Britain's role in Ireland, which it had actively opposed and against which the IRA had fought.

A century after their foundation, the two states whose legitimacy had been rejected by various iterations of Sinn Féin were still in existence. In the Republic, Fine Gael and Fianna Fáil, descended respectively from the pro- and anti-treaty cohorts of Sinn Féin, had long been the dominant parties. The contemporary Sinn Féin was the official opposition in Dáil Éireann, while also sharing power with unionists in Northern Ireland. It appeared to be on the road to becoming a normal political party, but still bore the stigma of its close relationship with the IRA during the bloody 30-years-long Troubles.

The first Sinn Féin

The journey towards the founding of what became known as Sinn Féin began with a set of policies developed by Arthur Griffith, a radical journalist, long-time independence activist and serial political entrepreneur. In November 1905, at a convention of the National Council, a group he had founded in 1903, he presented a set of policies for an independent Ireland.

At the heart of Griffith's proposals lay complementary sets of political and economic ideas: a political arrangement between Ireland

and Britain involving a dual monarchy (known as the 'Hungarian Policy'); and the development of Irish industries behind protective tariff barriers. One of his supporters, Máire Butler – a cousin of the unionist leader Edward Carson – dubbed his proposals 'Sinn Féin' ('Ourselves'), which became the party name.

The National Council was one of several loose nationalist coalitions with which Griffith was associated. He had founded Cumann na nGaedheal (society or association of the Gaels) in 1900 and the National Council in 1903. In April 1907 Cumann na nGaedheal merged with the republican Dungannon Clubs (established in 1905 by Bulmer Hobson and Denis McCullough), to form the Sinn Féin League, and in September 1908 the League and National Council amalgamated, becoming Sinn Féin, the political party.

The new party's aim was 'the re-establishment of the independence of Ireland' – but quite what this meant was ambiguous, according to historian F.S.L. Lyons. The wording was designed to satisfy the two broad categories of nationalists, says Lyons: 'those who would be happy with the restoration of the Kings, Lords and Commons of Ireland, as defined in the 1783 compact, and those of republican bent such as the Dungannon Clubs – two quite different concepts of Irish nationality'.[1]

Table 1: Emergence of first Sinn Féin party

1900	Arthur Griffith founds Cumann na nGaedheal
1903	Arthur Griffith establishes the National Council
1905	Bulmer Hobson & Denis McCullough found the republican Dungannon Clubs
1907	The Dungannon Clubs and Cumann na nGaedheal unite to form the Sinn Féin League
1908	The National Council and Sinn Féin League amalgamate to form the Sinn Féin party

Source: Various

---

1   F.S.L. Lyons, *Ireland since the Famine*, op.cit., p.256

A separatist and a realist

For Griffith the imprecision of Sinn Féin's aim was deliberate, recognising the prevailing reality. He said at the time: 'I am a separatist. The Irish people are not separatists. I do not think they can be united behind a separatist policy. But I do think it is possible to unite them on this policy.' [2]

If the grand political aim was vague enough to satisfy both royalists and republicans, the constitution's appendix offered a clear direction of travel in the form of practical proposals for economic development, establishing the institutions of an independent state, and breaking the link with British politics. The call for non-recognition of the British Parliament would assume major political importance after the party won a clear majority in the 1918 general election, abstained from taking their seats in London, and convened a parliament in Dublin.

The original Sinn Féin party might have gone the way of Arthur Griffith's other ventures, perhaps mutating into the next project, if events had not transformed the political environment. Initially Sinn Féin was just another group on the nationalist spectrum, but that began to change with London's heavy-handed response to the 1916 Rising (with which Griffith was not involved).

Lee summed up what happened: 'The home rule press and the British succeeded in investing Griffith's moribund Sinn Féin with a degree of authority it had never managed to achieve on its own, by the simple device of branding all rebels Sinn Féiners.' [3]

Before that re-branding Sinn Féin had made little impact. In the first by-election in Ireland after the rebellion – 'in the very representative nationalist constituency of West Cork in November 1916' – a candidate describing himself as a Sinn Féiner came bottom of the poll.[4] Then the tide started to turn: from February 1917 candidates running on the Sinn Féin ticket began winning by-elections.

Momentum was building, but few could have anticipated the electoral landslide of 1918, and it might not have occurred without the electoral reform implemented for the first time that year, or

---

2   Ibid., p.256
3   J.J. Lee, *Ireland 1912-1985: Politics and Society*, op.cit., p.38
4   R. Kee, *The Green Flag: A History of Irish Nationalism*, London, Penguin Books, 2000

without the takeover and professionalisation of the party by 1916 veterans, notably Éamon de Valera.

A new Sinn Féin

Two significant political conventions took place in 1917. Sinn Féin boycotted the first of these which, convened by the British government, met from July 1917 until March 1918 to consider the future administration of Ireland. Afterwards the leader of the southern unionists said that he would not have attended either if he had realised that it was committed in advance to partition of the island.[5]

A different convention, in October 1917, signalled the transformation of Sinn Féin into a potential new political force. Attended by some 2,000 representatives of Sinn Féin clubs, it adopted a new constitution and re-focused its direction. Arthur Griffith ceded leadership of the party he had founded to Éamon de Valera. De Valera's collaborator in the project, Michael Collins, barely scraped onto the executive, but his presence gave influence to the men secretly preparing for a military struggle.

The new constitution declared that the party would seek to secure international recognition of Ireland as an independent republic, adding that, having achieved that recognition, 'the Irish people may by referendum freely choose their own form of Government'.[6]

However, Sinn Féin's 'unresolved ambiguities' remained unresolved, says Robert Kee. The opposition to one proposal – that the party should make use of 'every available means to make impotent the power of England to hold Ireland in subjugation by military force or otherwise' – pointed to a fundamental fault line between those committed to constitutional means and those willing to resort to arms. De Valera placated the moderates, but the division between democrats and militarists would persist.[7]

Éamon de Valera wasn't just elected president of Sinn Féin in October 1917. At a concurrent convention, he also became president of the Irish Volunteers militia. Thus, says Joe Lee, 'blurring the

---

5   R. Kee, *The Green Flag: A History of Irish Nationalism*, op.cit., p.615
6   https://celt.ucc.ie/published/E900007/text002.html
7   R. Kee, *The Green Flag: A History of Irish Nationalism*, op.cit., pp.609-10

differences between the political and paramilitary movements'.[8] That symbiotic relationship between paramilitaries and Sinn Féin would continue to be crucial.

The reconstitution – or takeover – of Sinn Féin followed six months of bargaining between nationalist organisations. De Valera led the veterans of the Easter Rising into a new political struggle, says Fitzpatrick, adding: 'The creation of an open organisation not committed to violence, representing a broad coalition of nationalist factions, was an

Sinn Féin poster from the 1918 general election, the first in which women could vote.

astonishing sequel to a violent and conspiratorial insurrection'.[9]

De Valera was central to the machinations that rebooted Sinn Féin, to Sinn Féin's rise to political supremacy in 1918 and to Irish politics for some 40 years. He was, according to Ferriter, the 'most polarising and significant politician of twentieth-century Ireland'.[10] Lee considered him 'the most subtle Irish political intelligence of his generation',[11] although his political dominance from 1926 onwards occurred outside the confines of Sinn Féin.

Electoral triumph

The 1918 election was 'an act of largely peaceful secession' as Fintan O'Toole wrote on the century of the election that gave Sinn Féin a victory on a scale far beyond its expectations.[12] The results were

---

8   J.J. Lee, *Ireland 1912-1985: Politics and Society*, op.cit., p.38
9   D. Fitzpatrick, *The Two Irelands 1912-1939*, New York, Oxford University Press, 1998, p.66
10   D. Ferriter, *Judging Dev: A Reassessment of the Life and Legacy of Éamon de Valera*, Dublin, Royal Irish Academy, 2019, p.3
11   J. J. Lee, *Ireland 1912-1985: Politics and Society*, op.cit., p.150
12   F. O'Toole, 'The 1918 election was an amazing moment for Ireland', *Irish Times*, 14 December 2018

Members of the First Dáil Éireann, convened in 1919.

seismic but, as O'Toole added: 'Such is the drama of violence that it is easy to forget that the most important moment in the creation of an independent Irish State was a democratic election'.

Of Ireland's 105 seats in the Westminster parliament, Sinn Féin won 73 – though with less than 50% of votes cast – while the Irish Parliamentary Party took six and unionists 26 seats respectively, and Labour had stood aside to let the election be a plebiscite on independence. The actual number of Sinn Féin MPs elected was just 69, as some candidates contested and won more than one constituency. There were only two women among the Sinn Féin candidates and one was elected: Constance Markievicz became the first female MP in the history of the Westminster parliament but never sat in its chamber as, in line with Sinn Féin policy, she was committed to abstaining and, anyway, was still in prison for her part in the 1916 Rising.

The election results suggested a near total transfer of allegiance to Sinn Féin from the Irish Parliamentary Party, which had won 73 of Ireland's seats in December 1910; its seats tally had ranged from 69 to 85 over the previous 25 years. That perception was largely true, due to a substantial movement of IPP activists to Sinn Féin, but there was another highly significant factor.

Crucially, the 1918 Representation of the People Act gave the vote to men over the age of 21 without a property qualification and to women over the age of 30, though with property and residential conditions attached. This transformed the Irish electorate: the number eligible to vote soared from 700,000 in 1910 to 1.93 million in 1918. The new voters were 'primarily people who had had no voice in politics: women, the young and the poor'.[13]

Breakaway parliament

Having pledged to abstain from Westminster, Sinn Féin called its available MPs to a meeting in Dublin on 7 January 1919. Of those at liberty (35 were in prison) 29 attended and resolved: 'That we, the Republican Members of the Irish Constituencies, in accordance with the National Will, are empowered to call together the Dáil Éireann and proceed to act accordingly.'[14]

All elected MPs, including unionists, were invited to the opening session of the First Dáil on 21 January 1919, but foreign journalists reporting on the breakaway parliament outnumbered the 27 elected members in attendance, all of them Sinn Féin.[15]

The Dáil met openly until the British authorities banned it as a 'dangerous association' in mid-September, after which it operated in secret, as did its civil service. Sinn Féin was banned in November 1919, together with the Irish Volunteers, Cumann na mBan (a women's militia) and the Gaelic League (a cultural organisation).

Sinn Féin hoped to gain international recognition for an Irish Republic at the Allies' post-war Peace Conference but its delegates failed in that mission. It had better results at home, winning control of a majority of local councils in the 1920 elections, organised by the British authorities and held experimentally under proportional representation.

In London, the 1920 Government of Ireland Act legislated for the creation of two parliaments in Ireland while asserting Britain's sovereignty. It also provided for a Council of Ireland to facilitate cooperation and joint actions between the two parliaments and for a possible all-Ireland parliament by agreement.[16]

---

13   Ibid.
14   https://www.dail100.ie/en/timeline/
15   https://www.dail100.ie/en/people/
16   www. legislation.gov.uk/ukpga/1920/67/pdf s /ukpga_19200067_en.pdf

Partition was implemented and elections convened for the two Home Rule parliaments established by the Act. The result showed the polarising strength of the two main blocs. In southern Ireland there were no actual electoral contests: Sinn Féin took 124 seats unopposed, while the other four went to independent unionists representing the University of Dublin. In Northern Ireland the Ulster Unionist Party won 40 of 52 seats, to six each for Sinn Féin and the Nationalist Party (successor of the Irish Parliamentary Party).

The two parliaments were convened in June 1921. The Belfast body lasted until 1972, while the parliament in Dublin adjourned *sine die* and was dissolved in 1922, leaving an alternative story to play out.

Treaty and traumas

Meanwhile, from January 1919 guerrilla attacks had escalated into what became Ireland's War of Independence. It ended in a truce between the nationalist rebels and the British government in July 1921. The Second Dáil appointed plenipotentiaries to discuss final truce terms in London. The Irish delegation, led by Arthur Griffiths, signed a treaty on 6 December 1921, but did so without referring it

Irish delegation to the 1921 Anglo-Irish Treaty negotiations and their support staff. (© National Library of Ireland)

back to Dáil Éireann president and Sinn Féin leader Éamon de Valera for approval. When the Dáil ratified the treaty on 7 January 1922 (by 64 votes to 57), de Valera resigned his Dáil post and led the anti-treaty members of Sinn Féin out of the Dáil and into opposition.

The Irish delegation to the treaty talks had plenipotentiary powers but their decision to sign has been debated ever since. Would the outcome have been different if de Valera had gone to London? Probably not. De Valera had already met British PM David Lloyd George and failed to reach agreement with him. Interestingly, the then Sinn Féin leader appeared more interested in the oath of loyalty to the British monarch than in partition, which republicans have put centre stage ever since.

In the June 1922 election to the parliament of what was by then the Irish Free State, the pro-treaty wing of Sinn Féin, led by Michael Collins, won 58 seats while Éamon de Valera's anti-treaty bloc took 36. The Labour Party and others who accepted the treaty won a further 34 seats between them. The numbers pointed to a clear majority in favour of getting on with the business of building the new state, but anti-treaty Sinn Féin was not on board.

A vicious civil war ensued (June 1922 to May 1923) that left its mark on Irish politics for generations. The rift in Sinn Féin that led to the civil war only reached closure of a sort in 2020 when the parties descended from the two sides entered government together, blocking the ambitions of the contemporary iteration of Sinn Féin.

When the pro-treaty side constituted itself as a new political party it considered using Sinn Féin as its title but opted for Cumann na nGaedheal, the name of another nationalist group created by Arthur Griffith, founder of the original Sinn Féin. De Valera's anti-treaty side retained the Sinn Féin label for the immediate future.

De Valera splits

De Valera had an epiphany while imprisoned in 1923: tired of the mentality of the gunmen, he opted for constitutional politics. Sinn Féin must recognise the will of the majority and accept the new state, he concluded, or else face stagnation. He failed, however, to persuade a majority at a Sinn Féin convention that the oath of allegiance to the English Crown was merely an empty formula – one that could be changed if they gained power. He resigned his presidency of Sinn

Féin in 1926 and founded Fianna Fáil, which went on to become the most successful party in the southern state.

After the 1927 Dáil election, Sinn Féin was reduced to a purist rump that did not contest another southern election until 1957. For a time Sinn Féin and the IRA took different positions towards Fianna Fáil, with the IRA tending to support the new party electorally; but by 1936 relations had soured and a Fianna Fáil government banned the IRA.

The wilderness years

In Northern Ireland the Ulster Unionist Party established its hegemony and for half a century there was little political space for nationalists. In the Free State many republicans switched their support from Sinn Féin to Fianna Fáil, and expected their elected representatives – Teachtaí Dála (TDs) – to play a full part in parliamentary affairs.

Some republicans embraced left-wing activism during this interregnum, at times founding new groups such as Saor Éire (Free Ireland), launched in 1931 with the backing of the IRA leadership, with the aim of establishing a 'Workers' and Working Farmers' Republic'.[17]

The adoption of a new constitution in 1937 legitimised the Free State for some in Sinn Féin and the IRA, as acknowledged by the latter's former chief of staff Seán MacBride who left the IRA after the new constitution received the backing of a majority of voters in a referendum.

The tale took a fantastical turn in 1938. An increasingly isolated IRA wanted to launch an anti-partition military campaign and asked a group of former Sinn Féin TDs, ex-members of the Second Dáil who believed themselves to be the true government of all Ireland, to give them the right to 'declare war' on Britain. These intransigents duly passed on their 'governmental authority' to the IRA Army Council, which treasured it down the decades.

The IRA's 'war on Britain' took the form of a bombing campaign in English cities from January 1939 to August 1940. During the Second World War hundreds of IRA members were interned without trial, some were executed and others died on hunger strike.

---

17   M. McInerney, *Peadar O'Donnell, Irish Social Rebel*, Dublin, O'Brien Press, 1974, p.116

Having effectively retreated into elitist isolation for nearly 30 years, when Sinn Féin re-engaged with politics it was in association with an armed campaign by the IRA which had begun a focused revival in the 1950s, re-arming by raiding British Army barracks in the north and in England.

Sinn Féin won two seats in Northern Ireland in the 1955 UK general election, largely by shaming the Nationalist Party into standing aside to give it a clear run against unionist candidates.[18] Those electoral wins boosted the IRA's new campaign, launched in December 1956 with a series of attacks on targets in Northern Ireland. One by-product was the addition of new names to the pantheon of republican martyrs: Seán South and Fergal O'Hanlon, killed while involved in an attack on a barracks, received the ultimate accolade of huge funerals and adulatory ballads. The border and Northern Ireland, however, remained intact.

The campaign and deaths resuscitated republican emotions sufficiently for Sinn Féin to win four seats in the 1957 Dáil election, but their TDs refused to take their seats and lost them in 1961, by which time the border campaign had fizzled out. It had refreshed an old and anti-democratic undercurrent, the use of paramilitary action to achieve political aims, but it also led the IRA to reconsider its methods.

New direction, new split

In the 1960s a re-energised Sinn Féin began campaigning on social and socio-economic issues. This approach, in the republican socialist tradition, originated in the IRA but took operational form through Sinn Féin.

According to the historian Padraig Yeates, the republican movement at this time was 'entering its most experimental and least militaristic phase, not out of any conscious decision to abandon armed struggle but in order to find a role that would make it relevant in modern Ireland'.[19]

Campaigns such as fish-ins, housing protests, ground rent strikes, and an emigrants' rights campaign in Britain drew new blood into the

---

18   J. Bowyer Bell, *The Secret Army: A History of the IRA 1916-1970*, London, Sphere Books, 1972, p.318

19   P. Yeates, 'A Revolutionary Janus', op.cit.

old party. What worked was built upon, what didn't was discarded, says Yeates, who joined the republican movement in his teens. The most significant was the Northern Ireland civil rights campaign, which, Yeates claims, 'worked so well it plunged the whole country into crisis'.

To suggest that the civil rights campaign was responsible for the crisis is questionable, if that is what Yeates meant. Undoubtedly this new approach to old problems triggered a violent response from the entrenched sectarianism it was challenging, and the northern state was certainly plunged into crisis.

Early by-products of the emerging conflict included splits in the IRA and Sinn Féin. A group of hawkish hardliners left the main body of the IRA in December 1969 and a similar, possibly identical group walked out of the Sinn Féin Ard Fheis (annual conference) in January 1970. They became known as the 'Provisionals' or 'Provos' – Provisional Sinn Fein and Provisional IRA (PIRA) – while those remaining were dubbed the 'Officials'.

As Yeates notes, the republican movement was no more prepared than anyone else for the explosion of sectarian violence in Northern Ireland. He is probably right to suggest that the split within the republican movement in 1969/70 might have been delayed if it had been possible to defend Belfast's Catholic communities more effectively from sectarian attacks. However, as he also notes, 'a split was probably inevitable given the conscious decision of the IRA leadership in Belfast from the mid-1960s onwards to set its face against sectarianism'.

In August 1969, following the so-called Battle of the Bogside in Derry and vicious sectarian attacks in Belfast during which many, mainly Catholics, were forced to flee their homes, Britain deployed troops to Northern Ireland with a peacekeeping remit.[20]

Catholics initially welcomed the presence of British troops to enforce peace lines between Protestant and Catholic areas, but the welcome was short-lived. It quickly became clear that the UK government had 'provided the perfect target for traditional physical force nationalists, under the cover of protecting the Catholic community from the very real attacks by militant unionists'.[21]

---

20   https://cain.ulster.ac.uk/othelem/chron/ch69.htm
21   P. Yeates, 'A Revolutionary Janus', op.cit.

Conflicting journeys

The two claimants to the Sinn Féin title took dramatically different paths after their 1970 split. Official Sinn Féin faced firmly leftwards, fighting elections and moving ever further from militarism. Provisional Sinn Féin partnered paramilitaries through decades of violence that left thousands dead, while building a strong political base in its northern heartlands.

Official Sinn Féin continued the social agitation approach of its 1960s revival and won its first Dáil seat in 1981. Ideological and tactical debate led to name changes, first to Sinn Féin the Workers' Party (SFWP) in 1977, and simply The Workers' Party (WP) in 1982.

Following the collapse of the Soviet Union tensions between the Marxist-inclined and social democratic factions in the party came to a head. In 1992, six of the seven Workers' Party TDs left to form Democratic Left (DL). Joining the 1994-97 'rainbow coalition' government with Fine Gael and Labour gave DL some policy influence, such as an update of the social welfare system, and bolstered Dublin's anti-sectarian approach to Northern Ireland.

Proinsias de Rossa, the DL leader, sought opportunities to open communications with unionism and his stance was recognised when, on a visit to Belfast, Ulster Unionist Party leader David Trimble invited him to visit UUP headquarters. Trimble's invitation to this ex-IRA man was interpreted as a signal that the UUP would talk to those who had genuinely embraced constitutionalism.

Out of government after the 1997 election the DL's next significant step was a merger with Labour in 1999. A party descended directly from Sinn Féin joined the heir of a different but parallel tradition with which, by then, it shared social democratic views. This formal alliance carried some echoes of collaborative relationships during the early revolutionary period but signalled more practical political dilemmas on the cusp of the 21st century.

Rafter suggests that a lack of finance pushed DL towards this merger. However, the growing presence of Provisional Sinn Féin in the working-class communities that elected DL deputies – 'but within which, in the main, it was not organised'[22] – was likely to have been an important consideration.

---

22   S. Millar in *History Ireland*, May/June 2011, reviewing K. Rafter, *Democratic Left: the Life and Death of an Irish Political Party*, Irish Academic Press, 2011

Tomás Mac Giolla TD (1982-92) became president of Sinn Féin in 1962 and continued as leader of Official Sinn Féin after the 1970 split, and of The Workers' Party following the party's name change.

Democratic Left went on to play key roles in Labour, quickly providing a president, two party leaders and a deputy leader in what has been described as a reverse takeover. It may have been a marriage of convenience between two parties, both of them at a low point organisationally. Unsurprisingly, perhaps, the union was not all sweetness and light, with 'old' Labour stalwarts at times dramatically at odds with their 'DL' leadership.

The Workers' Party's sole remaining TD, former Sinn Féin president Tomás Mac Giolla, lost his seat in 1992. His much-reduced party achieved no further parliamentary success, and a dwindling number of local councillors suggested they had little prospect of future relevance.

The Provo path

After its launch in 1970, Provisional Sinn Féin positioned itself as a radically different alternative to the left wing and modernising Officials, although the latter continued to operate on the same terrain. Taunting their rival for being unable to protect Catholics against attacks by Protestant loyalists, the Provisionals were soon the dominant force.

Provisional Sinn Féin garnered growing support in beleaguered Catholic communities, mainly in urban working class areas where sectarian attacks were a constant risk. The symbiosis with the IRA – never clearer than during the Troubles – became a prime advantage to them, and recruitment to both wings of the republican movement, military and political, was often concurrent, reinforcing their claim to be protecting their communities from attack.

The conflict soon surged beyond the boundaries of inner city communities, engulfing all of Northern Ireland to varying degrees.

It also reached beyond NI's borders, including loyalist car bombs in Dublin and Monaghan in the Republic and IRA bombs in pubs in Birmingham and Guildford in England.

Sinn Féin and IRA membership soared as the conflict deepened, while the wider population lived in fear, caught between ruthless paramilitaries of opposing loyalties. British troops, sent in to keep the peace, failed to do so and too often worked with inadequate intelligence, facilitated loyalist terrorism or committed atrocities themselves.

Internment in August 1971, when the British Army and RUC rounded up 340 men overnight to be imprisoned without trial, acted as a recruiting agent for the IRA. Activist and journalist Éamon McCann claimed: 'the IRA had nowhere near 340 members that night. Potentially, though it had ten times that number the day after'.[23] The killing of ten innocent civilians in Belfast during August 1971 (the 'Ballymurphy Massacre') and the deaths of 13 civil rights marchers in Derry on 30 January 1972 ('Bloody Sunday') – in both cases by soldiers of the 1st Battalion of the Parachute Regiment – likely had the same effect.

The IRA's role as protectors of Catholics mutated into a war against Britain, presented as a struggle to get British troops out of Ireland. In reality, anyone not fully onside with that aim was seen as a legitimate target. This could include aggression against its political rivals such as the moderate nationalist SDLP (Social Democratic and Labour Party).

Tactics grew increasingly brutal. Both loyalists and Provisionals used car bombs, but some claimed that it was the IRA that invented the proxy bomb: the hijacking of a car and its driver who would be forced to drive the car filled with explosives to a target such as a military checkpoint. In the words of a character in Benedict Kiely's short novel *Proxopera*: 'Not even the Mafia thought of the proxy bomb'.[24]

Index of death

The full effect of the Troubles in its many forms may never be known, but there were more than 50,000 quantifiable crimes of extreme

---

23 D. Ferriter, *The Transformation of Ireland 1900-2000*, op.cit., p.625
24 B. Kiely, *Proxopera*, London, Quartet Books, 1979, p.58

violence, including more than 16,200 bombings and almost 37,000 shootings.

One source, in its dry comprehensive detail, helps to memorialise those who lost their lives. Malcolm Sutton has compiled a database of available information about the deaths that resulted from the conflict between 14 July 1969 and 31 December 2001. The information, known as the Sutton Index of Deaths, was first published in 1994 as *Bear in Mind These Dead: An Index of Deaths from the Conflict in Ireland 1969-93.* [25] He later expanded the database adding new information that emerged.[26]

The Sutton Index records 3,532 Troubles-related deaths. Republican paramilitary groups were responsible for 2,058 of them, loyalist paramilitaries for 1,027 and British security forces for 365. Five were attributable to Irish security forces and the identities of the killers of a further 77 were unknown.

Civilians accounted for 1,840 of the deaths; 1,114 were members of British security forces, 397 republican paramilitaries, 170 loyalist paramilitaries; and the Irish security forces lost 11 members.

O'Leary notes that were an equivalent proportion of deaths to occur in the United States they would amount to about half a million people.[27]

Table 2(a): Responsibility for Troubles-related deaths (14 July 1969-31 December 2001)

Summary of organisations responsible	Deaths
Republican Paramilitary	2,058
Loyalist Paramilitary	1,027
British Security	365
Irish Security	5
Not known	77
Total known deaths	3,532

Source: cain.ulster.ac.uk/sutton/index.html

25 M. Sutton, *Bear in Mind These Dead*, op.cit.

26 Ulster University hosts the online index at cain.ulster.ac.uk/sutton/index.html

27 B. O'Leary, *A Treatise on Northern Ireland, Vol. 3: Consociation and Confederation. From Antagonism to Accommodation*, Oxford University Press, 2020

Table 2(b): Troubles-related deaths - status of victims (14 July 1969-31 December 2001)

Summary status of those killed	Deaths
Civilian	1,840
British Security	1,114
Republican Paramilitary	397
Loyalist Paramilitary	170
Irish Security	11
Total known deaths	3,532

Source: cain.ulster.ac.uk/sutton/index.html

Having analysed the full data and considered the roles of the British state, the Irish state, the Royal Ulster Constabulary, the Ulster Defence Regiment, the British Army, Official Sinn Féin and IRA, Provisional Sinn Féin and PIRA, People's Democracy and others, Liam Kennedy concluded that the primary responsibility lay with 'the Provisional IRA and their associates'.

Kennedy and others say the conflict did not have to happen, because Northern Ireland was reformable.[28] By 1969, the British government had conceded most of the civil rights movement's objectives; it had made commitments to major reforms including of electoral laws, employment practices and housing allocations, but instead of a peaceful implementation of reforms, Northern Ireland got 30 years of terror.

Destination: Dáil power

With an eye to building a political power base in the Republic, in November 1986 Provisional Sinn Féin decided to abandon abstentionism in relation to Dáil Éireann. Martin McGuinness, a leading member of Sinn Féin described in media reports as being close to the leadership of the Provisional IRA, told delegates that when the IRA had met to discuss the issue a month earlier a minority

---

28   L. Kennedy, *Who was Responsible for The Troubles? The Northern Ireland Conflict*, Belfast, McGill-Queen's University Press, 2020

disagreed with the decision but pledged that they would not form a breakaway group.[29]

Despite that promise, a walkout by abstentionist hardliners occurred, led by names familiar from the 1970 equivalent. They proceeded to set up a new party, Republican Sinn Féin, but in contrast to 1970 they said they wanted to establish a 'democratic socialist republic'.[30]

The IRA may have given the seal of approval to dumping abstentionism, but they weren't about to dump their arms. Rather, support for the move was contingent – at least in part – on continuing the 'ballot and armalite' strategy of fighting elections while waging war – and continue they did.

In November 1987 one of the most notorious bombings of the Troubles occurred. During the annual Remembrance Day ceremony in Enniskillen, County Fermanagh, a bomb planted by the IRA exploded at the War Memorial killing 11 people and injuring 63 more, one of whom died later.[31] All of the dead were Protestants, most were elderly, and all were civilians apart from one off-duty policeman.[32]

Peace at last

The road to peace was long and tortuous. The most significant, most persistent promoter of peace talks with Sinn Féin and the IRA was John Hume, leader of the SDLP. Hume's Nobel Peace Prize citation notes that he 'devoted a great deal of energy to drawing the leader of the IRA, Gerry Adams, and the British Government, into the negotiations'.[33] This was despite the damage to his reputation and that of the SDLP and the harassment his own party suffered at the hands of the Provisionals.

The fact that Martin McGuiness and Gerry Adams were willing to hold talks indicated a new strategic outlook within the Provisionals' political leadership, if not necessarily on the military side. The realists amongst them had seemingly realised they could not win the war

---

29 D. Hearst, 'Sinn Féin votes to fight for seats in the Dáil: IRA political wing to take seats in Irish parliament', *The Guardian*, 3 November 1986

30 https://www.theguardian.com/theguardian/from-the-archive-blog/2020/feb/09/sinn-fein-votes-to-abandon-abstentionism-1986

31 https://cain.ulster.ac.uk/othelem/chron/ch87.htm

32 https://cain.ulster.ac.uk/cgi-bin/dyndeaths.pl?querytype=date&day=8&month=11&year=1987

33 www.nobelprize.org/prizes/peace/1998/hume/facts/

against the British forces. They had also realised that people wanted peace.

Following the December 1993 intergovernmental agreement known as the Downing Street Declaration,[34] talks led to an IRA ceasefire in August 1994. This ended in February 1996 when the IRA detonated a lorry bomb in London's Docklands.

When renewed negotiations were nearing completion McGuiness and Adams were at times wrong-footed by the Army Council. In September 1997, for example, after Sinn Féin had signed up to the Mitchell principles on democracy and nonviolence, the IRA issued a statement saying it 'would have problems' with sections of the principles[35] – a move that reportedly surprised the Sinn Féin representatives. The IRA's long delay in decommissioning weapons after the formal signing of the Belfast Agreement also proved problematic for all involved.

Finally, the peace accord was signed on 10 April 1998, in two parts: a multilateral agreement between the Irish and UK governments and the major parties in Northern Ireland including Sinn Féin (but not the loyalist DUP); and a bilateral international agreement between the two governments. Voters in Northern Ireland and the Republic backed it in separate referendums, by a majority of 71.2% in NI and by 94.5% in the Republic, which also dropped its constitutional claim to the northern territory.

There was one more major republican atrocity after the peace agreement was signed. In August 1998 a car bomb killed 29 people and injured 220 in the town of Omagh. The dead included children and two Spanish tourists. The perpetrators were dissident republicans, calling themselves the Real IRA, who opposed the ceasefire and peace agreement.

New realism, new treaty

The peace agreement became effective on 2 December 1999, and Sinn Féin became a party of political realists. After decades dedicated to opposing Northern Ireland's very existence as a political entity, it joined an Assembly and Executive operating under Westminster's

---

34 https://cain.ulster.ac.uk/events/peace/docs/dsd151293.htm
35 D. Godson, *Himself Alone: David Trimble and the Ordeal Of Unionism*, op.cit.

authority, effectively recognising the legitimacy of the northern state and of Britain's role in Ireland.

In 1998 the people of Northern Ireland wanted peace, and Sinn Féin knew this. Using electoral survey data Jocelyn Evans and Jonathan Tonge argue that Sinn Féin voters were leading the way and the party was following them; this turnabout helped it capture majority nationalist support.[36] The eventual result was the power-sharing partnership with the Democratic Unionist Party that began in 2007 when Ian Paisley and Martin McGuinness became first and deputy first ministers of Northern Ireland.

It looked as if the Sinn Féin of the long northern conflict might be on the road to becoming a mainstream party, following the well-trodden path of Éamon de Valera, Seán MacBride, and others who left behind their paramilitary past.

Electoral evolution

From an early stage in the Troubles both the new iteration of Sinn Féin and the Republican Clubs through which Official Sinn Féin operated in NI offered themselves to their communities as *de facto* local representatives. Ferriter describes this as 'both wings of the IRA ... offering advice on business normally the preserve of local authorities, a telling signal of the power vacuum that existed and republicans' determination to fill it'.

Ferriter also suggests that another actor influenced the political allegiance of Catholics in that period: 'the Catholic Church was quick to move to ensure the republican left did not control community associations in Belfast'.[37]

Provisional Sinn Féin was increasingly more successful than Official Sinn Féin at building a base to win the ballot box war, and its advantage began to pay serious dividends after 1998. In the first elections to the newly established Northern Ireland Assembly, the Provisionals – by then the sole owner of the Sinn Féin title – took 18 seats, making it the fourth largest party. Its vote share rose in succeeding elections and in 2007 Martin McGuinness became deputy first minister in the Assembly's Executive, sharing power with

---

36   J. Evans and J. Tonge, *From Abstentionism to Enthusiasm: Sinn Féin, Nationalist Electors and Support for Devolved Power-sharing in Northern Ireland*, 2012, pp. 39-57

37   D. Ferriter, *The Transformation of Ireland 1900-2000*, op.cit., p.624

the DUP, a hard-line unionist party that had not signed the peace agreement.

The party also won five seats in the 2010 UK general election, though it continued to abstain from taking its seats in Westminster.

While its direction of travel had been signalled in 1986 when it abandoned abstentionism it was only when the peace process was seen to be succeeding that Sinn Féin began to take off electorally in the Republic. From one seat in 1997, its Dáil presence rose gradually to 14 in 2011, a year of major political upheaval in the Republic when voters punished the established parties for the austerity that followed the financial crash of 2008. That wasn't, as some expected, a one-off for Sinn Féin, which went on to win 23 seats in 2016, though few, even within the party, foresaw their dramatic rise to 37 of the 160 Dáil seats in February 2020.

How did it manage that, and did it signify that Sinn Féin was on the final lap of a journey towards becoming a normal party and entering government?

Partly it was by appealing to a post-Troubles generation seeking solutions to contemporary problems, and also by providing tough-talking opposition to the establishment parties that had been tainted by their failure to solve those problems.

A fresh image helped too, epitomised in Mary Lou MacDonald, its leader since 2018. Described as 'the embodiment of educated, Dublin 6 middle-class privilege who peddles a persuasive anti-establishment line',[38] she began her political career in Fianna Fáil. In the Republic's 2020 election even unlikely voters were willing to 'give Mary Lou a chance' – invariably Mary Lou, not Sinn Féin *per se*.

Then there was the matter of a bank balance any party would envy, involving a multi-million pounds legacy from an eccentric Englishman, possible Irish-American donations, and perhaps, as some allege, a nest egg from its shady past.

Becoming a normal party?

Yet, the idea that Sinn Féin is no ordinary political party lingered. It still carried the baggage of the 30-year northern conflict during which it was an apologist for the Provisional IRA. Recent successes, however, suggest the reputational damage was fading.

---

38 K. Sheridan, www.irishtimes.com/life-and-style/people/kathy-sheridan-mary-lou-is-an-enigma-with-leadership-in-hersights-1.4596242

Sinn Féin leaders Martin McGuinness (left) and Gerry Adams (right) with their successors Mary Lou McDonald and Michelle O'Neill. January 2017. (© Sinn Féin)

Over time it has softened its public support for the PIRA, although party leaders continued to glorify 'heroes' of the 'struggle' and participated in militaristic funerals even when that involved flouting Covid-19 lockdown regulations. This tendency to praise superannuated or dead men of violence more than two decades after the peace treaty caused concern, but seemingly less so to many younger voters who grew up in peacetime.

On one side of the normality balance sheet the party supports the peace agreement, EU membership and progressive causes such as gay marriage and abortion rights, meaning it is in tune with a majority in the Republic. Promoting progressive causes doesn't necessarily endear them to a sometimes more conservative electorate in the north, however, which may be why their stance in the NI Assembly has not always been quite so liberal as across the border.

'Tiocfaidh ár lá' ('Our day will come') is a mantra frequently used by Sinn Féin. It looked as if their day had dawned when they won 37 seats (of 160) in the February 2020 general election to Dáil Éireann. They were already the second largest party in the Northern Ireland Assembly, sharing power with the lead unionist party, and a breakthrough into government in Dublin suddenly looked achievable

– but their prize in 2020 was the role of official opposition to a three-party coalition government.

The 2020 election showed that a sizeable slice of the electorate was prepared to trust Sinn Féin – or perhaps, as vox pop interviewees often said, to 'give Mary Lou a chance'. Mary Lou McDonald, its first female leader and a Dubliner, had rebranded Sinn Féin to an extent unimaginable under her predecessor Gerry Adams. The party tapped into widespread discontent on social issues from housing to childcare and offered itself to the electorate as the party of change.

When more than 5,300 voters across the state were asked in an exit poll[39] which issues most influenced their voting decision, most chose health or housing/homelessness. This seemed to suggest that the shock Sinn Féin breakthrough was mainly about frustration with establishment parties that had failed to solve such problems.

The Sinn Féin manifesto had made clear that its core political objective was 'to achieve Irish Unity and the referendum on Unity which is the means to secure this' and after the election the party proceeded to put the issue of national unification centre stage. They also made the most of their position as the official opposition to attack the government hard and often on issues of known public concern, although their position on climate change verged on populist and their opposition to construction proposals may have worsened the housing crisis they continually denounced.

It was increasingly assumed that Sinn Féin could enter government at the next scheduled election in the Republic, but forming a government in Dublin is no easy matter. For decades the electorate, though at times volatile, has mostly favoured the middle ground, resulting in coalitions and a sprinkling of minority governments. Parties have soared and sunk, and there was no certainty that Sinn Féin would be an exception.

There were lingering doubts about whether or not Sinn Féin could be trusted to behave as a normal democratic party. Some commentators were more scathing than others, suggesting, for example, that they had not cast off the habits of their years as the Provisional IRA's political voice. Others were more sanguine even if

---

39 *Irish Times*, 9 February 2020, https://www.irishtimes.com/news/politics/detailed-election-2020-exit-poll-results-how-voters-answered-15-questions-1.4167016

not convinced that those who voted Sinn Féin in 2020 would stay with the party.

Some argued that the main parties were dying and Sinn Féin was a strong player in the succession stakes. To grasp that opportunity they needed to convince enough voters that they had credible solutions to the problems that widened their appeal in 2020.

A symbolic breakthrough

On 5 May 2022 Sinn Féin became the first nationalist party to top the poll in a region-wide Northern Ireland election since the SDLP in 1998. Yet it did so without a dramatic rise in votes or representation.

The party's Assembly seats remained at 27 and its share of first preference votes increased only marginally compared with 2017, mainly at the expense of the moderate nationalist SDLP. However, the symbolism of beating the largest unionist party, the DUP, into second place was significant.

Becoming the largest NI party gave Sinn Féin the right to nominate the first minister, but that was a satisfaction delayed when the DUP refused to cooperate in enabling the NI Executive to function unless major changes were made to the NI Protocol to the EU Withdrawal Agreement.

Nevertheless, the Sinn Féin breakthrough in Northern Ireland in 2022, combined with its surge in the Republic in 2020, confirmed the party as a serious political challenger across the island. A significant junction had been reached in its long march from the supremacy of the 'armed struggle', a journey that began with the adoption of its 'ballot box and armalite' strategy in 1986. The next stage looked likely to be an all-out drive for simultaneous power in Dublin and Belfast, which, if successful, would give it a powerful dual platform. How might they win the double and what would they prioritise should they succeed?

Their history and stated aims suggest that a referendum on the border would be their priority, which their core supporters would expect. However, a premature border poll could be dangerously divisive even in the most benign of circumstances, to the extent of re-igniting violence – which would hinder genuine unity between peoples on the island.

As neither the Dublin nor Belfast government could initiate a border poll, how governments led by Sinn Féin might proceed on the matter appeared to be crucial: would they create circumstances to persuade the UK's secretary of state for Northern Ireland to do so, or argue that heading the poll in both jurisdictions gave them that right, despite the terms of the peace treaty? The latter would bring with it the additional risk of the Republic being drawn into any conflict as a protagonist rather than a mediator.

In a worsening global economic context, aggravated by the Russian invasion of Ukraine in February 2022, fears that chaos could be triggered again in Northern Ireland appeared not unreasonable. How Sinn Féin might perform in such a context – which would be more than challenging for even the most experienced party of government – looked as if it could become more central to how it pursues the next phase of its political drive, and to voters' perceptions.

Sinn Féin	
Founded:	Current party 1970; first iteration as a party 1908
Meaning of name:	Ourselves
Leaders:	Ruairí Ó Brádaigh 1970-83; Gerry Adams 1983-2018; Mary Lou McDonald 2018 -
In office:	NI Executive 1998-2002; 2007-11; 2011-16; 2016-17; 2020-
Affiliations:	The Left in the European Parliament - GUE/NGL
Elected representatives:	2022: 27 MLAs (12M, 15F); 7 MPs (5M, 2F) who do not take their seats in the Westminster parliament; 37 TDs (26M, 11F); 4 Senators (2M, 2F); 1 MEP (M)

4

The Irish Labour Party / Páirtí an Lucht Oibre

A responsible partner in many governments, in partial eclipse

Overview

Founded in the early 20th century, the Irish Labour Party, which operates only in the Republic, is the oldest continuously active political party in the state. Unlike most parties in Ireland it emerged from the trade union movement rather than the nationalist or loyalist traditions.

Labour stood aside in the 1918 general election to enable that to be a plebiscite on independence. It then polled well in the Free State's first election in 1922 becoming the official opposition in Dáil Éireann – thus, it claims, 'bringing constitutional politics to Ireland'.[1]

The third party in the politics of the southern state for most of its existence, Labour was often essential to government formation by one of the bigger parties, usually Fine Gael. Its role has been primarily managerial rather than revolutionary, its main achievement being the gradual improvement of conditions for the less well off or otherwise marginalised.

The party that was founded to represent the rights of workers has struggled at times to reconcile its loftier ambitions with its role as a responsible party of government. Rarely was that clearer than when, following the 2011 general election, a Labour and Fine Gael coalition inherited responsibility for salvaging the state from the worst financial crisis in its history.

Supporting larger parties in government, whether as a junior partner in coalition or in confidence and supply arrangements, has

---

1   www.labour.ie

been a Labour hallmark. At times this has been at great cost to itself. In the 2016 election it paid a high price for what many of its former supporters saw as acquiescence in the sweeping austerity measures inflicted on citizens, even though they were imposed at the behest of international institutions to avert national bankruptcy.

Its parliamentary fortunes have soared and slumped but never as dramatically as between 2011, when the it hit a high of 37 Dáil seats, and 2020 when it was reduced to just six. That calamitous experience left Labour in the political wilderness and possibly terminally wounded.

'Bolshevism in the air'

Arriving in Dublin in 1918, the new Lord Lieutenant of Ireland, Sir John French, was advised that Bolshevism was in the air and that Sinn Féin 'was heavily charged with Leninist spirit'.[2]

That analysis was unsurprising given the spread of militant trade unionism across the island, alongside a ferment of cultural, feminist and political activity. Class struggle and nationalist politics were coming together in places too, though not consistently, and the other kind of unionists, those loyal to the political union between Ireland and Britain, complicated the analysis.

The Lord Lieutenant worried that syndicalism might be a bigger threat than nationalism if workers were to collaborate across traditional religious and political divides.[3] Edward Carson, leader of the Ulster Unionist Party (UUP), took a decisive step to forestall that possibility: in June 1918, in association with the Ulster Unionist Council, he set up the Ulster Unionist Labour Association to win Protestant working class votes for the UUP rather than left-leaning parties.

Syndicalism, the 'new' trade unionism, had been on the rise in Ireland since earlier in the 20th century. The 1913 Dublin Lockout (August 1913 to January 1914) was its dramatic high point. With striking workers locked out by employers determined to smash militant unions, Dublin experienced what labour historian Padraig

---

2   M. Walsh, *Bitter Freedom: Ireland in a Revolutionary World 1918-1923*, London, Faber & Faber, 2015, p.165
3   Ibid., p.165

Statue of James Larkin, trade union leader and a founder of the Irish Labour Party, in Donegall Street Place, Belfast, near to where Larkin led a dockers' strike in 1907. (© Albert Bridge)

Yeates has called 'unbridled class war'.[4]

The Lockout brought tensions between radical trade unionism and elements of the nationalist movement to the fore. William Martin Murphy, who masterminded the Lockout, was a prominent supporter of Home Rule. As a major employer in several sectors, including transport, he had cultivated good relations with the craft unions, but he saw the Irish Transport and General Workers Union (ITGWU) as a threat to the competitiveness of Irish companies.

As class war raged in Dublin, labour leaders were also finding common ground with some nationalists, notably Pádraig Pearse, who would lead an armed uprising against British rule in 1916. Members of the Irish Citizen Army, founded during the 1913 Lockout to protect strikers, went on to fight side-by-side with militant nationalists in the 1916 Rising. James Connolly, commander of the Citizen Army and icon of the Irish left, was one of the 16 leaders executed for their role in the Rising.

By the time Lord French arrived in Dublin as Lord Lieutenant, the authorities had reason to fear the influence of the Russian Revolution on Irish workers. In 1919, strikes swept the country, hitting rail services, vital industries and less likely sectors: law clerks and shop assistants published pamphlets talking up workers' power. In small country towns, workers marched with red flags in defiance of police warnings.[5]

Strikers upgraded the significance of their local actions by declaring themselves Soviets. Warders at an asylum in Monaghan established the first, possibly unlikeliest, of these Soviets, inspiring an opera a century later.[6] Miners, foundry workers and tailors followed

---

4   P. Yeates, *The Dublin 1913 Lockout, in History Ireland* Issue 2 (Summer 2001) Vol. 9

5   M. Walsh, *Bitter Freedom: Ireland in a Revolutionary World 1918-1923*, op.cit., pp.166-7

6   *Irish Times*, irishtimes.com, 22 February 2021

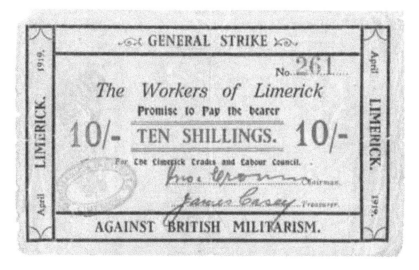

Paper money token issued by the Limerick Trades and Labour Council, which controlled the city during a 14-day strike in 1919 known as the Limerick Soviet.

the trend, but the most notable was in Limerick where strikers ran the city for two weeks.[7]

On the more directly political front, the Labour Party decided not to contest the 1918 general election.[8] This, they claimed, would allow the election to be, in effect, a national plebiscite on independence – which it was, gifting Sinn Féin a dramatic win – but the move was also a foretaste of a future in which the national question would take precedence over labour.

Nevertheless, the debt Sinn Féin owed to Labour did not go unrecognised. Labour Party leader Tom Johnson was invited to draft the Democratic Programme of the First Dáil. While his draft was too radically socialist for some, the version of the Programme adopted by the Dáil showed the influence of socialism as well as of Catholic social teaching, though expressed in nationalist language.[9] Any radical intent, though, was shelved by Éamon de Valera in April 1919 when, says Fitzpatrick, he 'regretfully explained that little effect could be

---

7   D. Ferriter, *The Transformation of Ireland 1900-2000*, op.cit., p.212

8   www.dail100.ie

9   www.oireachtas.ie

Countess Constance Markievicz (centre, holding flowers) in Liberty Hall, Dublin. Liberty Hall was the headquarters of the Irish Transport and General Workers' Union and the Irish Citizen Army, of which she was a founder.

given to the social programme so long as "they had the occupation of the foreigner in the country".'[10]

Foundation myths

Political parties, like states, tend to treasure their foundation myths. The Labour Party in Ireland is no exception. It's easy to understand, however, why it claims the charismatic Jim Larkin and the 1916 Rising leader James Connolly as founding fathers.

Fitzpatrick attributed the emergence of the Irish Transport and General Workers Union in 1908 to an uneasy blend of 'Larkin's inspirational syndicalism, with its evangelical and moralistic tone' and Connelly's 'more analytical socialism'.[11]

A third man, William O'Brien, is often left out of the narrative. Joe Lee describes him as 'a successful apparatchik combining fine administrative abilities with a domineering personality and a

10   D. Fitzpatrick, *The Two Irelands 1912-1939*, op.cit., p.42
11   Ibid., p.21

narrow mind'.[12] Perhaps it's understandable that his focus on the mundane tasks involved in improving workers' welfare makes him a less dramatically attractive founding father than leaders of strikes or rebellions.

Larkin's great contribution was to revolutionise Irish trade unionism, laying the basis of the modern Irish labour movement. Nonetheless, the image of him that lingers is his personification of Dublin workers as a 'risen people' during the Great Lockout of 1913, side-by-side with 'the idea of workers' solidarity as a code of honour'.[13]

The contrast between the 'radical, militant outlook' of Connolly and Larkin, and the 'cautious, reformist nature of the Labour Party from 1922 to the mid 1960s', says Gallagher, has led to claims that Labour would have been a very different party under the leadership of the former two. However, those radical men were 'decidedly atypical in their political beliefs'[14] and by the time the party got off the ground electorally Connolly was dead and Larkin was no longer in Ireland.

Claiming 1912 as the precise date of the Labour Party's foundation is also problematic. Little that could be classified as a political party of the working class existed in 1912. Those who could have become the catalysts of such a party were otherwise engaged building union membership and organising strikes.

The foundation date claim is based on a vague motion passed by the 1912 conference of the Irish Trades Union Congress (ITUC). This proposed only that 'the independent representation of Labour upon all public boards be and is hereby included among the objectives of the Congress'. Nothing practical happened until 1914 when the ITUC conference agreed a 'nominal conversion' into a party, changing its name to the Irish Trade Union Congress and Labour Party. A programme for the proposed party elicited an apathetic response at the 1916 conference. [15]

---

12   J.J. Lee, *Ireland 1912-1985: Politics and Society*, op.cit., p.241

13   D. Ferriter, *A Nation and not a Rabble: The Irish Revolution 1913-1923*, London, Profile Books, 2015, p.80

14   M. Gallagher, *Political Parties in the Republic of Ireland*, Manchester, Manchester University Press, 1985, p.62

15   Ibid., p.68

A Socialist Party of Ireland (SPI) was established in 1917 and most of the Congress leaders joined it, but then drifted away or were expelled after the SPI became a communist organisation in 1921.

A stronger case can be made for 1918 as the founding date, Gallagher suggests, as election candidates were selected and some work was done on a manifesto, though the general election was not contested after the decision to stand aside so that it could be considered a plebiscite on independence.

Gallagher argues that the party's real birth should be dated to the 1922 general election, which it contested on an 'entirely reformist' manifesto, with candidates who were often 'hard-working, locally oriented non-socialist men' of the kind who would dominate the party for the next 40 years.[16]

Northern complexities

At first glance Belfast appeared to be fertile ground for the 'new' trade unionism and a new party of labour. The most industrialised city in Ireland by far, it offered work for men in its shipyards and engineering shops and for women in its linen mills, but it had 'a notorious reputation for sectarian violence'.[17] Sectarian loyalties trumped tenuous class solidarity, says Fitzpatrick.[18]

Employment in the most industrialised corner of Ireland was less secure than is often assumed. Ferriter references a 1923 official memorandum that described shipbuilding as 'a notoriously unstable industry' while noting that, even during the war, Northern Ireland had higher unemployment than Britain; it cast doubt on the assumption that a revival in staple industry could bring unemployment down to the British level.[19]

The labour movement in Belfast, side-lined by the campaign against the Third Home Rule Bill, revived after the First World War. O'Connor characterises the period 1918-20 as Belfast's 'red years',

---

16   M. Gallagher, *Political Parties in the Republic of Ireland*, op.cit., p.68
17   E. O'Connor, 'A concise history of the Labour movement and the birth of Northern Ireland', sluggerotoole.com, 29 September 2019
18   D. Fitzpatrick, *The Two Irelands 1912-1939*, op.cit., p.20
19   D. Ferriter, *A Nation and not a Rabble: The Irish Revolution 1913-1923*, op.cit., p.311-12

involving a major engineering strike in 1919 and the election of 13 Labour councillors to the city Corporation in 1920.

This relatively comradely labour radicalism came to a dramatic end in the summer of 1920 with the expulsion of thousands of employees from the shipyards, mainly but not all on the basis of their religion. Historian David Fitzpatrick estimates that, in addition to some 5,500 Catholics, some 1,900 Protestants suspected of nationalism or socialism were violently expelled from Belfast shipyards in July 1920.[20]

Incipient Labour politics in northeast Ulster preceded the foundation of an Irish Labour Party; the Belfast Trades Council formed its own Labour Party in 1896. The Northern Ireland Labour Party (NILP) was founded in 1924 and remained active to varying degrees until 1987, though diminishingly so after the launch of the Social Democratic and Labour Party (SDLP) in 1970.

By the 1940s, the NILP had established formal links with the British Labour Party. It won four seats in the Northern Ireland Parliament in 1945 but lost them in 1949.[21] Having come out officially in favour of the Union with Britain in 1949, its appeal to Catholic voters had diminished, although it enjoyed a minor renaissance between 1958 and 1965 when it became the official opposition in Stormont.

A challenging Free State

Despite organisational weaknesses, Labour attracted 21.3% of first preference votes in the 1922 Free State election and won 17 seats in the 128-seat Dáil, suggesting a solid support base for a party dedicated to the interests of working people.

Even the best-organised, most focused party of the working class would have encountered many barriers to success in the early decades of the Free State. Not least the fact that most workers gave their allegiance to pro- or anti-treaty parties, and this continued despite the failure of governments to improve economic conditions until long after independence.

Lee suggests that Labour's spirit was broken by worsening unemployment in the newly independent state, indicated by the

---

20   D. Fitzpatrick, *The Two Irelands 1912-1939*, op.cit., p.7

21   B.M. Walker, *A Political History of the Two Irelands: From Partition to Peace*, Basingstoke, Palgrave Macmillan, 2012, p.38

fact that, by 1928, the number of working days lost by strikes had fallen to 5% of the 1923 level. 'Workers were being duly put in their place'.[22] By the 1943 general election, however, Labour appeared poised to emerge as a major party, but instead, in Lee's words, it 'rose to the challenge by tearing itself apart in internecine struggle between the old adversaries, William O'Brien and 'Big Jim' Larkin.'[23]

The 1940s had been difficult for Labour. A 'red scare' spooked its support base, the Irish Transport and General Workers Union disaffiliated from the party, and several TDs broke away to form the National Labour Party (NLP). The NLP won five seats in the 1948 election to official Labour's 14, but both joined the First Inter-Party Government. This experience of co-operation eased relations between the two factions, which reunited in 1950.

In government

The 1948-51 Inter-Party Government offers a freeze-frame of Irish Labour's recurring experience of coalitions: largely underwhelming, with some successes and a legacy of disappointed members and supporters.

In light of popular discontent about rationing and wage levels, and corruption allegations against the outgoing Fianna Fáil government, Labour believed their prospects were good in the snap election called for February 1948. Some also thought there was growing support for progressive politics, a belief bolstered by the emergence of a new republican-progressive party, Clann na Poblachta, viewed as a potential ally because of similar social and economic policies.

Hopes for a grand republican-Labour alliance melted when Labour won only 14 seats and Clann a disappointing 10. Approached by Fine Gael to form an inter-party government the two Labours and the other opposition parties agreed. Labour leaders appeared unconcerned about the lack of ideological compatibility in such a broad alliance – the electorate, they reasoned, had mandated them to 'put Fianna Fáil out' and they had to put the people's decision into effect.

---

22   J.J. Lee, *Ireland 1912-1985: Politics and Society*, op.cit., p.127
23   Ibid., p.240

The left of the party called for Labour to champion housing, transport, agriculture and social security as their key policy areas.[24] The Inter-Party Government did indeed prioritise housing and a comprehensive social security plan, but Clann na Poblachta leader Seán MacBride is credited with insisting on inclusion of the latter in the programme.[25]

As tánaiste, Labour's William Norton played a crucial role in keeping the 'makeshift majority' government together. He brought two important talents to the job, according to McCullagh: negotiation skills, and a feel for issues that could cause trouble for the government.[26] Niamh Puirséil suggests, however, that by becoming the government's trouble-shooter Norton was instrumental in Labour losing its identity in government.

The health minister in the Inter-Party Government, Clann na Poblachta's Dr Noel Browne, claimed that Norton supported the conservatism of Fine Gael,[27] This is accurate in relation to Norton's failure to back Browne's proposal to fund free healthcare for children and pregnant women, known as the Mother and Child Scheme. In March 1951 most of the cabinet, including Labour ministers, abandoned the scheme, caving in to opposition from the Irish Medical Association and the Catholic hierarchy.

The Mother and Child Scheme 'enjoyed massive support among ordinary Labour members and supporters' and it was difficult for them to understand why no one from the Labour Party in government defended a scheme 'which would have been of immeasurable benefit to the less well off', Puirséil notes.

Browne's accusation was not universally accurate, however. Notable progress was made on one of Labour's top priorities, building new homes. A brochure produced by the coalition proudly proclaimed 'Ireland is Building', as it inaugurated a 10-year plan to build 110,000 houses.[28] Puirséil lists other successes Labour could

---

24 N. Puirséil, *Labour and Coalition: The Impact of the First Inter-Party Government, 1948-51*, in *Saothar* Vol. 27 (2002), pp. 55-64, Dublin, Irish Labour History Society

25 D. McCullagh, *A Makeshift Majority: The First Inter-Party Government, 1948-51*, Dublin, Institute of Public Administration, p.31

26 Ibid., p.47

27 Ibid., p.48

28 D. Ferriter, 'A survival guide for coalition government in Ireland', *Irish Times*, 22 February 2020

claim, such as better wages for local authority workers, higher welfare benefits and a prices tribunal.[29] Yet failure to introduce a comprehensive social security scheme suggested there were limits to what could be achieved when in power with a conservative partner, according to McCullagh.[30]

Soon after the Mother and Child crisis the government lost its majority. In the general election that followed Labour faced the electorate as a united party for the first time since 1943, but its representation in the new Dáil fell and the party leadership failed to acknowledge any responsibility for the poor election result.

Labour was willing to join a new coalition with Fine Gael, but the bid failed to win majority Dáil support. One contribution to debate at the time illustrated the divide between the contrasting wings of the party: a deputy from Cork bragged about his efforts to lead a contingent to fight on the side of Franco's fascists in Spain – and nobody challenged him.[31]

A second inter-party government involving Labour was formed in 1954, lasting until 1957. After a further fall in representation the party decided to shun coalition, a stance it maintained for more than a decade.[32]

Junior partners

Five governments between 1973 and 1997 included the Labour Party. Fine Gael was lead party in all but one of these, a short-lived coalition with Fianna Fáil (1993-94), from which Labour segued into another with Fine Gael and Democratic Left (DL), known as the Rainbow Coalition.[33]

By the time the 1973 general election was called, Labour was ready to risk another stint in government. It agreed an electoral pact with Fine Gael, and the two parties campaigned jointly as an alternative government on a 14-point manifesto 'containing

---

29   N. Puirséil, *Labour and Coalition*, op.cit.

30   D. McCullagh, *A Makeshift Majority*, op.cit., p.197

31   N. Puirséil, *Labour and Coalition*, op.cit.

32   Ibid.

33   In 1999 Labour merged with Democratic Left, which had emerged from the Workers' Party, itself a direct offspring of Sinn Féin

promises for virtually everyone'.[34] The tactic worked and coalition was on again.[35]

The new government's honeymoon period lasted about a year, during which they made 'a large number of popular decisions',[36] but in October 1973 the Arab-Israeli war disrupted global oil supplies, sending prices soaring. This had a particularly strong impact in the Republic, which was almost entirely dependent on imports for its energy.

Government performance took a heavy hit, falling far short of the manifesto promise to 'stabilise prices, halt redundancies and reduce unemployment under a programme of planned economic development'. Instead, prices almost doubled, unemployment and inflation soared and the promised economic plan was not even drawn up.

On the positive side, over 100,000 homes were built, and the quality of local authority housing improved. The social welfare budget trebled, most welfare payments rose, and groups such as single mothers received benefits for the first time. Legislation was also passed to prevent unfair dismissal and to protect young workers, but the coalition came nowhere near achieving its promise to eliminate poverty and social injustice.[37]

In an echo of the Mother and Child Scheme's failure under the 1948-51 coalition, free hospital services failed to materialise because of failure to gain the medical profession's cooperation. The promised legislation to 'end all forms of existing discrimination against women' also fell by the wayside,[38] while the import and sale of contraceptives under licence was defeated on a free vote in the Dáil.[39]

Violence crosses the border

During the 1970s northern violence extended into the Republic. The Provisional IRA killed Fine Gael senator Billy Fox in March 1974[40]

---

34 J.J. Lee, *Ireland 1912-1985: Politics and Society*, op.cit., p.469
35 Ibid., p.468
36 M. Gallagher & M. Marsh, *Days of Blue Loyalty: The Politics of Membership of the Fine Gael party*, Dublin, PSAI Press, 2002, p.197
37 M. Gallagher, *The Irish Labour Party in Transition 1957-82*, Dublin, Gill & MacMillan, 1982, p.200
38 Ibid., p.208
39 Ibid., p.202
40 Ibid., p.205

and the British ambassador, Christopher Ewart-Biggs, in July 1976. On 17 May 1974, during the Ulster Workers' Strike, loyalist car bombs exploded in Dublin and Monaghan, killing 33 people including a woman with a full-term pregnancy. Separately, Provisional IRA supporters attacked two Labour TDs at their homes.

When legislation was introduced in April 1975 to prevent offenders in the north using the south as a safe haven, some in Labour had doubts about it, mostly on civil liberties grounds. Some described two further security Bills in 1976 as 'the politics of the last atrocity'. Labour TDs and senators were divided, voting for or against the Bills or abstaining, but only the iconoclastic Conor Cruise O'Brien TD spoke in support.

Although government responsibility for Northern Ireland lay with the taoiseach and the foreign affairs minister, Cruise O'Brien remained Labour's spokesperson on the north despite his controversial views, which had swung towards support for unionism.

Labour and Fine Gael again ran on a joint manifesto in 1977, but the results were disappointing for both: Fine Gael fell from 53 to 43 seats, Labour from 20 to 17. While Fine Gael made gains in 1981, Labour was still on a losing streak, winning just 15 seats. Meanwhile other parties of the left were emerging as possible challengers.

With a new leader, Michael O'Leary, Labour reluctantly decided to enter coalition with Fine Gael in 1981. Under Garret FitzGerald as taoiseach, O'Leary served as tánaiste, and Labour's Eileen Desmond was appointed minister for health and social welfare, only the second woman to hold a Cabinet post since the foundation of the state.

The government lasted only eight months, until February 1982, and O'Leary stood down as leader. His successor, former Ireland rugby international Dick Spring, became tánaiste in 1993, the only time the party shared power with Fianna Fáil. That partnership was short and controversial. Ferriter describes as 'scandalous' the tax amnesty granted by that government and endorsed by the Labour Party: 'tax defaulters were given a total amnesty on payment of just 15% of the tax they owed to the state, and a guarantee of absolute confidentiality (which undoubtedly benefited many who had contributed generously to the funds of political parties).'[41]

---

41   D. Ferriter, *The Transformation of Ireland 1900-2000*, op.cit., p.680

Labour transitioned from coalition with Fianna Fáil into a new government with Fine Gael and Democratic Left, dubbed the Rainbow Coalition.

When they took office in 1994 the economy was expanding at an unprecedented pace: exports were growing, inflation was low, and there was a firm exchange rate. This was due to a confluence of factors, some global, while others stemmed from policies implemented by previous governments. Inward investment by US corporations fuelled export expansion, investment in human capital was bearing fruit and, thanks to a social partnership with trade unions and employers, a stable operating environment boosted business confidence. Additionally, EU membership was paying off in the form of serious money for structural development and farming subsidies that eased the social impact of a radical restructuring of agriculture.

Breaking the glass ceiling

Though Labour was out of office in 1990 it was a historic year for the party and for women. Labour nominated Mary Robinson, a campaigning human rights lawyer and former party member, as a candidate for the presidential election. Against expectations she was elected, the first woman and first Labour nominee to hold the office of Head of State.

Robinson transformed the presidency from a staid sinecure for retired politicians into an active, outward looking role. Her meeting in London with Queen Elizabeth, the first such visit by an Irish President, was an important step towards improving relationships with the UK. Visiting Northern

Mary Robinson making her acceptance speech on her election as President of Ireland in November 1990, flanked by defeated candidate Brian Lenihan and Taoiseach Charles Haughey (r), both Fianna Fáil. (© National Library of Ireland)

Liz McManus TD represented Wicklow for Democratic Left 1992-99 and for Labour 1999-2011 after the merger of these two parties; she was Labour Party deputy leader 2002-07. (© William Murphy)

Ireland on several occasions she met political leaders including David Trimble of the UUP, the SDLP's John Hume and Sinn Féin president Gerry Adams.

Robinson's breakthrough paved the way for another female president, the Belfast lawyer Mary McAleese (1997-2011), nominated by Fianna Fáil, and later for a second Labour nominee Michael D. Higgins (2011-).

Further success was on the horizon for Labour under Dick Spring. In the 1992 general election the party more than doubled its seats in the Dáil, from 15 to 33. Leahy's verdict on the Spring years was fulsome: 'Spring and the group that surrounded him were perhaps the most important and dynamic force in Irish politics in the first half of the 1990s. They changed the national mood with the election of Mary Robinson and then changed the make up of the Dáil in the general election of 1992 [...] to give the country technocratic and policy driven governments of a type it never had before.'[42]

Leahy argues, however, that Spring's decision to lead his party out of coalition with Fianna Fáil and into a Rainbow Coalition with Fine Gael and the Democratic Left was a watershed in Irish political history because of its impact on the direction of economic policy. By pushing Fianna Fáil 'into the embrace of the Progressive Democrats', he claims, it also pushed the larger party's economic policy rightwards.[43]

Leahy also suggests that if Labour had been able to remain in government after 1997 'the years of the Celtic Tiger would have been guided by social democratic government, rather than economic liberalism and tax-cutting'.[44]

---

42   P. Leahy, *Showtime: The Inside Story of Fianna Fáil in Power*, Dublin, Penguin Ireland, 2010, p.124

43   Ibid., p.24

44   Ibid., p.61

Michael D. Higgins. The academic, poet and lifelong political activist was nominated for the presidency by the Labour Party in 2011; on seeking re-election in 2018 he won the largest majority in an Irish presidential contest. (© Irish Labour Party)

Crisis coalition

Éamon Gilmore rose to the top slot in the Labour hierarchy in 2007 and remained in that role until 2014. In his memoir Gilmore declared: 'Every leader has a vision and ambitions for their party. At the heart of mine was my sense that Labour itself had always lacked ambition.'[45]

In 2011 he led his party to its best ever election result, 37 seats in the then 166-seat Dáil. The campaign showed no lack of ambition. Buoyed by favourable opinion polls, which briefly put Labour in first place, the party campaigned on the slogan 'Gilmore for Taoiseach'.

The electorate didn't quite agree with that but did put the party into a strong position to negotiate a coalition deal with Fine Gael. After 14 years in the political wilderness, Labour entered government

---

45 É. Gilmore, *Inside the Room: The Untold Story of Ireland's Crisis Government,* Dublin, Merrion Press, 2016, p.8

Éamon Gilmore, tánaiste and Labour Party leader, meets US Secretary of State Hillary Rodham Clinton, 18 March 2011. (© US State Department)

and Gilmore became tánaiste, the deputy prime minister to Enda Kenny's taoiseach.

Although they knew the country was in dire financial straits, Gilmore and Kenny may have underestimated the extent of the challenge they faced: the toughest operating environment any Irish government had experienced since the foundation of the state.

Ireland was the first Eurozone country to fall into recession in the 2008 global financial crisis. In response, the Fianna Fáil-led government bailed out the banks and cut public sector pay. Tax revenues plummeted, the budget deficit soared and 300,000 people lost their jobs. Finally, in November 2010, the government requested help from the country's only available saviours, a Troika of the IMF, the European Commission and the European Central Bank. Help arrived, but at a very high price with strict and onerous conditions. There was never any doubt that the coalition partners faced defeat in the 2011 election. Labour and Fine Gael prepared for government.

Months before the general election, representatives of the Troika met Fine Gael and Labour to brief them on the implications of the bail-out that had been agreed for Ireland.[46] Their message was clear:

---

46   É. Gilmore, *Inside the Room*, op.cit., p.38

any new government would be bound by the promises made by its predecessors. In other words, the Troika required an incoming Fine Gael/Labour government to stick to the letter of the agreement with the outgoing Government of Ireland.

The key figures in the incoming administration did not at any stage discuss the possibility of walking away from the plan they had inherited, according to Leahy.[47] Issues high on the agenda included the requirement for the Irish state to compensate senior bondholders of the failed banks for their losses – one of the bailout conditions Labour sought to change.

The new government did, however, take some swift decisions on how to proceed with crisis management. Central to this was the establishment of an Economic and Monetary Council (EMC), a crisis war cabinet to be chaired by the taoiseach and managed by the tánaiste, Labour's Éamon Gilmore. Only two other politicians were involved, the minister for finance and the minister for public expenditure, the latter a newly created role filled by Labour's Brendan Howlin.[48]

Internal strife

When Gilmore took over as Labour leader in 2007, Bertie Ahern had just led Fianna Fáil to a third consecutive victory, following a general election in which Labour won 20 seats. Gilmore was one of those who had joined Labour from Democratic Left when the two parties merged in 1999. That merger was intended to create critical mass in left-of-centre politics and to a large extent it succeeded in doing so.

It wasn't a trouble-free marriage, though, as testified by the cracks that emerged in Labour ranks early in the 2011-16 coalition, epitomised in the worsening relations between Gilmore, as leader, and two senior 'old Labour' TDs. Joan Burton, the party's deputy leader, and Róisín Shortall, who had opposed the merger with Democratic Left, were both disappointed with the posts Gilmore offered them. Burton had expected the public expenditure job, but was made minister for social protection; Shortall had assumed she'd be made a full minister but was offered a junior ministerial position in health.

---

47   P. Leahy, *Showtime: The Inside Story of Fianna Fáil in Power*, op.cit., p.xi
48   É. Gilmore, *Inside the Room*, op.cit., p.82

Shortall's relationship with the senior health minister, James Reilly of Fine Gael, deteriorated rapidly. She felt stymied in her efforts to implement the health provisions of the programme for government. Reilly, himself a medical doctor who had become wealthy from his private practice, favoured a model with a large element of private medicine.[49] In the Celtic Tiger years Ireland had done what Aneurin Bevan did when establishing the NHS in the UK: bought the cooperation of the medical profession by 'stuffing their mouths with gold'. Shortall came to see Reilly as a representative of the men with mouthfuls of gold, in Leahy's opinion.[50]

The split between the senior and junior ministers came to a head, and became public, over where to locate 20 new primary care centres. Shortall wanted them placed in the poorest areas that needed them most. Reilly decided that three of them should be sited in key constituencies for Fine Gael, including his own.

Gilmore refused to bring down the government over the health centres standoff so Shortall, who believed she wasn't getting the support she needed from her party, made 'a devastating speech' in the Dáil which, the party chairman told the *Irish Times*, led to him being inundated with calls from members praising the speech. Shortall resigned, sat as an independent and later co-founded the Social Democrats in July 2015.

Joan Burton fought on and succeeded Gilmore as tánaiste and party leader in 2014, the first woman to lead Labour. She served until 2016, resigning after a disastrous general election when Labour won a mere seven seats. That the Labour vote plummeted from an historic high to an historic low was not surprising. Discontent was soaring inside the party and among voters long before the 2016 election. Demonstrators outside Gilmore's office shouting that he had betrayed James Connolly were indicative of sentiment on the left.[51]

Rock bottom?

By mid-2013 Ireland was experiencing the start of a fragile economic recovery. The budget for 2014 included €37m to start the roll-out

---

49 P. Leahy, *Showtime: The Inside Story of Fianna Fáil in Power*, op.cit., p.183
50 Ibid., p.183
51 Leahy, p.xiv

Ivana Bacik TD, elected to the Dáil in a by-election in July 2021, became leader of the Labour Party in March 2022. (© Irish Labour Party)

of free GP care, initially for children aged five and under.[52] Gilmore admits, however, that there was no blueprint for tackling the jobs crisis. The traditional approach of increasing government spending was not available because the public finances were still in crisis. 'We had to pioneer non-Keynesian solutions', Gilmore claimed, 'with government providing the leadership and opportunities, but with the private sector delivering the jobs.'[53]

For Labour, however, there was no sign of recovery. The 2016 result was shattering for the party, but worse was still to come. In 2020 it returned just six representatives to Dáil Éireann, the same number as the Social Democrats, founded in 2015 mainly by former Labour members. Alan Kelly, who replaced Brendan Howlin as leader, declared his hope for unity with the Social Democrats,[54] adding that he would not rule out talking to any party about cooperation, not even Sinn Féin.

Labour faced an uncertain future, 'eclipsed by populism in its various, very different manifestations'.[55] Some manifestations

---

52   É. Gilmore, *Inside the Room*, op.cit., p.143
53   Ibid., p.147
54   www.thejournal.ie, 10 July 2020
55   *Irish Times* (editorial), www.irishtimes.com, 6 April 2020

were represented in Dáil Éireann. Solidarity-People Before Profit, a Trotskyist electoral alliance, took three Dáil seats and one in Stormont. Their stated aim was to build a mass party of the left, though the history of political parties in Ireland suggests they are likely to be disappointed. The same history suggests that helping to form a government might not be totally beyond the bounds of possibility but how left-wing it might be is debatable.

Labour support also leached to the Green Party and to independents, but the most daunting challenge for the traditional party of the left lay in the Sinn Féin surge.

When Ivana Bacik won a by-election in July 2021, taking a seat formerly held comfortably by Fine Gael, Labour's hopes began to rise. Ms Bacik, a law professor and well-known campaigner, was elected unopposed as party leader in March 2022. However, the oldest continuously existing party in the Republic still faced a daunting task to make itself credible again in a crowded field of centre left contenders.

The Labour Party / Páirtí an Lucht Oibre	
Founded:	Decision taken 1912; functioning as a party by 1918
Leaders:	Tom Johnson 1922-1927; T.J. O'Connell 1927-1932; William Norton 1932-1960; Brendan Corish 1960-1977; Frank Cluskey 1977-1981; Michael O'Leary 1981-1982; Dick Spring 1982-1997; Ruairi Quinn 1997-2002; Pat Rabbitte 2002-2007; Éamon Gilmore 2007-2014; Joan Burton 2014-2016; Brendan Howlin 2016-2020; Alan Kelly 2020-2022; Ivana Bacik 2022-
In office:	In coalition with Fine Gael 1948–51; 1954–57; 1973–77; 1981–82; 1982–87; 1994–97; 2011–16; in coalition with Fianna Fáil 1993-1994
Affiliations:	PES Socialists and Democrats
Elected representatives:	2022: 7 TDs (6M, 1F), 5 Senators (1M, 4F)

5

Fianna Fáil

Populism, power and crash: what next for the Soldiers of Destiny?

Overview

Fianna Fáil exemplifies the Irish road from rebel to realist, to political power and beyond. Its story has been central to that of the larger of the two juristictions on the island of Ireland, and at times crucial in Northern Ireland's destiny.

From 1926 to 2022 Fianna Fáil had just eight leaders, all men, each one a taoiseach. Inevitably those leaders were central to the party's story, but success was primarily due to a faithful membership and a solid local organisation focused on winning power.

Historically the party was associated inextricably with Éamon de Valera, its austere founder. Party bosses would probably prefer to keep it that way, in order to banish voter memory of the corruption of Charles Haughey, or the ineptitude of those who led the country to the brink of bankruptcy and Fianna Fáil to the verge of oblivion.

Founded in 1926, when Éamon de Valera and others in the anti-treaty faction of Sinn Féin came to terms with the reality of an established Irish Free State, Fianna Fáil emerged as the largest party in Dáil Éireann in 1932. It remained dominant until 2011 when it hit rock bottom following the country's brush with bankruptcy that occurred on its watch.

The party wasn't averse to U-turns while in power. When it became clear in the late 1950s that its experiment in economic protectionism had failed, a Fianna Fáil government embraced free trade and assiduously courted foreign investors. This set the direction of travel for all succeeding governments, culminating in the Republic of Ireland having one of the world's most open economies, one that was also open to the charge of acting as a tax haven.

The 1937 constitution, Bunreacht na hÉireann, drawn up by Éamon de Valera, provided a political framework that, on the whole, served democracy well. It also, however, set conservative Catholicism above democracy, infringed significantly on the rights of women and enshrined a territorial claim to Northern Ireland that was at best problematic until removed by referendum in 1998.

The reunification of Ireland remained Fianna Fáil's official aim, but one that was mostly low down the priority list compared with winning power in the Dublin government. Whenever northern affairs took centre stage, however, most party leaders reacted more pragmatically than might have been expected from Fianna Fáil's early history, and some contributed significantly to the process that brought peace to Northern Ireland.

Led by the nationalist ideologue Éamon de Valera for three decades, some of its later leaders had little ideology but were very interested in power. Their populist political formula worked well and was adapted to the shifting aspirations of new generations. Some also seemed to have found a formula that facilitated their personal enrichment.

From being the most successful political party in the state's history, Fianna Fáil collapsed to small party status in 2011, punished by the electorate for the 2008 financial crisis and the austerity it triggered – and, by implication, for policies that left the country exposed to that catastrophe.

A partial comeback under Micheál Martin saw Fianna Fáil form a coalition government in 2020 with Fine Gael, its traditional rival for the top slot – suggesting a possible squaring of the political circle broken by the 1922-23 civil war, or at least a truce. The historic 2020 deal added a modern dimension with the inclusion of the Green Party in the tripartite government. This left the latest iteration of Sinn Féin as the lead opposition party and potentially an obstacle to Fianna Fáil's ability to flourish again.

The road to power

Launched in May 1926, Fianna Fáil had its roots in Sinn Féin, the party that topped the poll across Ireland in the 1918 UK general election and then, abstaining from Westminster, convened the First Dáil in Dublin. More precisely, it was a breakaway from the faction of Sinn Féin that opposed the 1921 Anglo-Irish Treaty.

While Sinn Féin leader Éamon de Valera had held post-ceasefire talks in July 1921 with British Prime Minister David Lloyd George, he purposefully did not take part in the formal treaty negotiations later that year. He subsequently rejected the deal done by the official Irish delegation, claiming it should have been referred back for approval.

Why de Valera stayed in Dublin rather than leading the treaty team in London is still debated. One possibility is that, based on his talks with Lloyd George in July 1921, he knew that a republic was not on the cards. Lloyd George's secretary and companion, Frances Stevenson, in her diary entries about these opening 'talks about talks', records an exchange in which Lloyd George said to de Valera: 'Why do you insist upon Republic? Saorstat [Free State] is good enough'.[1]

When Dáil Éireann voted to approve the treaty, de Valera resigned his presidency of the parliament. Several years and a civil war later he led a breakaway from the anti-treaty side and this element contested Dáil elections under a new label, with a view to changing the constitutional settlement from the inside.

De Valera had revised his approach while imprisoned for his part in the civil war, but he failed to persuade a majority in Sinn Féin to treat the taking of the oath of allegiance to the English monarch as a necessary tactical step rather than a principle. The result was a split from Sinn Féin and the establishment of Fianna Fáil – The Republican Party, described by co-founder Seán Lemass as 'a slightly constitutional party'.

Éamon de Valera got 'his first real taste of the mentality of the gunman' during the civil war, according to historian Joe Lee. Serving in the anti-treaty forces he 'came face to face with the authentic militarist mentality' and 'drew the lesson'. Lee also argues that he 'would prove the real reaper of the harvest of death in the civil war'.[2]

The 'Dev' brand of politics

In terms of electoral reality there was clearly a constituency for the de Valera ('Dev') approach. Fianna Fáil won 44 seats in the June 1927 general election, coming a close second to the ruling Cumann na nGaedheal. The new opposition deputies took their seats in Dáil Éireann on 11 August 1927, having sworn an oath of allegiance to

---

1   J. Bowman, 'When Lloyd George met de Valera', *The Irish Times*, 10 July 2021
2   J.J. Lee, *Ireland 1912-1985: Politics and Society*, op.cit., p.150

Still comrades before the 1921 Anglo-Irish Treaty tore Sinn Féin apart: (left to right) Harry Boland and Michael Collins (pro-treaty) and Éamon de Valera (anti-treaty).

the English Crown that they simultaneously dismissed as an empty formality.[3]

With Fianna Fáil's entry into Dáil Éireann, a majority on both sides of the civil war had accepted the Anglo-Irish Treaty, even though it had led to partition of the island and the southern state was not a republic. In effect, they also accepted the ongoing connection with Britain, whatever the semantic distinctions drawn by the latest rebels turned parliamentarians, and despite accusations of betrayal levelled at them by those in the IRA/Sinn Féin who continued to reject the legitimacy of the post-treaty Dáil and Free State.

---

3   D. Ferriter, *Judging Dev*, op.cit., p.103

In the 1932 election Fianna Fáil emerged as the largest party with 44.5% of first preference votes, giving them 72 seats. Fearing that Cumann na nGaedheal would try to hold on to power, some leading Fianna Fáil members carried guns into the chamber when the Dáil met on 9 March 1932. Cumann na nGaedheal leader William Cosgrave was not prepared to flout the democratic will, however, and handed over power to those he had defeated in the civil war.[4]

Nevertheless, Fianna Fáil had to rely on Labour Party support to govern. De Valera fixed that by calling a 'snap' election in 1933 and won his majority. Maurice Walsh sums up what happened next: De Valera 'set out to achieve what Collins had promised could be done by dismantling the treaty bit by bit'.[5]

The Fianna Fáil founder didn't have the ultimate satisfaction of turning the Irish Free State into a republic, though, as Fine Gael, the new electoral vehicle of his pro-treaty opponents, beat him to it. The First Inter-Party Government (1948-51) withdrew from the British Commonwealth and legislated to establish the Republic of Ireland, thus ending the formal constitutional connection to the English Crown.

The Fianna Fáil agenda wasn't all about constitutional matters, however. Mary Daly describes it as 'an amalgam of nationalist and quasi-socialist policies' drawn from an eclectic range of sources, from left wing republican and Labour Party manifestoes to Papal encyclicals.[6] Branding Cumann na nGaedheal a 'government by the rich for the rich', and demanding homes and jobs, Fianna Fáil's 1932 campaign materials could have come from the presses of the radical left.

Despite his dreamier speeches about national ideals, 'Dev' had a pragmatic streak and was very much aware of the need to address people's basic needs. In a speech to the League of Nations in September 1932, for example, he declared the provision of adequate food, clothing and housing to be the primary aims of economic policy.

---

4   S. Collins & C. Meehan, *Saving the State*, op.cit., p.25
5   M. Walsh, Bitter Freedom: *Ireland in a Revolutionary World 1918-1923*, op.cit., p.431
6   'The Fianna Fáil Economic Revolution', in M.E. Daly, *Industrial Development and Irish National Identity, 1922-1939*, Syracuse, Syracuse University Press, 1992, pp.59-74

In office, Fianna Fáil did try to tackle some of the social ills they had condemned while in campaign mode, although this was done side-by-side with overt discrimination against women, cultural censorship and sexual morality laws.[7]

One problem they began to solve was slum housing, amongst the worst in Europe at the time. The period from the early 1930s to mid-1950s could be regarded as the golden age of social housing, according to Michelle Norris, when 'for the first time significant progress was made in clearing the extensive and wretched slums which had heretofore blighted the inner areas of most Irish cities and towns.'[8] Fianna Fáil could not claim full credit, though, as the period also included two Fine Gael-led administrations that gave a high priority to housing.

Protectionist experiment

Fianna Fáil began to roll out the Sinn Féin economic self-sufficiency policy after 1932. The target was economic development; the armoury included a system of tariffs and laws to restrict foreign ownership of Irish manufacturing companies.[9]

This period became one of 'lavish and indiscriminate industrial protection', according to Ken Whitaker, the non-politician behind the Fianna Fáil economic U-turn that would begin in the late 1950s.[10]

The concept of protectionism to support indigenous industrial development was far from new. Alexander Hamilton, the first US Treasury secretary, had proposed it. Ireland's great 19th century leaders, O'Connell and Parnell, had supported it. Arthur Griffith made it central to the policies of the party he founded, and Sinn Féin's spin-off parties adopted it.

Cumann na nGaedheal, which governed the Irish Free State prior to 1932, had attempted a less full-blown form, described by

---

7   D. Ferriter, *The Transformation of Ireland 1900-2000*, op.cit., p.360
8   M. Norris, *Financing the Golden Age of Irish Social Housing, 1932-1956 (and the dark ages which followed)*, Working Papers 201901, Geary Institute, University College Dublin, 2018
9   The Control of Manufactures Acts 1932 and 1934, Legislation.ie
10 Quoted in, A. Chambers, *T. K. Whitaker: Portrait of a Patriot*, Dublin, Doubleday Ireland, 2014, p.31

Fitzpatrick as half-hearted, with protective tariffs applied to selected products, often haphazardly and in response to lobbying.[11]

Overall, the result of the Fianna Fáil experiment in self-sufficiency was underwhelming, but the party could claim some successes particularly in urban employment creation. It could also claim that success was inhibited by events – but some of those were of their own making.

Churchill's offer to Dev

The 'Economic War' with Britain was a saga foretold in Fianna Fáil's election manifesto, which opposed payment of land annuities, the annual repayments to Britain arising from loans to tenants who benefitted from pre-independence land reforms.[12] De Valera duly stopped the payments in 1934, Britain imposed a 20% duty on most imports from Ireland, and Dublin retaliated in kind. The 'war' ended with the Anglo-Irish Trade Agreement of 1938, under which Ireland made a one-off payment of £100 million and Britain returned to Irish control the ports it had retained under the 1921 Anglo-Irish Treaty.[13]

The Economic War and its settlement boosted Fianna Fáil's electoral popularity, which hit a high in 1944, particularly in Dublin. As economic historian Cormac Ó Gráda notes: 'Cheap food, a by-product of the Economic War, and a post-1932 industrialization drive that created considerable employment, benefited workers in the towns and cities most.'[14]

The Free State remained neutral throughout the Second World War, termed the 'Emergency' in Ireland. In a context that was complex and controversial, the state faced a political and economic emergency: Britain and the US applied strong pressure to abandon neutrality, and the degree of self-reliance required during the war put the Irish economy's very survival at stake. The Free State was highly dependent on imported fuel and manufacturing inputs but

---

11   D. Fitzpatrick, *The Two Irelands* 1912-1939, op.cit., p.212
12   The payments were part of the 1923 Anglo-Irish Financial Agreement
13   Anglo-Irish Trade Agreement, April 1938
14   C. Ó Gráda, *Five Crises: Central Bank of Ireland T.K. Whitaker Lecture*, 29 June 2011, p.8

London was willing to supply only those raw materials it considered essential to ensure Irish agriculture could produce food for Britain.

London also quickly regretted handing back the 'treaty ports' to Ireland. De Valera's refusal to let the British war fleet use these Irish ports provoked a retaliatory embargo by Britain.[15] It also led to a high-stakes proposition by Winston Churchill that could have changed the course of Irish history.

Twice during the war the British prime minister offered an end to partition if Dublin would abandon neutrality and join the war on the Allied side,[16] and twice Éamon de Valera ignored his offer.

The first proposal, in a memorandum to de Valera on 26 June 1940, promised to 'seek to obtain the assent' of the Northern Ireland government to unification. De Valera doubted that the NI government would give that assent.

Churchill's second offer arrived in a late night telegram during the Japanese attack on Pearl Harbour in December 1941: 'Following from Mr. Churchill to Mr. de Valera. Personal. Private and Secret. Begins. Now is your chance. Now or never. "A Nation once again." Am very ready to meet you at any time. Ends.' De Valera took this to mean 'now is the chance for taking action which would ultimately lead to the unification of the country'.[17] He ignored the telegram, however, allegedly believing that Churchill was drunk when he sent it, though some dispute the drunkenness charge.[18]

As a result, the border between the two states remained in place and partition continued to trigger political discord, and worse.

Radical rivals

Although Fianna Fáil comfortably won the 1944 general election, the cumulative effects of wartime deprivation, persistent economic stagnation and emigration, and issues such as slum housing and a marked rise in tuberculosis, were setting the scene for a post-war political drama.

---

15   A. Chambers, *T. K. Whitaker: Portrait of a Patriot*, op.cit., p.59
16   D. Ferriter, *Judging Dev*, op.cit., pp.153-4
17   The Earl of Longford and T.P. O'Neill, *Éamon De Valera*, London, Hutchinson, 1970, pp.392-93
18   See e.g. D. Freeman, *Finest Hour 147*, Summer 2010, winstonchurchill.org

A radical new party, Clann na Poblachta, emerged in 1946, challenging Fianna Fáil from the left – both on social issues and its commitment to republicanism. As Ferriter amongst others notes, much of Clann's rhetoric about the need for radical social and economic change echoed that of Fianna Fáil in 1932.[19]

When Clann won two out of three by-elections in the winter of 1947, de Valera called a general election for February 1948 in an attempt to halt their march before they could organise adequately. The tactic worked insofar as it stunted the Clann surge. Though the newcomers won just ten seats, that was enough to enable the opposition parties to form a government, blocking Fianna Fáil from office until 1951. Politically this period was important in demonstrating that coalition governments could work effectively and that Fianna Fáil's hold on power could be broken.

De Valera spent much of his time in opposition rallying support abroad. In his absence the state's first coalition government, led by Fine Gael and influenced by Clann na Poblachta, declared that the Free State would become a republic and withdrew from the British Commonwealth. In its title at least, and its constitutional relationship with the UK, a paramount Fianna Fáil aim had been achieved by others.

Importantly too, the 1948-51 coalition's 'Keynesian lite' approach to economic policy eased the way for a change of direction by Fianna Fáil, one that would have a major influence on Ireland's economic future.

Éire passé wakes up to reality

In office again in 1957 with an overall majority – and at the start of a long run of election wins – Fianna Fáil faced what had become an unavoidable impasse: how to move on from policies that had patently failed to achieve the economic security expected by the idealists who had fought for independence.

Ireland was haemorrhaging people. The 1956 census showed a sharp fall in population over the five years from 1951, which didn't come as a surprise to Seán Lemass, who would soon inherit responsibility for the problem. Net emigration had peaked at 10.4 per thousand in 1937, then 15.5 per thousand in 1943, and reached a

---

19   D. Ferriter, *The Transformation of Ireland 1900-2000*, op.cit., p.481

Seán Lemass, taoiseach from 1959 to 1966, was instrumental in ending protectionism and moving the Republic towards a modern open economy; he is also remembered for his ground-breaking summit meeting with Northern Ireland premier Terence O'Neill in 1965.

new high of 20.3 per thousand in 1958.[20]

By then the aging de Valera was seen as part of the problem, 'a symbol of *Éire passé*',[21] in the words of a non-politician who was about to become more influential than most politicians. De Valera stepped aside from the daily fray, moving on to become President of the Republic. He was succeeded as party leader and taoiseach by Seán Lemass, a veteran of the 1916 rebellion and of Fianna Fáil governments, who had already begun nudging his party away from protectionism, the policy he himself had implemented.

Lemass feared that Ireland was at a tipping point politically. On the eve of his election as taoiseach, he declared that the historic task facing him was 'to consolidate the economic foundations of our political independence'. Fail to do that, he said, and 'everything else goes with it'.[22]

In deciding to break with his party's failing economic policy Lemass was aided or, it can be argued, guided by an outstanding civil servant, T.K. 'Ken' Whitaker. Recently appointed secretary of the Department of Finance, Whitaker had already begun a major research exercise mapping the economic state of the country. He had also developed relationships in the World Bank and International Monetary Fund, believing that Ireland would need their expertise.

In May 1958 Whitaker and his colleagues completed their report, entitled *Economic Development*. Lemass agreed it should be published

---

20 C. Ó Gráda, *Five Crises*, op.cit., p.20
21 A. Chambers, *T. K. Whitaker: Portrait of a Patriot*, op.cit., p.121
22 Lemass, 3 June 1959, quoted in Lee, J.J. Lee, *Ireland 1912-1985: Politics and Society*, op.cit., pp.372-3

in Whitaker's name, an unprecedented move that had the advantage of giving his political masters the option, if necessary, of distancing themselves from its contents. It wasn't, and they didn't.

In November 1958 the Houses of the Oireachtas approved a White Paper, *Programme for Economic Expansion* (known as 'the First programme'), based heavily though not consistently on *Economic Development*. A new direction had been officially endorsed.

This is often referred to as the moment when protectionism was abandoned in favour of free trade, the active pursuit of foreign investment, and the shifting of public expenditure from social to 'productive' investment. Though largely true, the reality is more complex, particularly regarding Whitaker's intent in relation to public expenditure priorities. Whitaker emphasised that knowing what needed to be done, and how, should be central to investment decisions:

'What is urgently necessary is not to know that more resources should be devoted to productive rather than non-productive purposes but rather to know what are the productive purposes to which resources should be applied and what unproductive, or relatively unproductive, activities can, with the minimum social disadvantage, be curtailed to set free resources for productive development.'[23]

The new direction for economic development earned a place in history and public opinion, for Whitaker the analyst and Lemass the political risk-taker. It did no harm to Fianna Fáil's reputation either, but it would take time for improvements to be felt in real life, and Whitaker's advice was forgotten at crucial moments.

There were ups and downs along the way to the hoped-for modern economy. Emigration slowed and rose again in line with economic fortunes, until Ireland became a destination for global migrants in the late 20th century. By then the state was experiencing a level of prosperity unimaginable in the era of Éamon de Valera. It seemed to many that there was no longer a need to worry about the danger Lemass had feared – the loss of everything – but danger was lurking on the horizon, largely because of Fianna Fáil decisions.

In the shorter term another historic decision was about to bear fruit. A Fianna Fáil government completed negotiations for Ireland's accession to the European Economic Community (EEC) in 1973 under the leadership of Jack Lynch, who succeeded Lemass. Backed by more than 83% of voters in a constitutional referendum, membership of

---

23   *Economic Developent*, p.227

the EEC (later the European Union – EU) opened new opportunities for development and trade. Ireland joined when it did because of its close economic ties with the UK, but a crucial result of membership was diversification of trade away from heavy dependence on the UK market, and European funding provided much-needed development assistance.

Northern conflict

Jack Lynch, an eminent sportsman from Cork who had been a reluctant entrant to politics, succeeded Lemass who retired for health reasons in 1966. When hard-line unionists reacted violently against the Northern Ireland Civil Rights Association's campaign for an end to discrimination against Catholics, Lynch found himself at the heart of external and internal political storms. While confronting the island's greatest political crisis since partition, he also had to handle internal dissent and get his party to back solutions acceptable to both communities in Northern Ireland.

Rioting erupted in Derry, a majority Catholic city, in October 1968, and again in August 1969 when it turned into what became known as the 'Battle of the Bogside'.[24] The unrest spread across Northern Ireland. Six people were killed in Belfast on 15 August in sectarian attacks and many families, mainly Catholics, were forced from their homes. British troops were deployed on 14 August 1969, at the request of the NI government.

In Dublin, in a televised statement on 13 August, the taoiseach had opposed deployment of British troops. He called for a United Nations peacekeeping force and announced that the Irish army had been directed to establish field hospitals along the border.

Describing the situation as 'the inevitable outcome of the policies pursued for decades by successive Stormont governments' he said that the Irish Government 'can no longer stand by and see innocent people injured and perhaps worse'.

The taoiseach's public statement differed considerably from Lynch's original draft, having been amended during prolonged argument around the Cabinet table, according to party insider

---

24   'A Chronology of the Conflict', cain.ulster.ac.uk, details events relating to the NI conflict

Noel Whelan.[25] Something was stirring in Fianna Fáil: a rekindling of territorial nationalism, reaching into the highest echelons of government.

On 20 September 1969 Lynch gave a speech to party members with the intention of calming tensions. He stressed support for the principle of unity, but unity by consent; not a forced unification but 'a free and genuine union of those living in Ireland, based on mutual respect and tolerance'. Of its nature, he said, this was a long-term policy.[26]

At that point the taoiseach was seemingly unaware that some of his ministers had a more short-term, urgent and secretive agenda – one that involved an Irish army intelligence officer, meetings with the IRA and a gun-running plot.

Word of arms trafficking allegations reached Lynch in early May 1970 and on 6 May he sacked two of his ministers, Charles Haughey and Neil Blaney. The two went on trial charged with conspiring to import arms with the intention of smuggling them to Northern Ireland for use by the IRA. Though they were acquitted, Lynch's swift action appeared to signal his commitment to a peaceful resolution of the conflict – but the taoiseach's troubles and the Troubles in the north were only beginning.

When British paratroopers shot dead 13 unarmed civilian protesters in Derry on 30 January 1972 ('Bloody Sunday'), it sparked widespread protests. Leaders of the three main political parties in the Republic united in condemning the killings. Ireland recalled its ambassador from London and an estimated 90% of the state's workforce stopped work to honour the victims. The British embassy in Dublin was burnt to the ground.

The taoiseach called for calm but pulled no punches: 'The government is satisfied that British soldiers recklessly fired on unarmed civilians in Derry yesterday and that any denial of this continues and increases the provocation offered by present British policies both with the minority in Northern Ireland and to us here'.[27]

He asked Britain to end internment without trial[28] and to declare its intention to achieve a final settlement of the Irish question. Such

---

25 N. Whelan, *Fianna Fáil: A Biography of the Party*, Dublin, Gill Books, 2011
26 Ibid.
27 Taoiseach's address to the nation, 1 February 1972, www.rte.ie archives
28 G. Moriarty, *Internment explained: When was it introduced and why?*, *Irish Times*, 9 August 2019

a 'final settlement' would prove considerably more elusive than Lynch or his colleagues could have imagined, but most Fianna Fáil leaders who came after him would approach Northern Ireland matters through diplomacy and a commitment to unity by consent as outlined in Lynch's September 1969 speech to party members.

Lynch faced turmoil inside the party, led by Blaney and Boland. Noel Whelan recalls that de Valera and Lemass had led 'united, disciplined and cohesive parliamentary parties' and 'had never experienced the division and mistrust that characterised Lynch's time'.[29] Eventually, loyalty to the party prevailed, perhaps in part because one man stayed out of the fray, quietly building his network for a power bid.

Devaluing democracy

Charles Haughey's dismissal from the front bench as a result of the 'Arms Trial' affair in 1970 had paused but not halted his rise to the top. He won the party leadership in December 1979 and held onto power until February 1992, while simultaneously amassing a large personal fortune.

Haughey lived in style. An Ascendancy mansion, 150-acre stud farm, a private island, helicopter, racing yacht, monogrammed shirts made in a Parisian atelier – how was that possible on a TD's income of £7,000 a year?[30] The whispers didn't, however, shake the party.

The Inquiry into Payments to Politicians and Related Matters (known as the Moriarty Tribunal), set up in 1997 after Haughey had retired, found that he lived a life vastly beyond the scale of what was affordable on what he earned as a public representative.[31] It concluded that payments received by Haughey during his political career 'devalued the quality of a modern democracy.'[32]

Haughey also played fast and loose with sensitive political matters. Des O'Malley, a senior Fianna Fáil TD and three times a cabinet minister, described Haughey as an opportunist, with little

---

29   N. Whelan, *Fianna Fáil: A Biography of the Party*, op.cit.

30   Salary quoted in *The Irish Times*, 25 July 2000

31   Moriarty Tribunal, *Report of the Tribunal Into Payments to Politicians and Related Matters*

32   'Haughey severely criticised by Moriarty', www.rte.ie, 19 December 2006

or no ideology.[33] One of his clashes with Haughey involved the report of the New Ireland Forum,[34] which sought to identify how a lasting peace in Northern Ireland and island-wide stability could be achieved by democratic means. All parties in the Dáil had signed the report but, according to O'Malley, 'half an hour after signing it, Haughey repudiated the kernel of it'.

Expelled from Fianna Fáil when he refused to vote against a Bill to liberalise the availability of contraceptives, O'Malley founded a new party, the Progressive Democrats (PDs), in which other disillusioned TDs joined him. Going on to partner Fianna Fáil

Charles Haughey, taoiseach three times between 1979 and 1992, was found by a Tribunal of Inquiry to have 'devalued' democracy. (© European Communities)

in coalition governments the PDs had an impact out of all proportion to their size on the future direction of Ireland's economic policy.

Fianna Fáil was by then also tapping into a lucrative new source of party finance, the republic's bourgeoning business class. Through an organisation called TACA, an Irish word meaning support or backing, 'businessmen were given access to ministers in return for contributions to party (and personal) coffers'.[35] The practice was reined in – or at least carried on more discreetly – following media focus on rumoured deals with speculative property developers. That category of entrepreneur gained considerable influence and played a major role in the events that led to the fall of the Celtic Tiger economy that was then gestating.

Other facets of the close relationship between high-ranking government figures and major business bosses emerged in media

33 D. O'Malley, in L. Weeks and A. Clarke, *Radical or Redundant: Minor Parties in Irish Politics*, Dublin, History Press, p.80

34 New Ireland Forum Report, Dublin, The Stationery Office, 2 May 1984

35 D. Ferriter, *The Transformation of Ireland 1900-2000*, op.cit., p.561

reports and from various official tribunals of inquiry. Such tribunals became a long-running and expensive feature of Irish political life, which brought to light corruption by politicians, especially some in Fianna Fáil.

Bands, beef and an IRA ceasefire

Albert Reynolds, Haughey's successor as taoiseach (February 1992-December 1994) could more readily account for his wealth. From the late 1950s he and his brother ran a chain of dance halls, capitalising on the 'showband' craze sweeping the entire island (until the killing of 'Miami Showband' musicians in July 1975 by loyalist paramilitaries also took the life out of that phenomenon).[36] A classic example of the business sector from which Fianna Fáil drew much support, after the dance band boom Albert Reynolds made his money from pet food manufacturing, food processing and exporting, and local media.

It was food exports that brought Reynolds, by then taoiseach, into the orbit of a tribunal of inquiry into illegal activities in Ireland's beef industry, but the tribunal's focus was on his time as a minister under Haughey.[37] The tribunal probed the relationship between Goodman International, a large meat export company headed by Larry Goodman, and Taoiseach Charles Haughey. It found that, by underwriting Goodman's beef exports to Iraq, the Fianna Fáil government of 1987-89 had placed at risk large sums of public money, for no economic benefit to the state.

As minister for industry and commerce, Reynolds was involved in decisions relating to the awarding to Goodman of state-funded export insurance that was considerably above the amount Ireland's Industrial Development Authority (IDA) thought appropriate. Yet the key overall decisions were taken at Cabinet under Charles Haughey with whom, it emerged, Goodman met several times while in conflict with the IDA about the amount of insurance he had demanded for his exports to Iraq.

---

36   A BBC documentary, *Showbands: How Ireland Learned to Party*, examines the phenomenon and the 'Miami Showband' murders; first broadcast BBC Four 15 March 2019

37   Convened in 1991, the tribunal reported in 1994

Taoiseach Albert Reynolds at the Dáil on 15 December 1993 after his return from London where he and Prime Minister John Major agreed their approach to peace in Northern Ireland, outlined in the Downing Street Declaration. (© National Library of Ireland)

One thing the tribunal, the first of its kind, did not probe was the extent of corporate donations Fianna Fáil received from beef companies that had benefited from the Haughey government's decisions. 'In one fortnight in 1987 alone, the party got £105,000 from three companies: Goodman International, Master Meats and Hibernia. Donations of £25,000 or £30,000 sometimes coincided with key moments in the process of conferring large public benefits on these companies'.[38]

In November 1992 the beef tribunal had a direct political impact on the fate of the government led by Reynolds, which collapsed after he and Des O'Malley, leader of coalition partner the Progressive Democrats, clashed about the evidence each had given to the tribunal.

The positive high point of Reynolds' short tenure as taoiseach was his contribution to the Northern Ireland peace process. Working with British Prime Minister John Major and SDLP leader John Hume, he helped persuade the IRA/Sinn Féin to begin peace negotiations.

---

38 F. O'Toole, 'Failures of beef tribunal haunt us yet', *The Irish Times*, 25 June 2001

The Downing Street Declaration issued by Major and Reynolds in 1993, which affirmed that Irish unity would happen if a majority in Northern Ireland agreed, laid the grounds for an IRA ceasefire in 1994. Reynolds memorably claimed: 'The IRA have nowhere to go. I've stripped away all their excuses, one by one.'[39]

The 'Teflon' taoiseach

With Bertie Ahern at the helm after Reynolds, the efforts to find a peace formula for Northern Ireland continued. His younger aides couldn't imagine how that focus could offer payback for the party, believing Sinn Féin would eat into their electoral base. Ahern's commitment remained unwavering[40] and in 1998 he was vindicated when he signed the Belfast Agreement with UK Prime Minister Tony Blair and Northern Ireland's main political parties (apart from the DUP).

Ahern's approach to the peace process has been described as calm and patient, as it had been at other key moments – such as when negotiating national agreements with the trade unions and employers, deals that delivered industrial peace for almost a decade in the Republic and were vital to the success of the Celtic Tiger economy.[41]

Ahern knew how to win power as well as peace. Taking over the leadership of Fianna Fáil in 1994, he modernised and re-energised the party in opposition (1994-97). Having pre-agreed a coalition deal with the Progressive Democrats, he led his party to success not just in 1997, but also in two more successive general elections.

He had honed his skills during the years spent building his local base in Drumcondra, a working class area in north Dublin that he and his loyal inner circle turned into a fortress for Fianna Fáil. The Drumcondra operation was outstanding even in a party renowned for dedicated and disciplined local activists. Noel Whelan, a Fianna Fáil insider, noted that Ahern 'designed, built and led the most formidable and well-resourced urban political machine ever seen in Ireland'.[42]

---

39   Various sources e.g. BBC, 21 August 2014
40   P. Leahy, *Showtime: The Inside Story of Fianna Fáil in Power*, op.cit., p.37
41   D. Ferriter, *The Transformation of Ireland 1900-2000*, op.cit., p.659
42   N. Whelan, *Fianna Fáil: A Biography of the Party*, op.cit.

Bertie Ahern was also the protégé of Charles Haughey, whose name became synonymous with corruption in politics. Initially Ahern was able to rise above that association, seemingly untouchable despite recurring questions about his finances. Eventually, it was his inability to explain satisfactorily how he had come into possession of considerable sums of money that ended his long run as the 'Teflon taoiseach'.

Bertie Ahern, taoiseach 1997-2008, played a key role in the Northern Ireland peace talks that led to the Belfast Agreement. (© European Communities)

The Tribunal of Inquiry into Certain Planning Matters and Payments (known as the Mahon Tribunal) was set up to investigate payments to politicians in the context of planning decisions. Its terms of reference were expanded to include other suspect payments to politicians. Bertie Ahern was one of those politicians. His financial offences turned out to be minor compared to Haughey's, but as details slowly emerged, the tide of public opinion began to turn against this formerly very popular politician.

Remaining public and party sympathy for Ahern dissipated in the face of his low-paid former secretary's clear distress when questioned about bank lodgements she had made on his behalf. Gráinne Carruth finally told the tribunal that in all probability she might have lodged large sums of cash in sterling to his accounts.

When the Mahon Tribunal published its report[43] in 2012 it did not accuse Ahern of corruption, but rejected his evidence about the sources of monies in his own and related bank accounts. By then Bertie Ahern had resigned as taoiseach and leader of Fianna Fáil, the Irish economy was in 'special measures' under IMF oversight, and Fianna Fáil had fallen to a fraction of its former strength in the 2011 general election.

---

43   The Final Report of the Tribunal of Inquiry into Certain Planning Matters and Payments, Dublin, The Stationery Office, March 2012

Riding the Celtic Tiger

Bertie Ahern became taoiseach while the Celtic Tiger[44] was roaring, giving him an advantage not available to his predecessors: governments from 1997 to 2007 had a current-account surplus,[45] which offered them unique freedom. The first two Fianna Fáil-led coalitions of the period implemented policies that pleased both right and left by cutting taxes dramatically while simultaneously raising social welfare to one of the most generous levels in Europe.

Ahern's great skill lay in winning elections, not in economic or fiscal policy detail. In 1997 he appointed Charlie McCreevy as his finance minister and left him to get on with the job. McCreevy knew what he wanted to do with the most powerful position in the Cabinet. He and his friend Mary Harney, leader of the PDs, were in different parties but they had shared priorities: to 'remake the tax system, incentivise business and transform the economy'.[46]

McCreevy moved swiftly in the direction he and Harney favoured. In his first budget he reduced taxes all round, cutting the rate of capital gains tax from 40% to 20% with immediate effect, and almost halved interest rates. It was a classic right wing move but public spending also increased substantially, with rises in old-age pensions, child benefits and the minimum wage proving understandably popular.

The tax cuts seemed 'a little less Thatcherite' given that they 'were demanded, lobbied for and lauded by the trade unions'[47] which were influential thanks to successive social partnership agreements brokered by Ahern. Additionally, Leahy notes, Labour was the first party to call for tax cuts during the 2007 election campaign, but by then the economic context was changing – the current account was heading into deficit and economic meltdown was just over the horizon.

McCreevy and the PDs were able to set the agenda in 1997 in large part because Bertie Ahern lacked a strong ideology and was happy with whatever worked[48] – i.e. whatever kept Fianna Fáil in

---

44   Ireland's economic boom period known as the Celtic Tiger era is usually considered to have lasted about a decade from the mid-1990s

45   R. Lyons, *Irish Economic History & Lessons for the Future*, IGEES Conference, March 2016

46   P. Leahy, *Showtime: The Inside Story of Fianna Fáil in Power*, op.cit., p.133

47   Ibid., pp.255-6

48   Ibid., pp.134-5

Supreme Commander of the Irish Defence Forces President Mary McAleese meets Irish troops prior to their deployment to Chad on a peacekeeping mission (16 December 2009); McAleese, a professor of law, was nominated for the presidency by Fianna Fáil in 1997 and was elected unopposed when she sought a second term in 2004. (© Irish Defence Forces)

government – and government satisfaction ratings were booming with the good times.

Five years of rapid growth raised living standards, more and higher-paid jobs were created, and the flourishing economy seemed set to give Fianna Fáil a majority in 2002. However, yet again they fell short of a majority and formed another coalition with the PDs.

Once more in 2007, this time against expectations, Ahern led Fianna Fáil to first place in a general election but not to a majority. In a new twist, in addition to the PDs he invited the Green Party into coalition. The rationale for that move has been much debated but may have reflected Ahern's skill at spotting the significance of shifts in public opinion, however slight a six-seat Greens breakthrough may have appeared to others.

Things fall apart

On 2 April 2008, after his grilling by the Mahon Tribunal, Ahern announced that he intended to resign as taoiseach. Brian Cowen moved from finance minister to taoiseach and would spend most of his premiership fire-fighting the greatest financial failure in the history of the state – one caused by a combination of a global crisis and the added effects of its Irish variant.

Ireland's open economy was highly exposed to global disturbance, but domestic characteristics put it into a higher risk category. As the IMF noted: 'Ireland was swept up in the global financial crisis, but its problems were home-grown.'[49] Economic historian Cormac Ó Gráda summarised the Irish experience as, in one sense, 'just an extreme version of what a poorly regulated, perversely innovative, get-rich-quick banking culture produced in many economies'.

Deepening integration with Europe hadn't stopped Ireland making serious mistakes. 'One might have hoped that the European project had removed our freedom to score economic own goals – and so it seemed for a while – but economic integration did not extend to regulation. And thus, the excesses of our banking system were facilitated by a home-spun regulatory regime'.[50]

The banking system had become overexposed to the property sector, to which it had been excessively accommodating and insufficiently challenging. The Joint Committee of Inquiry into the Banking Crisis would note in its 2016 report that the Central Bank and Financial Regulator 'were aware as early as 2003 that the Irish banking sector was placing increasing reliance on lending to the property sector, and that different lending practices were being adopted'. Yet, as it also noted: 'No independent in-depth 'deep dive' investigation of the banks had been commissioned by the authorities before September 2008.'[51]

Having been finance minister since 2004, Brian Cowen might have been expected to be familiar with such problems. His department had prepared a 'Financial Stability Issues' paper in January 2008. In February it had warned against providing an open-ended, legally binding State guarantee to underwrite a bank's solvency position. That, it said, could only be justified if the entire financial system was at risk of collapse.[52]

When the crunch came and the system was actually at risk of collapse, Cowan's government responded by bailing out the

---

49 IMF, *Ireland from Tiger to Phoenix*, www.imf.org
50 C. Ó Gráda 2011, *Five Crises*, op.cit., pp.26-7
51 Report of the Joint Committee of Inquiry into the Banking Crisis, Houses of the Oireachtas, January 2016
52 Ibid.

banks at enormous cost to the public purse. Having announced on 30 September 2008 that it would guarantee the liabilities of the country's six major banks, the government pumped €46 billion into them over the next two years and nationalised two of them.

Bailing out the banks, however, simply delayed the day of reckoning. As the banks were kept alive with emergency loans from the European Central Bank (ECB),[53] the working population bore the cost: public sector pay was cut by 14% and by the end of 2010 one in every seven workers – some 300,000 people – had lost their jobs.

The harsh reality remained, though, that the deep spending cuts couldn't counterbalance the effect of plummeting tax revenues and higher spending on social services. On 27 November 2010, the government formally applied to enter a programme with the European Commission, the ECB and the International Monetary Fund (IMF) – the Troika.

The governor of Ireland's central bank broke the news of the coming bailout on national radio on the morning of 18 November 2010, announcing that the state would be receiving a loan package worth tens of billions of euros from the IMF.[54] Those loans eventually totalled €67.5 billion over three years, and technical experts from the Troika moved into government buildings to advise Ireland on how to put its house in order.

Paying the price

Brian Cowen resigned on 9 March 2011 after Fianna Fáil's worst ever general election when it won a mere 17.45% of first preference votes. Having been able to muster only 75 candidates, party morale was at an all-time low. Cowen's successor as leader, Micheál Martin, swiftly initiated remedial treatment and five years later the party was out of intensive care and seemingly on the road to recovery.

Having won a mere 20 seats in 2011, Fianna Fáil began its comeback in 2016 when it captured 44 seats, finishing in second place to Fine Gael. The two parties reached a confidence and supply deal to let Fine Gael remain in power, with Fianna Fáil agreeing to abstain on key votes in return for policy concessions. In the next general election the political dynamic changed again, dramatically.

53   www.imf.org
54   M. Minehan, *A Deal with the Devil: The Green Party in Government*, Dunboyne, Maverick House, 2011, p.193

In the February 2020 election Fianna Fáil edged into first place, but only just, one seat ahead of Sinn Féin whose surge shocked the political system. Drawn-out negotiations led to a genuinely historic five-year coalition deal between Fianna Fáil, Fine Gael and the Green Party. The deal included rotation of the taoiseach's position between the bigger two parties, with Fianna Fáil's Micheál Martin leading for the first two and a half years.

Uncertain destiny

Born from a bloody civil war, Fianna Fáil – the 'Soldiers of Destiny' – embraced the political reality open to them in the 1920s, took the oath of allegiance to the English king to start the journey towards achieving its republican aims, and went on to become the most dominant party in the state. It faced many challenges in its long life, but never a death threat until it led the country to the verge of bankruptcy and near loss of sovereignty.

Having come back from the brink and back into government, the challenge facing Fianna Fáil was not just how to survive but to find a *raison d'etre*, perhaps a 21st-century version of the party's founding aims, as Ferriter has suggested.[55] Nearly a century after its birth, in a world its founders would not recognise, could the founding aims offer a workable and vote-winning template?

Did the party simply need a new leader? Micheál Martin was closer in style to Jack Lynch, another quiet man from Cork, than to the party's more charismatic leaders. He struggled to establish himself as taoiseach when he assumed office during the Covid-19 pandemic, but his ratings rose as his government's handling of the pandemic response gained wide approval.

Leadership challengers – exclusively men – tested the wind, but the mostly realistic membership knew that a leadership contest would destabilise not just the party but also the finely balanced coalition government it led. They also knew that the latest iteration of Sinn Féin was gunning for power as forcefully as even Fianna Fáil at its peak.

Might ideological realignment be the right option? A backbencher called for a 'modern centre-left alliance' with Labour – but Labour too was suffering an existential crisis. An assumed leader-in-waiting

---

55   D. Ferriter, 'Fianna Fáil identity crisis driven by pretenders Sinn Féin', *The Irish Times*, 2 October 2020

Fianna Fáil leader Micheál Martin TD leading his party's contingent in the Dublin Pride parade, 2019. (© Shutterstock)

suggested presenting itself as a 'centre-left national party' that would prioritise unity, public housing, welfare of the vulnerable, the environment and rewarding 'hard work and business' – issues of the day and something for everyone.

Taking back the republican terrain from Sinn Féin appealed to some – but was that a feasible or desirable tactic? Micheál Martin wasn't convinced.

When he became leader, Martin's initial prescription for his wounded party included an appeal to their origins, but realism has permeated Fianna Fáil throughout its history and Micheál Martin appeared to be a realist. Perhaps the party really needed to broaden its horizons, become open and inclusive, to prepare for a transformed island's next phase, either as a single constitutional unit or in a federal neighbours-together arrangement.

Boxing clever?

As the possibility of a referendum on Irish unification began to dominate political chatter after the 2016 Brexit vote in the UK, and more so following Sinn Féin's electoral surge in 2020, Martin chose the 'sensible party' route.

Rather than join in the clamour for an early border poll, the new taoiseach ruled out a referendum during the tripartite government's five-year term.[56] Instead, echoing Jack Lynch's conciliatory approach during the emerging conflict in Northern Ireland and the peace efforts of Reynolds and Ahern, he opted to reach out to all communities and traditions with a Shared Island initiative.[57]

The 2020 Programme for Government included plans for 'all-island approaches to the strategic challenges facing Ireland, North and South'. This was to involve strengthening cooperation and developing the all-Ireland economy, investing in the border regions and 'fostering constructive and inclusive dialogue'. A mammoth task, made harder by the ongoing dispute regarding the UK's exit from the EU, especially the Northern Ireland Protocol.

Nevertheless, from its base inside the Department of the Taoiseach and with a €500 million budget, the Shared Island Unit began rolling out its various strands. Practical projects started to emerge, such as a bridge across Carlingford Lough to boost tourism and connect east coast border communities,[58] with cash from the unit and cross-border, cross-party backing. The political question remained, as ever; however successful such initiatives, would voters acknowledge Fianna Fáil's contribution.

Back in 2007 Bertie Ahern had a plan to remodel the party on an all-Ireland basis. Fianna Fáil registered as a political party in Northern Ireland, but little came of the intention to contest NI local authority and Assembly elections. Neither did much come of a 2010 proposal for a merger with the SDLP, although the two parties agreed a policy partnership.

Home game

In reality, though, the party once famed for its election-winning ways knew all too well that to thrive or even survive it had to win back voters – and recruit members – in the Republic.

---

56   *The Irish News*, 22 October 2020
57   Dept. of the Taoiseach, www.gov.ie
58   Dept. of the Taoiseach press release, www.gov.ie, 29 June 2021

In a political field that was more competitive than ever, Fianna Fáil wanted to attract under-represented groups to its under-representative and dwindling membership. Visitors to the party website may be invited to join Fianna Fáil's LGBTQI+ Network, or directed to policies for a fair economy or a more equal Ireland. The low number of women amongst its elected representatives, however, suggested there remained a long way to go.

The dynamics of post-crash politics put everyday problems at the heart of what the electorate expected from political parties. Not just promises but actual policies, actually implemented. Problems like housing – Micheál Martin launched his government's multi-billion euros housing plan in September 2021,[59] and solving a problem like that could have the bonus of undermining Sinn Féin's southern power push.

Who would benefit at the ballot box from successes during Fianna Fáil's agreed stint as lead party of government? Fine Gael or the Green Party could equally claim credit. Which brings up the matter of the relationship between Fine Gael and Fianna Fáil – a merger remained unlikely but a close relationship might be the only realistic option while Fianna Fáil's identity and survival conundrum remained unresolved.

	Fianna Fáil **The Republican Party / An Páirtí Poblachtánach**
Founded:	1926
Meaning of name:	Soldiers of Destiny
Leaders:	Éamon de Valera 1926-59; Seán Lemass 1959-66; Jack Lynch 1966-79; Charles Haughey 1979-92; Albert Reynolds 1992-94; Bertie Ahern 1994-2008; Brian Cowen 2008-11; Micheál Martin 2011-
In office:	1932-33; 1933-37; 1937-38; 1938-43; 1943-44; 1944-48; 1951-54; 1957-61; 1961-65; 1965-69; 1969-73; 1977-81; Feb-Nov 1982; 1987-89. In coalition governments: 1989-92; 1993-94; 1997-2002; 2002-07; 2007-11; 2020-
Affiliations:	Alliance of Liberals and Democrats for Europe (ALDE)
Elected representatives:	2022: 38 TDs (33M, 6F), 21 Senators (15M, 6F), 2 MEPs (2M)

---

59   *Housing for All - a New Housing Plan for Ireland*, www.gov.ie

6

Fine Gael

Conservative patriots to social modernisers

Overview

Founded as 'The United Ireland Party – Fine Gael' in September 1933 from three pre-existing groups, Fine Gael's main precursor was Cumann na nGaedheal, the re-named faction of Sinn Féin that accepted the Anglo-Irish Treaty and governed the Irish Free State until 1932. Another was the Centre Party, mainly representing the interests of farmers, but it was the controversial decision to link up with the 'para-fascist' National Guard that earned Fine Gael the derogatory tag of 'Blueshirts', an insult that has endured down the decades.

When Fine Gael achieved its big electoral breakthrough in 1948, after 15 years in opposition, it was as lead party in the state's first coalition government. This became the template: Fine Gael led several more coalition governments but failed to become the largest party until 2011, after Fianna Fáil suffered meltdown in the aftermath of the 2008 financial crash.

Getting into government required willing political partners. These sometimes drove a hard bargain when negotiating the pre-nuptials but could be more pliant in the *realpolitik* of government. Overall, left-leaning coalition partners tended to influence specific policy areas but did not shift Fine Gael far from its core centre-right position.

Adapting to changing times has marked Fine Gael's political history. It moved from early social and economic conservatism, through a mid-20th century flirtation with social democracy and Keynesianism, to growing liberalism on social issues and economic neoliberalism when that was in the ascendant in mainstream politics.

It could also surprise as when, in 1948, Taoiseach John A. Costello declared that Ireland was to leave the British Commonwealth and become a republic. Or when, in negotiations with Garret FitzGerald, Margaret Thatcher agreed to a role in Northern Ireland for the Dublin government.

Though never winning a clear parliamentary majority, and never developing as strong an electoral machine as its main rival, Fine Gael beat Fianna Fáil into opposition sporadically, and outstripped its civil war rival in 2011.

The dynamic changed when a modern version of Sinn Féin pushed Fine Gael into third place in the 2020 general election. Fine Gael formed a government with its lifelong rival Fianna Fáil for the first time but to do so had to rely on a third partner, the Green Party, symbolising a new challenge in a new era for Fine Gael and other traditional parties.

Putting the case for the Anglo-Irish Treaty, signed 6 December 1921; a civil war followed the treaty's later ratification by the new Dublin parliament.

Fine Gael: the PR version

Fine Gael was launched in 1933 by amalgamating three organisations into a revamped electoral vehicle for Cumann na nGaedheal, which was itself formed in 1923 by the pro-treaty faction of Sinn Féin and governed until defeated by Fianna Fáil in 1932.

The version of its history presented for public consumption by Fine Gael highlights its nationalist pedigree and spotlights people who had been involved in the Easter Rising and the War of Independence. However, the degree of emphasis on its roots has shape-shifted in line with the exigencies of the times, becoming more low key, for example, when wooing unionists in Northern Ireland.

Its self-image includes the fond belief that Michael Collins, the 'marketable, romantic'[1] independence leader who signed the 1921 Anglo-Irish Treaty, would have been a party member had he not been assassinated in August 1922 before even Cumann na nGaedheal was founded.

The declaration of the Republic and Ireland's departure from the British Commonwealth are top of Fine Gael's claimed achievements. Key moments in economic development, international relations and the Northern Ireland peace process follow. Then comes the social progress narrative, with the party taking credit for advances in modernising Irish society. These include access to abortion and contraception, divorce and marriage equality, breakthroughs that occurred during periods when Fine Gael was the lead party in government.

One aspect passed over lightly is its 1933 foundation, which it describes as 'the amalgamation of a number of groups: the pro-treaty Cumann na nGaedheal party, the Centre Party, and the National Guard'.[2] That summary glosses over a dark moment in Fine Gael history, the serious political misjudgement that saw the presidency of the new party offered to the National Guard's Eoin O'Duffy, leader of the fascist-leaning 'Blueshirts'. O'Duffy didn't last long and is missing from the official list of leaders; instead, the reader's eye is directed to the role of Cumann na nGaedheal leaders in the independence struggle and the foundation phase of the Irish Free State.

Building the state

On 16 June 1922, pro-treaty Sinn Féin won 58 of 128 seats in the new parliament, Dáil Éireann, with 34 seats going to Labour and other non-Sinn Féin candidates. Anti-treaty Sinn Féin took just 36 seats. Two significant aspects of the outcome are often overlooked: the pro-treaty side won twice as much of the popular vote as those opposed to the treaty, while Labour and others had a combined total that was greater than either of the Sinn Féin factions.

Public opinion had accepted the Anglo-Irish Treaty or at least, as Ferriter suggests, had tired of debate about oaths and symbols

---

1   S. Collins & C. Meehan, *Saving the State*, op.cit., p.44
2   www.finegael.ie/the-party/history-of-fine-gael/

Government of the Irish Free State, 1922-23, led by W.T. Cosgrave (3rd from left, front row) who was also leader of Cumann na nGaedheal when that party was formed from pro-treaty Sinn Féin members. (© University College Dublin)

and prioritised bread-and-butter issues.[3] The violence wasn't over, however, and civil war broke out, lasting from 28 June 1922 to 24 May 1923.

As the vicious war raged the pro-treaty side established a new political party to fight elections. Delegates to a December 1922 conference considered using the Sinn Féin name, but opted instead for Cumann na nGaedheal, the name of another organisation established by Arthur Griffith in 1900 – thus maintaining a link with their separatist past.[4]

In the Irish Free State election held on 27 August 1923, soon after the civil war had ended, Cumann na nGaedheal won 41% of seats. Led by W.T. Cosgrave it formed a government whose performance, in uncharted waters for the recent rebels, could be described as pragmatic, conservative and often ruthless: they did not hesitate to jail or execute opponents in their zeal to impose order and build a viable state.

---

3   D. Ferriter, *The Transformation of Ireland 1900-2000*, op.cit., p.254
4   M. Farrell quoted in, S. Collins & C. Meehan, *Saving the State*, op.cit., p.13

Tackling Ireland's socio-economic challenges, whether these were due to pre-existing conditions such as the dire poverty prevalent in both rural and urban areas, or to external factors, called for informed, imaginative and bold policies. With few exceptions the rulers of the new state were not up to this challenge. They didn't lack firmness – they were as focused and ruthless in government as in their pursuit of independence – but their approach to governing was cautious, favouring balanced budgets and free trade. Radical social reform was barely on their horizon and, consciously or unconsciously, the conservative Catholic ethos of those times tended to guide decisions.

War damage to the country's infrastructure aggravated an already enormous task and, as Collins and Meehan note: 'The financial burden of repairing the destruction undermined the prospect of realising the lofty aspirations that had inspired the independence movement'.[5]

Economic protectionism was not yet in the mainstream, despite its centrality to the original Sinn Féin policy platform. Protective tariffs were imposed sporadically, often in response to lobbying, but a comprehensive approach to economic development was lacking. The Shannon Hydro Scheme, one of the largest civil engineering projects in the world at the time and still generating electricity today,[6] was the outstanding exception in the record of what Ferriter has called 'a cautious government which was loath to tinker with free-trade orthodoxy or scare vested interests'.[7]

Fine Gael's reputation for hard-hearted social policies emerged during this period. One example was cutting old age pensions by a shilling a week, which, according to Ferriter, reflected the finance minister's determination to balance the books regardless of the social cost. Another was a comment by economy minister Patrick McGilligan during a Dáil debate on unemployment: 'There are certain limited funds at our disposal. People may have to die in this country and may have to die through starvation'.[8]

---

5   S. Collins & C. Meehan, *Saving the State*, op.cit., p.12

6   www.ice.org.uk/what-is-civil-engineering/what-do-civilengineers-do/shannon-hydro-scheme

7   D. Ferriter, *The Transformation of Ireland 1900-2000*, op.cit., p.316

8   Dáil Éireann debate, 12 Jun 1924, Vol. 7 No. 23

Flirting with fascism?

Ousted from office by Fianna Fáil in 1932, Cumann na nGaedheal found itself adrift and organisationally weak. Casting about for ways of strengthening its party machinery, it merged with two other organisations, the National Centre Party and the National Guard, formerly known as the Army Comrades Association, to form the United Ireland Party – Fine Gael.[9]

Merging with the National Centre Party, a resurgence of the old Farmers Party, was a logical move given Cumann na nGaedheal's centrist ideology and rural support. The National Guard was a different matter. Rafter describes it as having 'offered energy and organisation

The governing Cumann na nGaedheal party ran a negative campaign in the 1932 election, using posters such as this to highlight the recent violent past of its Fianna Fáil opponents.

to a demoralised Cumann na nGaedheal', but the cost was high. The National Guard leader, the controversial and militaristic Eoin O'Duffy, became president of the new party. O'Duffy's tenure was brief but it left a toxic legacy from which the party has never been able to escape.

The Army Comrades Association, formed in 1931 and renamed the National Guard a year later – though widely known as the Blueshirts – sought to establish 'a fascist system of government', according to Rafter.[10] Others are less absolute in their assessment, while recognising the group's easy resort to mob violence. Ferriter describes the Blueshirts as possessing 'certain fascist traits', but says they were not fascist in the sense of German or Italian fascism.[11] Lee claims that, though the Blueshirts had 'vaguely corporatist'

---

9   S. Collins & C. Meehan, *Saving the State*, op.cit., p.33

10   K. Rafter, *The Road to Power: How Fine Gael Made History*, Dublin, New Island, 2011, p.61

11   D. Ferriter, *The Transformation of Ireland 1900-2000*, op.cit., p.416

policies[12] they possessed few of the essential characteristics of fascist movements 'as distinct from a small number of largely incidental similarities' and that 'it would be a travesty of the history of ideas to dignify these mobs ... as fascist'.[13]

Nevertheless, adopting a uniform of blue shirts suggested a deliberate modelling on the Brownshirts and Blackshirts of Germany and Italy respectively, however politically naïve most of its members were in reality.

The Cumann na nGaedheal leadership was a different matter. That they found the Blueshirts' alleged organisational expertise attractive enough to over-ride any qualms about their use of violence and their dubious politics suggests either a degree of sympathy with fascism or an underestimation of its sinister implications. Either raises serious questions about Ireland at that time as well as about authoritarian tendencies within Cumann na nGaedheal and, ultimately, the early Fine Gael.

The first coalition

1948 marked an important bridging moment, if not quite a turning point, for Irish political parties: it was the year in which the concept of coalition government was pioneered and normalised.

Fianna Fáil called an election in 1948, banking on the opposition parties not being well prepared to fight it: Fine Gael appeared to be on the verge of collapse; Labour had split into two parties; and the recently formed Clann na Poblachta, seen as a serious threat to the ruling party, needed more time to build an organisation.

What Fianna Fáil didn't foresee was cooperation between the diverse opposition parties. Lacking the numbers in the new Dáil to form a government alone it had to watch as Fine Gael became the lead party in Ireland's first coalition. Partnering it in the Inter-Party Government, as it was termed, were the two Labour parties, Clann na Talmhan (a farmers' party), six independent TDs and Clann na Poblachta, the newcomer that had spooked Fianna Fáil into calling an election.

Fine Gael's hope of spearheading a ruling coalition faced an initial roadblock: its leader, General Richard Mulcahy, was anathema to Clann na Poblachta, mainly because of his role in the execution

---

12   J.J. Lee, *Ireland 1912-1985: Politics and Society*, op.cit., p.178
13   Ibid., p.182

of republicans during the civil war. John A. Costello TD reluctantly accepted nomination as Taoiseach. Costello was not only more acceptable than Mulcahy but also more sympathetic than many in Fine Gael to the other parties. He had persuaded Clann leader Seán MacBride to take up constitutional politics, and his father had been friendly with Jim Larkin, a legendary Labour leader.[14]

The parties agreed a ten-point programme for government, the detail of which mainly originated with Clann and Labour. It committed the government to enhanced public investment, a substantial increase in social welfare benefits, an extensive programme of new social housing, and the building of hospitals and sanatoria for tuberculosis sufferers. This signalled a break with the past by prioritising social commitments and introducing Keynesian elements into economic policy.

While the coalition was still in its infancy, Costello surprised his Cabinet colleagues as well as the country – and shocked Britain – by declaring that Ireland intended to become a republic and withdraw from the British Commonwealth. Costello's announcement was made by apparent chance: he confirmed during a press conference while in Canada that it was his government's intention to take this constitutional step. No record of a Cabinet decision has been found but record keeping was lax at the time. As well as boosting its own nationalist credentials and forestalling potential friction with Clann na Poblachta, the move allowed Fine Gael to outflank its historic rival, Fianna Fáil.

Nevertheless, there were many other tensions in the coalition Cabinet, according to McCullagh, with ideological dividing lines between parties and particularly between Fine Gael and the rest.[15] Despite this, there was sufficient Cabinet accord to implement some key commitments, including an extensive social housing programme, establishment of an Industrial Development Authority and unprecedented healthcare investment.

Although the policies most associated with the first coalition government originated with Clann na Poblachta and Labour, they could not have been implemented without the cooperation of Fine Gael as the senior partner.[16] In one key area, however, ideology did intrude: a proposal to provide free medical care to children and pregnant women, known as the Mother and Child Scheme, was the

---

14   D. McCullagh, *A Makeshift Majority*, op.cit., p.33
15   Ibid., p.43
16   Ibid., pp.179-181

coalition's most controversial failure and 'has remained one of the great *causes celebres* of Irish politics'.[17]

Proposed by health minister Dr Noel Browne (Clann na Poblachta) this scheme fell victim to ministerial conservatism in the face of opposition from two powerful lobbies, doctors who feared loss of income and the Catholic hierarchy that saw in the scheme the thin edge of a socialist wedge. Most cabinet ministers, like the majority of their constituents, were deeply religious and would not flout the will of their bishops. Noel Browne found himself opposed not just by Fine Gael but also by the other parties and even his own party leader. The scheme fell and Browne resigned, but the coalition limped on.

That the 1948-51 government was in a position to adopt an expansionary investment policy, while simultaneously cutting tax rates, was due in large part to an external source of finance and the approach to post-war recovery in Europe. Access to US Marshall Aid offered windfall funding for some of the coalition's ambitious goals and smoothed economic differences between the parties.[18] It also brought Ireland closer to mainstream developments in the UK and across Europe. Fine Gael found itself moving from conservative custodian of limited resources to acceptance of a serious role for the state in investment and citizens' welfare.

Fianna Fáil won the 1951 election but Fine Gael led a second coalition government in the 1954-57 period, though this was generally considered a weaker and less significant administration. Collins and Meehan, however, argue that this second coalition laid the foundations for later economic transformation.[19]

Although Taoiseach John Costello was unwilling to stand up to Catholic bishops on the matter of free medical care, there is some evidence that he was open to fresh thinking. He was interested in new economic theories and appointed a Keynesian economist, Patrick Lynch, as his personal adviser. Lynch influenced not just the taoiseach but also the finance minister Patrick McGilligan. 'The scourge of mere humanitarianism' 25 years earlier, McGilligan 'became an intellectual as well as a political convert to the potential of a moderate Keynesianism in Irish circumstances'.[20]

---

17   J.J. Lee, *Ireland 1912-1985: Politics and Society*, op.cit., p.313
18   D. McCullagh, *A Makeshift Majority*, op.cit., p.140
19   S. Collins & C. Meehan, *Saving the State*, op.cit., p.68
20   J.J. Lee, *Ireland 1912-1985: Politics and Society*, op.cit., p.312

Ideological vacuum

While the governments led by Costello in 1948-51 and 1954-57 had engaged with some key challenges, any edge its successes might have given Fine Gael over Fianna Fáil was short-lived.

By the 1960s the party was struggling to prove it had a distinct ideology, according to Diarmaid Ferriter. Its new leader, James Dillon, appeared to be unaware of the party's organisational weaknesses, to the extent that he assumed electoral success was inevitable and confided in a colleague that he found the idea of Fine Gael becoming the largest party 'an alarming prospect'.[21]

Nor did Dillon believe there was a need for serious ideological differences in Irish politics, unlike the frustrated members of the party's emerging social democratic wing. One of these impatient young men, Garret FitzGerald, was blunt in his criticism: 'Fine Gael does not understand what is meant by the formation of economic, social and cultural policies under modern conditions'.[22]

This leftward-leaning faction set about filling the policy vacuum. Declan Costello TD (son of former Taoiseach John A. Costello) produced a position paper, 'Towards a Just Society',[23] that set out eight areas for action including economic planning; government control of prices and of the banks' credit policies; investment in industry; and social capital investment.

In echoes of the 1948 Inter-Party Government, the paper recognised 'the very wide areas in our society where great poverty exists', and aimed for a society in which freedom and equality are 'expressed in real and tangible conditions which all our people can enjoy'. Heavily referencing Christian Socialist principles, the 'Just Society' paper has also been described as a social democratic charter and was adopted as Fine Gael's 1965 general election manifesto, though this was largely by default due to the absence of alternative proposals. The election was its test, the opportunity to convince voters that Fine Gael offered solutions for left-behind sectors of society, that it could end perpetual high unemployment, emigration, and economic stagnation.[24]

---

21   D. Ferriter, *The Transformation of Ireland* 1900-2000, op.cit., p.558
22   Ibid., p.558
23   Fine Gael Policy 1965, *Towards a Just Society*, Fine Gael, 1965
24   R. McCord, www.theirishstory.com, 'A Just Society for Ireland (review), 16 December 2013

It was an offer that failed to enthuse voters. Crucially, it did not enthuse many Fine Gael candidates either or convince the leadership. At its press launch, leader James Dillon made clear that his party was not turning socialist: 'We shall rely on private enterprise,' he declared to journalists. 'We are a private enterprise party'. This was both a summary of Fine Gael's bedrock beliefs and a warning to Costello and his associates in the nascent social democratic wing that the party he led was not for turning.

Declan Costello had succeeded in setting Fine Gael's policy agenda but it was a partial and temporary win, not a commitment to a new direction. The wider party was not ready to embrace change.[25] The social democrats would continue trying to reform policy and rebrand the party, but little was done to advance any of Costello's proposals until Garret Fitzgerald became leader.

Waves of hope

Ireland joined the European Economic Community (EEC) on 1 January 1973, on a wave of hope for a future better than anything delivered during the dreary post-independence decades. 1973 was also a year of optimism for Fine Gael, which entered government with Labour in March. This coalition, led by Liam Cosgrave, as well as those that would be led by Garret FitzGerald (1981-82 and 1982-87), challenged some entrenched political attitudes in different but overlapping ways, but particularly regarding Northern Ireland.

In September 1973, Cosgrave and British Prime Minister Ted Heath met at a military airport near Dublin, where they agreed to convene the conference that would lead to the Sunningdale Agreement.[26] Attended by delegations from the Irish and British governments and the Northern Ireland Executive (designate), the agreement ratified a power-sharing Northern Ireland executive and, significantly, a Council of Ireland.

Prompted by the growing violence in Northern Ireland, both Fine Gael and Labour had been engaged in a fresh analysis of their northern policy, focusing on divided communities rather than partition as the central problem. In addition to the Sunningdale

---

25   C. Meehan: https://ciarameehan.com/2013/06/06/declancostellos-just-society-a-fine-gael-symbol-of-progress-or-of-division/

26   S. Collins & C. Meehan, *Saving the State*, op.cit., p.151

negotiations, Taoiseach Liam Cosgrave made a significant statement in the Dáil: that Northern Ireland's constitutional position could not be changed without the consent of a majority of its people.[27] This espousal of the consent principle signalled effective abandonment of the territorial claim to the north in the Republic's constitution, though the constitution would not be revised until after the 1998 peace accord.

While economics had dominated the 1973 election campaign, and the shift in Northern Ireland policy was significant, it was fiscal policy that brought about the downfall of Cosgrave's government.

The 1973-77 coalition succeeded in boosting house building and tried to protect social welfare, despite the impact of the global oil crisis that began in 1973. It also introduced a wealth tax, the brainchild of foreign affairs minister Garret FitzGerald who proposed it as 'a more effective method of limiting the accumulation of wealth in too few hands'.[28] The wealth tax contributed to the coalition's undoing: Fianna Fáil, in its 1977 'razzmatazz' election campaign, promised to abolish it and did so when back in office.

Unlike most Irish political leaders, FitzGerald was an intellectual whose writings and actions suggest someone in search of solutions. When he succeeded Cosgrave as leader in 1977 he injected a degree of enthusiasm and organisational vigour into Fine Gael that would lead to another spell in government in 1981.

The crusades of 'Garret the Good'

Garret Fitzgerald, who considered himself a social democrat, had supported Declan Costello in developing the Just Society policy in the 1960s.[29] According to his adviser and speechwriter, Michael Lillis, he had joined Fine Gael to change the party, take it into power and change the country, even though 'ideologically his sympathies would have suggested' he should join Labour.[30]

FitzGerald's family background was impeccably nationalist: both his parents had fought in the 1916 Easter Rising – the rebellion

---

27   CAIN https://cain.ulster.ac.uk/othelem/chron/ch74.htm

28   G. FitzGerald, *All in a Life*, Dublin, Gill & Macmillan, 1992, pp.300-301

29   C. Meehan, 'The Constitutional Crusade', *A Just Society for Ireland? 1964–1987*. London, Palgrave Macmillan, 2013

30   M. Lillis, 'The Good Statesman', *Dublin Review of Books* (Issue 124), July 2020

Taoiseach Garret FitzGerald and UK Prime Minister Margaret Thatcher signed the 1985 Anglo-Irish Agreement which gave the Republic a voice in Northern Ireland affairs while agreeing that unification would require the support of the people of NI. (© European Communities)

against British rule that forms the cornerstone of the republic's foundation story – but his mother was a Belfast Presbyterian and he grew up in close contact with her family in Northern Ireland, an experience that influenced his approach to north-south relations. He sought constitutional change and social liberalisation in order to make a united Ireland attractive to Ulster Protestants.

When he became taoiseach in 1981 FitzGerald declared a crusade 'to make this a genuine republic on the principles of Tone and Davis'.[31] He wanted to create a pluralist society, 'a society within which people of different religious, cultural or linguistic traditions would be treated as equal citizens',[32] with the aim of reuniting Ireland during his time in power.

According to Lillis, FitzGerald was concerned with 'righting the injustices that the unionists, with the unspoken support of London, systematically visited on the Catholic nationalist minority' in the north. Ending religious bigotry in the south was the key to reunification, he believed, and would require a new legal and social framework in the republic that 'would make our society less alien to northern unionists'.[33]

Under FitzGerald's leadership Fine Gael began to adopt an openly liberal stance on social issues, particularly on individual rights, setting the party and the country on a path that would transform 'Catholic

---

31   Quoted in C. Meehan. The reference is to Theobald Wolfe Tone of the United Irishmen, and the Young Irelander Thomas Davis.

32   G. FitzGerald, *Towards a New Ireland*, Dublin, Gill & MacMillan, 1972

33   M. Lillis, 'The Good Statesman', op.cit.

Ireland' into a more modern and progressive state, although this would not happen until decades after Fitzgerald's time as taoiseach.

Implementing a socially liberal agenda in Ireland even as recently as the final quarter of the 20th century was hugely challenging, as FitzGerald discovered. A proposal to legalise divorce was defeated in a referendum in 1986,[34] although a second proposal in 1995 was successful under a later Fine Gael–led government.

'A modest concession to reality'

As a key step in his constitutional crusade, FitzGerald established the New Ireland Forum, to consult on 'the manner in which lasting peace and stability can be achieved in a new Ireland through the democratic process'.[35] Reporting in May 1984, the Forum suggested three options for a new relationship between the two states on the island: a unitary state, a federal or confederal state, or a joint British/ Irish authority under which the London and Dublin governments would have equal responsibility for all aspects of the government of Northern Ireland.[36]

Margaret Thatcher, the British prime minister, initially dismissed all three alternatives but Fitzgerald persisted and was vindicated when he and Prime Minister Thatcher signed the landmark Anglo-Irish Agreement in November 1985.

In Lillis' version of events FitzGerald 'persuaded the most pro-unionist and least pro-Irish British prime minister of the twentieth century [...] to give a substantial role to the Irish government in the processes of government of Northern Ireland.' This, he claimed, made the 1985 Anglo-Irish Agreement FitzGerald's most important achievement.

Although it fell short of the Forum's aspirations, the Anglo-Irish Agreement gave the Republic a voice in Northern Ireland affairs through an intergovernmental conference. The British government thus recognised the legitimacy of the Republic's interest in Northern Ireland, and of its potential contribution to the resolution of the so-

---

34   This was precipitated by a Private Member's Bill introduced by Michael O'Leary, then a FG backbencher but previously leader of the Labour Party
35   Dáil Éireann debate, 11 May 1983
36   New Ireland Forum Report, 2 May 1984; 8.1

called 'Ulster question'. Historian Joe Lee remarked: 'To that extent it was a modest, but not insignificant, concession to reality.'[37]

While recognising the significance of the Anglo-Irish Agreement, Lee took a less positive view of FitzGerald's crusade to achieve 'a pluralist consensus embracing Catholic and Protestant religious traditions equally'. In Lee's view 'his pluralism was too anaemic, his vision of Ireland too devoid of any sense of a distinctive national identity to arouse mass support'.[38] Instead, what he did arouse was resistance by conservative Catholics in the Republic, who, in 1983, showed their resentment at the FitzGerald government's liberal direction by voting to enshrine in the Irish constitution an even more restrictive approach to abortion than had existed since 1861.

During FitzGerald's later period in office the economy fell into recession and the optimism generated by EEC membership dissipated. The Fine Gael/Labour government was defeated in the 1987 general election.

A Rainbow Coalition

Fine Gael got through another three leaders during the 15 years following FitzGerald's resignation in 1987. Neither Alan Dukes (1987-90) nor Michael Noonan (2001-02) succeeded in leading their party into government but, in December 1994, John Bruton (1990-2001) formed an unlikely alliance, dubbed the Rainbow Coalition, with the Labour and Democratic Left parties.

The collapse of a Fianna Fáil/Labour coalition in late 1994 created a novel scenario: President Robinson used her prerogative to facilitate formation of a new government without calling a general election on the grounds that a proposed new three-party government had a parliamentary majority.[39]

The arrangement was also unusual in an ideological sense. While Fine Gael appeared to have more in common with the neoliberal Progressive Democrats, it chose Democratic Left as a government partner despite its more radical policies.

Fine Gael leader John Bruton had initially favoured a four-party arrangement including both the Progressive Democrats and

---

37   J.J. Lee, *Ireland 1912-1985: Politics and Society*, op.cit., p.457
38   J.J. Lee, *Ireland 1912-1985: Politics and Society*, op.cit., p.653
39   K. Rafter, *The Road to Power: How Fine Gael Made History*, op.cit., p.70

Democratic Left, which he thought would have created a centrist administration. That plan came to nothing, however, as neither of the smaller parties wanted this, believing that one of them would lack influence.

Nor was it a matter of parliamentary arithmetic – involving the Progressive Democrats would have given a more solid majority. The clincher was Labour's preference for Democratic Left (with which it would later merge) and, according to Rafter, there were also good personal relationships between key Fine Gael and Democratic Left TDs.[40]

The Rainbow Coalition took office in 1994 at a unique moment in the state's economic history. The economy was expanding at an unprecedented pace: Irish growth rates were notably above the European average, exports were growing, inflation was low, and the exchange rate was firm. This was the result of a confluence of factors: global and domestic policies (in particular inward investment by US corporations), investment in human capital, a social partnership with trade unions, and EU membership.

Meanwhile, as the prospect of unprecedented economic prosperity entranced voters in the Republic, in Northern Ireland the peace process suffered a huge blow when the IRA ended its ceasefire in 1996 by exploding a massive bomb in London's Docklands. The Dublin government continued to engage with northern affairs, officially and via freelancing by individual party leaders – but the Rainbow Coalition would be out of office before the Belfast Agreement was signed in April 1998.

Although progress towards peace was slow on John Bruton's watch as taoiseach, his administration could claim some social policy achievements, including a successful divorce referendum in 1995.

The Rainbow Coalition partners agreed to contest the 1997 general election on a joint programme while also producing their own manifestoes, but they had already written the script for their coming failure by resisting pressures to deliver a populist pre-election budget. Fianna Fáil and the Progressive Democrats had no such scruples and defeated the Rainbow parties by wooing voters with promises of tax cuts.

---

40   Ibid., p.72

Pragmatism and power

The upswing in Fine Gael membership and activist engagement in the early 1980s, driven by Garret Fitzgerald's leadership, didn't lead to a long-term transformation. The party still lacked an electoral machine to rival that of Fianna Fáil, which consistently outperformed Fine Gael when it came to organisation and elections – until 2011.[41] That was the year in which, under Enda Kenny's leadership, Fine Gael became the largest party in the Dáil for the first time, with 76 seats to Fianna Fáil's 20.

A major study undertaken in 1999 showed that Fine Gael had about 1,000 branches and 20,000 members, down from a high of over 33,000 under FitzGerald in the early 1980s.[42] This analysis, the first of any Irish political party, confirmed that the typical member was male, middle-aged, middle-class and attended church regularly. Members were generally non-ideological although they tended to describe themselves as centre-right and relatively liberal – a description with which the man who led Fine Gael between 2002 and 2017 might have been expected to feel personally comfortable.

Enda Kenny was a political technocrat, the antithesis of the academic Garret FitzGerald. Kenny had enjoyed a low-key career but also personal popularity across political divides. His easy manner hid his organisational talent. On election as party leader in 2002 Kenny proceeded to build a party machine capable of winning, but it would take him almost a decade to achieve his aim of leading a government.

Kenny promised consensus and team building but gave 'no sense that there was an ideology in his approach to politics', according to Rafter.[43] Yet he would go on to prove that he was not lacking in deeply held beliefs and his humanity shone through in a number of memorable speeches. Just a few months into his time as taoiseach, in July 2011, he launched an unprecedented attack on the Vatican for failing to protect children from paedophile priests, accusing the Catholic Church of dysfunction, disconnection and elitism.

A different speech drew global attention in 2017, shortly before Kenny ended his tenure as taoiseach. During the traditional St. Patrick's Day presentation of a bowl of shamrock to the US President,

---

41   Ibid., pp.75-76
42   M. Gallagher & M. Marsh, *Days of Blue Loyalty*, op.cit.
43   K. Rafter, *The Road to Power: How Fine Gael Made History*, op.cit., p.44

Taoiseach Enda Kenny presents Barack Obama with a hurley, used in the Irish sport of hurling, during the US President's visit to Ireland. Dublin, 23 May 2011.

he lectured the incumbent, Donald Trump, on immigration. Ireland's national saint was an immigrant, he noted, and the Irish had been 'the wretched refuse on the teeming shore', looking for shelter in America and 'believing in the compassion of America'. Delivered on the day when Trump's travel ban on six predominantly Muslim countries had been due to be rolled out, the message could hardly have been clearer.

When, in February 2011, Fine Gael became the largest political party in the Dáil for the first time in its history, the success wasn't entirely due to Enda Kenny's party-building skills. Nor was Fine Gael's parliamentary party big enough to govern alone, meaning Kenny had to form a coalition with the Labour Party.

While the new parties of government benefitted electorally from Fianna Fáil's handling of the 2008 banking crisis they also inherited the fallout from the worst financial crash suffered by any EU member state, and thus faced the greatest challenge.

Managing a complex crisis

In 2011 Fine Gael and Labour inherited an economy on the rocks, a country in hock to international lenders, and a population reeling from the austerity measures introduced to deal with the crisis triggered by the combination of a global financial crisis and a home-grown meltdown due to construction sector and banking failures.[44]

The real government of Ireland by then was a Troika composed of the International Monetary Fund (IMF), the European Commission and the European Central Bank (ECB). In pre-election meetings with Fine Gael and Labour, the Troika had warned that any new government would be bound by the promises already made by the outgoing government.

That message was reiterated when Enda Kenny, the new taoiseach, attended his first European Council meeting. European leaders made clear that the bailout conditions were not for overturning – or at least not unless Ireland was willing to forfeit its low corporation tax rate. Kenny's answer to that option was a firm 'no'.[45] He argued that losing this pillar of the Republic's economic strategy would make recovery harder.

The incoming Fine Gael / Labour administration did not consider walking away from the deal they had inherited, according to Leahy,[46] but they did try to renegotiate terms. Kenny asked, unsuccessfully, for the interest rate on loans to be cut in line with the deal agreed for Greece. At an IMF meeting, Ireland's finance minister sought to have senior bondholders for the broken Anglo Irish Bank accept that they would not get all their money back. The proposal was vetoed by the European Central Bank, yet Ireland would go on to recover more quickly and strongly than Greece.

The framework in which the new coalition had to operate had been set by the 2011 budget, passed before the general election. The coalition's own first budget aimed to reduce the deficit by €3.8 billion, of which €2.2 billion would come from spending cuts and €1.6 billion from extra taxation.

The negative reactions were predictable and would continue, exemplified in mass protests against property taxes and water charges. Some protests turned nastily personal as ministers were

---

44 For consideration of why Ireland experienced a systemic banking crisis see report of Oireachtas inquiry: *https://inquiries.oireachtas.ie/banking/*

45 É. Gilmore, *Inside the Room*, op.cit., p.110

46 P. Leahy, *The Price of Power: Inside Ireland's Crisis Coalition*, Dublin, Penguin Ireland, 2013, p.xi

attacked, one in her car by water charge protesters, another at home with his three-week-old baby.

With signs of recovery starting to show, the government presented a mildly expansionary budget for 2015. This, say Collins and Meehan, was a calculated gamble. The gamble paid off and economic performance improved. Crucially, unemployment fell, from a 15.1% peak to under 5% in 2019.

In late 2015 Ireland became the first European Union (EU) country to leave the financial bail-out process. Collins and Meehan argue that, with hindsight, the actions the government took in its first year to implement the bailout programme put the economy on the road to recovery.

21ˢᵗ century alliances

The coalition lasted until Labour withdrew in July 2014, after which Kenny led a minority government until the February 2016 election. Fine Gael emerged from that contest as the largest party once again but, with its seats total reduced to 50, it had limited options. With a mere seven seats, 30 fewer than pre-election, Labour could make no useful contribution to a new coalition, even if it had wanted to do so – voters had punished that party for what they saw as complicity in austerity. Sinn Féin had emerged as the third largest party, with 23 seats, but was definitively unacceptable to Fine Gael as a political partner.

Another option was the diminished but recovering Fianna Fáil. A coalition between the two traditional rivals was still a step too far for either party, but a deal with independent TDs plus a confidence and supply accord with Fianna Fáil enabled Fine Gael to form a minority government. That accord eased the way towards the historic relationship that would be reached in 2020.

From Kenny to Varadkar

Enda Kenny tendered his resignation as Fine Gael leader and taoiseach in June 2017 and was succeeded by Leo Varadkar. In 2015, just months before Ireland's historic marriage equality referendum, Varadkar had come out as gay, the first Irish government minister to do so. When he became leader of a party viewed as conservative for most of its history, his sexuality and ethnic background attracted

Taoiseach Leo Varadkar and Helen McEntee, minister of state for European affairs, in Brussels, 12 December 2019. (© Shutterstock)

widespread attention. How had the gay son of a self-styled socialist from India and a mother from a Fianna Fáil family ended up as leader of Fine Gael and of the Irish government? Also, what did that say about the changing nature of Ireland and Fine Gael in particular?

Rafter presents Varadkar as a force to be reckoned with from his earliest involvement in Fine Gael.[47] Like Garret FitzGerald decades earlier he was outspoken in his criticism of his party's policies and performance, but his approach to widening the party's appeal focused at least as much on presentation as policy.

After Fine Gael lost the 2007 general election Varadkar, a first-time TD, went on the offensive: 'We did not win the policy debates. We showed an unwillingness to take clear positions. We did not demonstrate competence to run the economy ... we were unable to stand over our own promises ...'[48] He called on the party to adopt a more modern cosmopolitan image and develop policies that could appeal to the 'hundreds of thousands of uncommitted swing voters in cities, county towns and commuter belts across Ireland'.[49]

---

47   K. Rafter, *The Road to Power: How Fine Gael Made History*, op.cit., p.244
48   Ibid., p.241
49   Ibid., p.244

Combining PR and policies targeted at a new generation of voters appeared to have an impact. Fine Gael became the largest party in the Dáil in 2011 for the first time in its history – though the reasons went far deeper than Leo's PR offensive. It didn't retain the top slot, but while in prime political position it oversaw some significant social policy changes – reforms that were in tune with Varadkar's approach to wooing younger voters.

As party leader and taoiseach from June 2017 Leo Varadkar focused again on updating Fine Gael's image, making a pitch to members in spring 2019 to add personal liberty, Europe and openness, protection of the environment and compassion to Fine Gael's official values.[50] The last of these four, defined as affirming the role of the state 'in offering a helping hand to those that need it', would soon be put to the test in unimaginable circumstances: the Coronavirus pandemic which would dominate the concerns of the Irish government, like most other governments, from early 2020.

Social progress and political setback

In a May 2015 referendum the electorate voted to extend full marriage rights to same-sex couples, making Ireland the first country in the world to legalise gay marriage by popular vote.

Three years later a bigger majority approved repeal of the Eighth Amendment to the Constitution, which had restricted abortion to extreme circumstances where the life of a pregnant woman was at risk. The 'at risk' clause hadn't saved Savita Halappanavar, who died from septicaemia in 2012 after being refused an abortion while miscarrying her first child. In response to a public outcry Enda Kenny introduced the 2013 Protection of Life During Pregnancy Act, legalising abortion in limited circumstances.

The next step would be to repeal the Eighth Amendment. While the majority of Fine Gael TDs and Senators were in favour, the party was divided. Opponents of liberalisation included Lucinda Creighton TD, who left Fine Gael and later co-founded the conservative (and unsuccessful) Renua Ireland party.[51]

After an intensive campaign that owed less to political parties than to civil society groups and widespread revulsion at Savita's

---

50   www.finegael.ie/our-policies/introduction-from-an-taoiseachleo-varadkar-td/
51   www.renuaireland.com

death, 66.4% of voters backed the proposal, a larger majority than that for equal marriage.[52]

Taoiseach Leo Varadkar hailed the result as a 'quiet revolution' but it was a revolution that had taken place over several decades, as Ireland modernised, grew in wealth and confidence, and adopted more liberal social attitudes. It's also fair to note that governments led by Fine Gael contributed significantly to that change.

Fine Gael might have expected voters to show some appreciation at the ballot box for the delivery of those two controversial reforms, and it is likely that some did. They might also have expected some reward for leading the state out of the recession sparked by the 2007-08 financial crisis and Ireland's home-grown extra dimension linked to a construction industry dominated by out-of-control property developers. However, while economic recovery was comparatively swift, the austerity measures introduced to achieve it triggered a tsunami of political after effects.

That the crisis exploded under a Fianna Fáil/Green Party government was of little interest to voters by 2016, and less so in 2020. Voters blamed Fine Gael for the ongoing impact of the austerity measures introduced to achieve the recovery, measures arising from conditions imposed by the Troika to deal with imminent insolvency.

The Fine Gael government was widely seen to have performed well on another international issue, winning strong EU backing for Ireland's interests when faced with the UK's decision to leave the European Union. Brexit, the outstanding economic and political issue post-2016, unified the main parties and the vast majority of the electorate, and the very fact that there was cross-party consensus neutralised the potential for Fine Gael to gain from its creditable performance.

More immediate concerns dominated voters' decisions in February 2020, especially when some were still smarting from their economic losses *en route* to exiting the recession. Social problems, which were skilfully highlighted and exploited by Sinn Féin, dominated the political agenda and swamped the government's achievements.

Varadkar and his Fine Gael colleagues appeared seriously out of tune with public opinion on a range of everyday concerns. Their handling of a significant shortfall in affordable housing and associated high rental costs left voters underwhelmed and many

---

52   www.bbc.co.uk/news/world-europe-44256152

angry. Their approach towards implementing Sláintecare,[53] a proposal for reform of health and social care services, appeared far from urgent. Just days before the 2020 general election thousands of childcare providers and parents protested against high costs and underfunded infrastructure in early years education and care.[54]

The denouement came with a 'could do better' verdict by voters. A near dead-heat result saw Sinn Féin emerge as the second largest party in the Dáil with 37 seats, just one seat behind Fianna Fáil's 38, with Fine Gael in third place on 35. However, at 50 seats, 'Others' – the small parties and independents - were the largest single category, though not one with enough in common to form a coherent bargaining bloc. Three months of talks led to a tripartite government with leadership rotating between Fianna Fáil and Fine Gael, with the Green party forming the third pillar of the partnership.

Between the February election and formation of a new government, Fine Gael's Leo Varadkar continued to act as taoiseach, and found his standing with the public soaring thanks to his handling of the early period of the Covid-19 pandemic.

Ideological (con)fusion

Is Fine Gael right wing? Not always, but often. Mostly it has hovered around the right of centre mark, though with a social democratic phase and leaning leftwards more recently on social issues like gay marriage and abortion.

It has been accused of neoliberalism and Thatcherite austerity, but a notable degree of pragmatism has marked its political positions and economic policies. This was due in part at least to having to go beyond its comfort zone in order to seal coalition deals.

Its economic policies have moved with the times but rarely far from a conservative core: a firmly 'good housekeeping' approach during the state's formative years, moderate Keynesianism in the mid-20th century, and later a largely unquestioning adoption of neoliberalism, by then dominant in Ireland as in most of the western world. Throughout, however, they have deviated little from James Dillon's description in 1965: 'a private enterprise party'.

---

53 www.gov.ie/en/campaigns/slaintecare-implementationstrategy/

54 www.irishtimes.com/news/education/tens-of-thousandsprotest-in-dublin-over-crisis-in-childcare-sector-1.4162763

Is Fine Gael nationalist? Yes, but softly so, usually. Its nationalism has had a pragmatic tinge since its main predecessor, Cumann na nGaedheal, chose to focus single-mindedly on building the 26-county state, often ruthlessly.

The party's original title, The United Ireland Party – Fine Gael, reflected the centrality of the reunification question in 1933, barely a decade after partition. The emphasis has oscillated but could never have been described as radically republican, even though it was under Fine Gael that the state formally declared a Republic.

By the 1980s, under Garret FitzGerald's leadership, Fine Gael was wooing northern unionists with efforts to end constitutional and social obstacles to re-unification. Via the New Ireland Forum, it sought recognition for the validity of both Irish and British identities.

Is Fine Gael conservative or progressive? It can legitimately claim to have helped modernise Irish society: reforms such as access to contraception, divorce, abortion, and marriage equality were implemented, or passed key milestones, when Fine Gael was the lead party in government.

New era, old aims?

Leo Varadkar has been accused of being too nationalistic in how, as taoiseach, he dealt with Brexit and the related Northern Ireland Protocol, but most parties in the Republic supported his government's efforts to get the best deal for Ireland and preserve peace in the north.

While he waited impatiently for his turn as taoiseach to come round again after the 2020 power-sharing deal, he seemed to be ramping up his nationalism, telling his party's 2021 annual conference: 'I believe in the unification of our island and I believe it can happen in my lifetime'.[55] He went on to say the views of unionists must be 'acknowledged, understood and respected' but that 'no one group can have a veto on Ireland's future'.

While nodding to the 2020 tripartite government's 'Shared Island' strategy, what he said harked back to his party's foundation as The United Ireland Party – Fine Gael. Commentators gave it a modern interpretation, as a reminder that Sinn Féin wasn't the only party with unification credentials.

---

55   L. Varadkar, speech to Fine Gael conference, 15 June 2021

Leo Varadkar's, and Fine Gael's, real challenge, though, was closer to his Dublin home: how to convince electors who decided to 'give Mary Lou a chance' by voting Sinn Féin in 2020 that Fine Gael had listened, learned and was on the way to solving the major problems of everyday life that underpinned the shift away from the Republic's traditional parties of government.

Fine Gael	
Founded:	1933
Meaning of name:	Family, tribe or race of the Irish
Leaders:	W.T. Cosgrave 1934-44; Richard Mulcahy 1944-59; James Dillon 1959-65; Liam Cosgrave 1965-77; Garret FitzGerald 1977-87; Alan Dukes 1987-90; John Bruton 1990-2001; Michael Noonan 2001-02; Enda Kenny 2002-17; Leo Varadkar 2017-
In office:	In coalition: 1948-51; 1954-57; 1973-77; 1981-82; 1982-87; 1994-97; 2011-16; 2016-20; 2020-
Affiliations:	European People's Party
Elected representatives:	2022: 34 TDs (28 M, 6F); 16 Senators (11M, 5 F), 5 MEPs (2M, 3F)

7

Clann na Poblachta

Radical, influential and disappointing

Overview

Clann na Poblachta was a radical Irish republican party with progressive social policies and was an influential member of Ireland's first coalition government. Founded in July 1946, it swiftly attained a high profile, but is often cited as a warning to smaller parties about the perils of coalition. Its political and social agenda, and its successes and failures won it a place in Ireland's political history and folk memory disproportionate to its size and short lifespan.

The party found itself in office two years after its launch, forming part of Ireland's first coalition government (1948-51) on whose programme it had a major influence. It is associated closely with withdrawal from the British Commonwealth and a definitive declaration of the state's status as a republic, as well as the near total eradication of tuberculosis (TB) and a failed attempt to introduce free health and social care for mothers and children.

Effectively a coalition of two strands in Irish politics, Clann na Poblachta attracted republicans disillusioned by the failure of Fianna Fáil, the then ruling party, to end partition, and social radicals inspired by Keynesian-style economics and the welfare state model emerging in Britain.

There had been other attempts to forge a radical republican party as an alternative to Fianna Fáil and the dormant Sinn Féin[1] – such as Saor Éire (Free Ireland) founded in 1931 – but Clann na Poblachta was the first that Fianna Fáil saw as a serious electoral threat. Eithne MacDermott argues that the Clann 'represented the first major attempt since Fianna Fáil won office in 1932 to reproduce something more republican in its constitutional integrity and more impatiently

---

1   Sinn Féin did not contest elections between 1927 and 1957.

concerned with addressing social affairs than anything offered by Fianna Fáil'.[2]

The party's founder, Seán MacBride, had attractive credentials for republican voters. The son of iconic independence movement figures Maud Gonne[3] and Major John MacBride, who was executed by British forces following the 1916 Rising, he was himself a former IRA Chief of Staff who had become a barrister and turned to constitutional politics. He would eventually enjoy a distinguished international career and win the Nobel Peace Prize in 1974 for his efforts to promote human rights.

A radical new force

Clann na Poblachta achieved early political successes, winning two out of three Dáil by-elections called in late 1947. Fianna Fáil, to thwart what it saw as a serious threat from Clann's combination of strong nationalist credentials and progressive politics, called a snap election for February 1948. The election pitted Fianna Fáil, in government for 16 years, against an array of parties united by little more than their shared determination to oust the government.

Clann's election slogan was simple – 'Put Them Out' – but its campaign was far from ordinary. With broadcaster Noel Hartnett as director of elections it broke new ground in Irish political campaigning, making clever use of what Ferriter describes as the first modern political 'spin doctors' and producing Ireland's first party political broadcast – a film called 'Our Country'.

Following veiled threats by a Fianna Fáil government minister the major cinema chains refused to show the film, but Clann took it on the campaign trail, projecting it onto walls, thus adding a 'touch of exotica'[4] (for the times) to the election.

The film exposed the darker aspects of contemporary Irish life of which there were many: severe unemployment, low incomes and high food prices, a rising rate of emigration, poor housing conditions,

---

2   E. MacDermott, *Clann na Poblachta*, Cork, Cork University Press, 1998, p.5
3   Known to some as W.B. Yeats' muse, she was an influential republican leader in her own right
4   E. MacDermott, *Clann na Poblachta*, op.cit., p.57

Clann na Poblachta founder Seán MacBride (r) in February 1948, with his son and his mother Maud Gonne, a radical republican, suffragette and the muse of poet W.B. Yeats.

widespread poverty, and an extraordinarily high rate of illnesses associated with poverty, including the omnipresent tuberculosis.[5]

In the film a young doctor called Noel Browne, who worked in a TB sanatorium, described the shortage of facilities for patients suffering from this terrible illness. Before long he was minister for health and his mission to eradicate TB led to one of the Inter-Party Government's major successes.

The first coalition government

The general election came too soon for Clann, which overstretched itself by fielding 93 candidates without a strong organisational base. It won 13% of first preference votes but just ten of the Dáil's 147 seats, although that was enough to deny Fianna Fáil a majority, forcing it into opposition.

---

5   D. McCullagh, *A Makeshift Majority*, op.cit., p.10

The result was the formation of the state's first coalition government. Known as the Inter-Party Government, it was led by Fine Gael with John A. Costello as taoiseach and Labour Party leader William Norton as tánaiste. All other parties except Fianna Fáil were involved: the Labour Party, Clann na Poblachta, Clann na Talmhan, National Labour, plus several independent TDs.

Although a minor partner in numeric terms, it was Clann na Poblachta that provided the government with some of its key policies as well as acknowledged passion and focus. It also provided two of the most high profile ministers, Seán MacBride as minister for external affairs, and Dr Noel Browne as health minister. Browne carried the flag for the social progressives in Clann and would provide a great deal of the passion for change in the coalition government.

MacBride insisted on the inclusion of four points in the coalition's 10-point programme for government: more public investment in Irish resources; a doubling of forestry planting; the release of funds[6] to build hospitals and sanatoria; and a very substantial increase in social welfare benefits. All parties agreed.[7] MacBride later claimed that there was a collective sigh of relief that he had not mentioned the External Relations Act 1936 or political prisoners although he had campaigned for release of the latter and reform of the former. To have done so, he said, would have put an impossible strain on the other parties.[8]

Constitutional shock

The outgoing Fianna Fáil government had ensured that aspects of the 26-county state's constitutional position were nebulous enough to let Ireland claim to be a republic while remaining a member of the British Commonwealth. The 1937 Constitution[9] masterminded by Fianna Fáil leader Éamon de Valera declared the state to be a republic. Yet the 1936 External Relations Act,[10] also promoted by de Valera, left the door open to Commonwealth membership, retained the King of England as head of state and allowed Britain the right

---

6   These were to come from the Hospitals Trust, which had been founded to raise finance for Irish hospitals by means of an international lottery known as the Irish Sweepstake

7   Ibid., p. 31

8   Quoted in McCullagh, Ibid., p. 31

9   www.irishstatutebook.ie

10   Ibid.

As health minister in the 1948-51 Inter-Party Government, Dr Noel Browne implemented measures that almost eliminated TB in the state, but vested interests blocked his plan to offer free healthcare to children and pregnant women.

to accredit Ireland's diplomatic and consular representatives,[11] matters resented by republicans and decried by Clann.

Although MacBride had not insisted on repeal of the External Relations Act as part of Clann's price for joining the coalition government, events brought this to the fore. In a lecture in Canada in September 1948 the taoiseach said the 1936 Act was full of discrepancies. When asked at a later press conference if it was to be repealed he replied affirmatively. This took politicians in Dublin by surprise and, although the Cabinet was not opposed to its repeal, it was speculated that an impatient MacBride had forced the matter. No evidence has been found, but if true he was successful.

By the end of the year the Oireachtas had passed the Republic of Ireland Act 1948.[12] This decreed that the description of the state should be the Republic of Ireland and that the President of Ireland would assume the right, until then held by the King of England, 'to exercise the executive power or any executive function of the State in or in connection with its external relations'.

Unexpectedly, the 'rag-tag' coalition government had clarified the state's constitutional status and formally established the Republic. The matter might not have risen up the political agenda, or at least not so quickly, without Clann na Poblachta's participation. A key Clann aim had been achieved swiftly and smoothly, but achieving some of its social objectives would prove much more challenging.

---

11 '...for the purposes of the appointment of diplomatic and consular representatives and the conclusion of international agreements, the king so recognised may, and is hereby authorised to, act on behalf of Saorstát Éireann for the like purposes as and when advised by the Executive Council so to do.'

12 Ibid.

Health challenge

The new health minister, Dr Noel Browne, entered politics and government determined to revolutionise health and social services. Dr Browne brought knowledge, urgency and single-minded leadership to his role. Personal suffering added fire to his mission: he had lost his parents and five siblings to tuberculosis (TB), spent two years in a sanatorium himself recovering from the illness and suffered recurring bouts, including while in government.[13]

Within a few years the Department of Health had all but eradicated TB, a disease that had long been rampant across the state, especially but far from exclusively in urban slums.[14]

The necessary legislation to proceed with tackling TB was already on the statute books in the form of the Health Act 1947 and the Tuberculosis (Establishment of Sanatoria) Act 1945. Section 38 of the 1947 act granted the minister for health sweeping powers to address urgent public health matters. The outstanding barriers were lack of finance and political will.

Browne knew that what needed to be done would be expensive, and impossible within the confines of the normal health budget.[15] Thanks to Clann's insistence on access to funds held by the Hospitals Trust as a condition for joining the coalition, the health budget rose from under £700,000 in 1947 to more than £5 million by 1951. Hospitals and TB sanatoria were quickly built.

Cause célèbre

Browne's attempt to introduce the Mother and Child Scheme was a dramatic failure, however, and would become the saga for which Clann na Poblachta is best remembered – what Lee calls 'one of the great *causes célèbres* of Irish politics'.[16]

Browne sought access to full free health care for all pregnant women as well as children up to the age of 16. His efforts pitted vested

---

13   Interview with Browne, www.rte.ie/archives
14   Breathnach: Statistics from the 1880s through to the 1950s showed that TB/consumption/phthisis was a primary cause of death and those living in over-crowded urban areas were more vulnerable to the disease
15   Breathnach: the Bacillus Calmette-Guérin (BCG) vaccine had been discovered by the 1920s; the efficacy of penicillin was known by 1944
16   J.J. Lee, *Ireland 1912-1985: Politics and Society*, op.cit., p.313

interests against the welfare of women and children and divided the Cabinet.

This scheme, like the legislation enabling action on TB, had been proposed under the previous administration, but had failed. The immediate opposition from the medical profession halted progress then and prefigured the reaction to Browne's later decision to reactivate it.

After an acrimonious battle that included a standoff with the medical profession, which feared loss of income, and Catholic bishops who saw it as creeping socialism, as well as opposition within the Cabinet even from his own party leader, Dr Browne resigned in April 1951. Two months later the government fell.

A very divided Clann supported the second Inter-Party Government (1954-57) from the Opposition benches. It lost eight of its 10 Dáil seats in 1951 and MacBride lost his seat in 1957. Merger talks with Labour came to nothing, MacBride left Ireland, and the party was wound up in 1965.

Disappointing or influential?

Ferriter describes Clann as 'an acute disappointment' that promised much but sank 'under the weight of individual members' arrogance'. He goes further, claiming that it was searching for a 'populist' issue of social concern in order to 'emphasise ideological purity in a hybrid government', a charge that may be unfair to individuals like Browne who were strongly motivated by social justice; it is also hard to sustain in light of the issues on which the party campaigned, at least initially. More fairly, Ferriter also notes that they lacked the skills to handle government or inter-party relations effectively.

Browne himself said in his memoir that he was not quite sure what the party stood for. Yet its conditions for joining the coalition were clear and some were successfully implemented, and enabled Browne to pursue his campaign to eliminate TB. Though Browne lost the battle over the Mother and Child Scheme a similar Bill was passed with minor concessions by the next Fianna Fáil government.

Factors outside its control contributed to Clann's failure to reach its potential, including Fianna Fáil's tactic of rushing it into a premature election. Seán Lemass, who would later become Fianna Fáil leader and taoiseach, claimed that Clann na Poblachta could have succeeded in eclipsing his own party if it had played a longer game instead of entering government at the earliest opportunity. This should be set beside Clann's success in achieving key policies, including MacBride's aim of extricating the state from the British Commonwealth and ending Britain's right to accredit Ireland's diplomatic representatives.

The successes and failures of both Clann and the coalition nudged the state towards change and in some cases prefigured future patterns in Irish politics. The Inter-Party Government's economic policies made it easier for Lemass to steer Fianna Fáil towards abandoning protectionism and opening the economy. The battle over health policy, however, continued to cast a shadow.

The coalition of MacBride's republicans with Browne and others who prioritised social progress may have carried within it the seeds of its own destruction. This is the position of Eithne MacDermott who argues that the party was divided from the start. It's a view that finds echoes in efforts before and since to combine republicanism with progressive or radical social policies within one Irish party.

Clann na Poblachta	
Founded:	1946
Dissolved:	1965
Meaning of name:	Family of the Republic
Leader:	Seán MacBride
In office:	Inter-Party Government: 1948-1951

8

The Alliance Party of Northern Ireland

A radically moderate party

Overview

The Alliance Party of Northern Ireland (APNI) was founded in 1970 during a period of intense civil unrest, inter-community strife, and growing paramilitary and military activity. It aimed to bridge the gap between the polarised Catholic and Protestant communities by offering an alternative to the region's traditional republican and unionist political parties.

Its political programme was moderate, in the liberal tradition, but its approach was radical in the context of Northern Ireland's political history and contemporary reality. In attempting to forge an alternative political path between unionists and nationalists it challenged the inherited political beliefs of the majority of the population.

Success was limited during the decades of strife and continued to be elusive after the 1998 peace agreement. The party's fortunes began to look up under Naomi Long, its first female leader, with gains in the 2019 Westminster and European Parliament elections. In 2022 it more than doubled its representation in the NI Assembly, reflecting what appeared to be a significant shift in favour of an alternative to nationalism and unionism.

Filling the vacuum

The concept of a non-sectarian party materialised in a period in which the Northern Ireland Civil Rights Association protests of 1968/69 had shaken up the region's politics as never before. The British government had responded to the civil rights movement with a series of initiatives. These included requiring the NI government to take immediate action to reorganise the police, create a ministry of community relations, reform the local government franchise, and introduce measures to prevent sectarian discrimination in the distribution of public posts and social housing. The ruling Ulster Unionist Party found itself having to implement these measures while facing strong opposition to them from much of the unionist community.

The British assumption that these reforms would reconcile Catholics to the existing political structure and lead to a new normality proved ill-founded. Although the crisis had been managed, local politicians lacked strategies for a new future, and civil rights leaders had no specific plans for further political activity. As historian Joe Lee noted, this political vacuum needed to be filled 'because it would inevitably be some time before any concrete consequences of the reform programme, even assuming no resistance, could be felt at grass roots level'.

One attempt to fill the vacuum came from the New Ulster Movement (NUM), launched in January 1969 with the aim of involving both Catholics and Protestants in moderate, cross-community politics. 'Chaos was at hand, and it was up to the Northern Ireland people themselves to put aside their sterile divisions and build the solution', was how one founding member, Denis Loretto, described the context for the NUM's launch.[1]

Some of those behind the inauguration of the New Ulster Movement had another – and secret – aim: to launch a new political party.

Oliver Napier, a founder of both the NUM and the Alliance Party, disclosed that he had always intended the NUM to be the launch pad for a new liberal non-sectarian party, but the truth about the driving force behind this aim had to be kept secret: 'We did our best to hide the fact that a group within the Liberal Party was handling it, which would be the kiss of death'.[2]

As the New Ulster Movement expanded across the region, behind the scenes Napier and his group were secretly using its structure to put in place the building blocks for their new party. According to Napier, it all worked like a dream and 'no one suspected a Liberal foundation'.[3]

---

1   D. Loretto, 'Alliance, Liberals and the SDP, 1971-1985: a personal memoir', in *Journal of Liberal Democrat History* (Winter 2001–02), p.33
2   Quoted in B. Eggins, *History and Hope: The Alliance Party of Northern Ireland*, Stroud, The History Press, p31
3   Ibid., p36

Alliance launch

On 16 April 1970 the radical Protestant Unionist Party[4] defeated the ruling Ulster Unionist Party (UUP) in two by-elections, gaining its first seats in the Northern Ireland legislature. However, in another by-election, an unknown independent backed by New Ulster Movement activists took more than 25% of the vote, raising confidence in the embryo moderate party that the time had come to go public.

On 20 April 1970 they launched the Alliance Party of Northern Ireland. Its founders judged correctly that some sections of society felt increasingly disenfranchised as the region's main parties moved towards more extreme unionist or republican positions. Significantly, the new party attracted members from the long-dominant UUP, people who were concerned that the UUP was becoming too extreme.

When it came to the nationalist segment of its target audience, however, timing at least was against the Alliance Party. Unknown to Napier and his colleagues, arrangements were underway to form another new party, the Social Democratic and Labour Party (SDLP), launched the following August. While Alliance garnered some support from middle class Catholics, the SDLP offered a stronger counter attraction for nationalist voters concerned about the emergence of a militant new manifestation of republicanism in the the Provisional IRA and Sinn Féin .

The Ulster Liberal Party (ULP), meanwhile, had expelled those of its members who helped to form the New Ulster Movement. This, and Alliance's success in capturing a section of the middle ground, hastened the ULP's decline and its formal demise in 1987.

Electoral record

The Alliance Party contested its first elections in 1973, winning 12% of local council seats, spread thinly across all but four of the 20 electoral areas. A slight surge in 1977, when Alliance benefitted from the Peace People movement,[5] was not sustained and its local government presence remained at around 7% until 2019 when it rose to 11% of local councillors.

---

4   A precursor of the Democratic Unionist Party
5   B. Eggins, *History and Hope*, op.cit., p.66

In elections to the new Northern Ireland Assembly[6] held on 28 June 1973, Alliance won eight of the 78 seats, the same number as the Democratic Unionist Party. The SDLP, the other new party of 1970 and a rival for the nationalist centre vote, won 19 seats.[7] Or, as summarised by Diarmaid Ferriter, 'The assembly elections resulted in seats being won by 22 power-sharing unionists, 28 anti-power-sharing unionists, 19 SDLP, eight Alliance and one Labour.'[8]

The Ulster Unionist Party, the SDLP and the Alliance Party agreed to form a cross-community coalition and, following the Sunningdale Agreement,[9] joined in establishing a power-sharing Executive from 1 January 1974. Alliance leader Oliver Napier served as justice minister and head of the Office of Legal Reform in this short-lived Executive. The Executive and Assembly collapsed in May 1974, partly under the weight of opposition from within the UUP but more specifically and dramatically as a result of a strike organised by the Ulster Workers Council (15-28 May) in opposition to power sharing and in particular to the cross-border cooperation provision of the Sunningdale agreement. The strike was successful in undermining Sunningdale, and direct rule from Westminster resumed.

The Alliance Party did not win representation in the UK House of Commons until 40 years after its foundation, although the defection from the UUP of Stratton Mills MP gave it a brief Westminster presence in 1973-74.[10] The breakthrough came in 2010, when Naomi Long became MP for East Belfast, defeating Peter Robinson, the then leader of the DUP, with a 22.6% swing. However, she failed to retain the seat in 2015, thanks to an electoral pact between unionist parties, or to regain it in 2019. A different electoral pact in 2019, between anti-DUP parties, helped Alliance win the North Down constituency, a result also partly attributed to the party's staunch opposition to the United Kingdom's exit from the European Union (Brexit).

Given its lacklustre performance in local authority and Westminster elections, Alliance needed the re-establishment of a legislature in Belfast to raise its profile and electoral fortunes. Yet

---

6 The Northern Ireland parliament was suspended in 1972 and formally abolished in 1973

7 Ibid., pp.54-5

8 D. Ferriter, *The Transformation of Ireland 1900-2000*, op.cit., p.629

9 Signed on 9 December 1973

10 B. Eggins, *History and Hope*, op.cit., p.55. Robin Baillie also left the UUP for Alliance in 1973.

US President Bill Clinton addressing the Northern Ireland Assembly with (left to right) David Trimble (UUP), UK Prime Minster Tony Blair, Séamus Mallon (SDLP) and Lord Mayor of Belfast David Alderdice (Alliance). 3 September 1998.

when that happened in 1998 the party benefitted little from the new settlement. It languished at six to eight Members of the Legislative Assembly, never rising above the position of fifth party until 2017 when it retained its eight seats in an Assembly slimmed down from 108 to 90 Members. The Alliance breakthrough came in 2022 when it more than doubled its Assembly presence, from eight to 17 seats, making it the third largest party.

Beyond Good Friday

Throughout the decades of violence the Alliance Party actively supported efforts to restore devolved government to Northern Ireland, taking initiatives and cooperating in those of others, even when doing so was detrimental to their hopes for political success. They were equally committed to achieving peace, and Walker notes that they were the first non-nationalists to enter discussions with Sinn Féin after the 1994 IRA ceasefire.[11]

Finally, in 1998, the Belfast Agreement opened up the prospect of a new normality in Northern Irish politics. A devolved legislature

11   B.M. Walker, *A Political History of the Two Irelands*, op.cit., p.142

and power-sharing Executive were established, but once again the Alliance Party was to be disappointed.

Writing in the *Fordham International Law Journal* in 1998, Stephen Farry and Alliance's then leader Seán Neeson described the Agreement as 'little more than a "Band-Aid" approach to the Northern Ireland conflict' that would not by itself produce long-term peace and stability.[12]

It didn't produce a new era of success for Alliance either. The party never held more than two ministerial positions in the NI Executive between 1998 and 2022 because it lacked the necessary percentage of Members of the Legislative Assembly (MLAs) to qualify for office under the power-sharing mechanism that was a central tenet of the 1998 accord.

Alliance can claim that it made a political sacrifice in supporting the Agreement. The consociational[13] power-sharing formula regulating the make-up of the Executive runs counter to the Alliance party's anti-sectarian principles by institutionalising a unionist-nationalist dichotomy within Northern Ireland politics, Jonathan Tonge argues.[14] Alliance itself argued that the consociational formula would deepen the sectarian divide but accepted it as a necessity to achieve the peace agreement. It chose to designate as 'other' in the Assembly rather than as 'unionist' or 'nationalist', although this considerably limited its influence and access to power.[15]

Brexit shock

In the June 2016 UK-wide referendum on European Union (EU) membership, Northern Ireland voted to remain in the EU by a majority of 56% to 44%. Alliance Party supporters voted overwhelmingly to

---

12   S. Farry and S. Neeson, 'Beyond the Band-Aid Approach: An Alliance Party Perspective upon the Belfast Agreement', in *Fordham International Law Journal* (Vol. 22 No. 4), pp.1221-49

13   Consociational power-sharing was intended to promote cross-community consensus and forge a moderate centre by managing the competing aims of unionism and nationalism. See: R.B. Andeweg, 'Consociational Democracy', in *Annual Review of Political Science*, Vol. 3:509-536, June 2000.

14   J. Tonge, 'Victims of Their Own Success? Post-Agreement Dilemmas of Political Moderates in Northern Ireland', *The Global Review of Ethnopolitics* (Vol. 3, No.1), September 2003, pp.39-59 Special Issue: Northern Ireland

15   The Green Party and the People before Profit Alliance also designate as 'Other'

remain (an estimated 83%), as did SDLP and Sinn Féin supporters, while a majority of unionist voters preferred leave (although the strength of the leave vote varied by party, with the UUP being the most evenly balanced).[16]

Reflecting the preference of their supporters, Alliance continued to campaign for a 'soft' Brexit, in the belief that 'Northern Ireland only works based on sharing and interdependence', and that Brexit 'exposes contradictions and ambiguities that are otherwise being managed through the Good Friday Agreement'.[17]

Voters gave Alliance a parting gift in the May 2019 European Parliament elections, presumably in recognition of its pro-EU stance: Naomi Long became her party's first MEP, in what was to be a very short tenure before the UK exited the EU on 31 January 2020.[18] The victory came too late to enable Ms Long, widely acknowledged to be an impressive political performer, to use the role to boost her party's profile. As Northern Ireland was one single constituency for European elections the result cannot be easily interpreted as a harbinger of an ongoing upturn for Alliance, but it was certainly part of a suite of electoral successes in 2019.

Reality check

From its beginnings in 1970, the Alliance Party succeeded in attracting support from across the political middle ground, irrespective of religion or traditional political affiliation, but the success was limited in terms of the ambitions of its founders.

Timing and the political climate militated against it. Even if it had not initially underestimated the strength of traditional allegiances, the militarisation of the political sphere heightened cross-community suspicions and deepened the polarisation that Alliance had set out to counter.

In the febrile political atmosphere of late 20th century Northern Ireland, the cross-community, non-sectarian messaging of the

---

16 J. Garry, 'The EU referendum Vote in Northern Ireland: Implications for our understanding of citizens' political views and behaviour', Knowledge Exchange Seminar Series 2016-17. Based on data from a large-scale survey conducted by IpsosMORI at the time of the referendum.

17 www.allianceparty.org/brexit

18 For the first time the region returned an all-female cohort of MEPs; the others were the DUP's Diane Dodd and Martina Anderson of Sinn Féin.

Alliance party did not play well with the majority of electors, many of whom either adhered to customary voting patterns or threw in their lot with emerging radicals. Alliance did gain, though to a limited extent, from sharpening polarisation amongst unionists.

By the 1970s, the Ulster Unionist Party, in power since Northern Ireland's emergence as a political entity in 1921, was increasingly unable to hold together what had always been a 'broad church' party. Faced with competition from new, stridently unionist parties, it gravitated towards more extreme positions, which failed to satisfy its hardliners and simultaneously alienated its moderates, some of whom saw the Alliance Party as an alternative political home.

Analysis of transfers under the Single Transferable Vote system of proportional representation suggests that a limited range of voters saw Alliance as an acceptable but lower option on the ballot paper. In the Assembly election of 1973, for example, 94% of the SDLP surplus and 50% of the Northern Ireland Labour Party surplus transferred to Alliance candidates. Alliance Party surplus transfers 'went in all directions', however, confirming the 'catch-all' nature of its middle ground position and the electoral limits of that position.[19]

Prior to its 2022 breakthrough, the Alliance's best performance to date occurred in 2019, nearly 50 years after its foundation, when it won a seat in the UK House of Commons and one of Northern Ireland's three seats in the European Parliament, and saw a 65% rise in its representation on local councils.

Historian Joe Lee argues that the Alliance Party could hardly have hoped for more than 10% electoral support 'in view of the inherited animosities'.[20] The party's electoral record supports this view. While it benefitted from the Single Transferable Vote proportional representation system in use in Northern Ireland elections (other than those to the Westminster parliament), it rarely rose above fifth place in party rankings until it became the clear third party in 2022.

The identity enigma

In the context of traditional Northern Ireland politics the Alliance Party can look like an anomaly if not an enigma. Is it unionist or 'pan-nationalist' as critics have variously claimed, or simply 'a perfectly

---

19   B. Eggins, *History and Hope*, op.cit., p.56
20   J.J. Lee, *Ireland* 1912-1985: *Politics and Society*, op.cit., p.431

David Ford, Alliance leader 2001-16, represented South Antrim in the Northern Ireland Assembly from 1998 to 2018 and in 2010 became Northern Ireland's first justice minister for 30 years, holding the office until 2016. (© Alliance Party)

sensible, social democratic party with liberal views' as a more recent commentator has described it?[21]

Its founding principles gave credence to the claim that it was in reality a unionist party: these included a statement of support for the constitutional link between Northern Ireland and the rest of the United Kingdom.[22] On constitutional questions, Tonge argues, Alliance 'has always been pro-consent and thus pro-union' while refusing to label itself as a unionist party.[23]

Despite its early signalling of support for the union with Great Britain, which may have been shrewdly targeted at wavering UUP supporters, Alliance has generally tried to avoid being labelled either unionist or nationalist. Yet it has been flexible when politically necessary, notably in November 2001 when three of its MLAs temporarily re-designated themselves as 'unionist' to break a deadlock in the Assembly and thus ensure the re-election of the UUP leader, David Trimble, as first minister.

Significantly, its own members are divided. In a survey of Alliance members, Evans and Tonge found that 27% of those questioned believed it to be a party of soft unionism while 48% disagreed;

---

21 S. Creighton, 4 May 2019, www.sluggerotoole.com

22 APNI, 'Guideline Statement for all news media on the formation of The Alliance Party of Northern Ireland' , cain.ulster.ac.uk

23 J. Tonge, 'Victims of Their Own Success? Post-Agreement Dilemmas of Political Moderates in Northern Ireland', *The Global Review of Ethnopolitics* (Vol. 3, No. 1), September 2003, pp.39-59 Special Issue: Northern Ireland, p.58

only seven per cent saw their organisation as a nationalist party. [24]

The media sensation – and consternation within her party[25] – sparked by one prominent member, Anna Lo MLA, when she said she favoured Irish unification highlighted that open support for Irish nationalism really was an uncommon stance for an Alliance member. The declaration did no electoral harm to Ms Lo or her party in 2014, however, as she went on to produce Alliance's best European election result up to that date.[26]

Religion appeared to be less controversial than Irish unification in the Alliance party

Anna Lo, elected as MLA for South Belfast in 2007, was the first parliamentarian of Chinese heritage in the UK; she cited online racist abuse as a major reason for her retirement from politics in 2016. (© Sinn Féin)

credo and dynamics. Some of the party's leaders have been Catholic, others Protestant, with no obvious link between that and the party's electoral fortunes.[27] Its members are drawn from Catholic and Protestant communities, but Evans and Tonge found that only 20% identified as Catholic.

More interesting for the party's campaign gurus may be the fact that as many as half of Alliance voters claim to be of neither religion, a high percentage when compared with the general population. They may be looking with some hope towards a growing lack of religious affiliation as reflected in the annual Northern Ireland Life and

---

24   J. Evans & J. Tonge, 'The Future of the 'Radical Centre' in Northern Ireland after the Good Friday Agreement', Political Studies (Vol. 51, Issue 1), March 2003, pp.26-50,

25   www.sluggerotoole.com

26   44,432 votes, 7.1% vote share: www.belfasttelegraph.co.uk

27   In the 1973 Assembly election Alliance ran the Catholic Oliver Napier in largely Protestant East Belfast and the Protestant Bob Cooper in largely Catholic West Belfast and both were elected - D. Loretto, 'Alliance, Liberals and the SDP, 1971-1985, op.cit., p.36

Under the leadership of Naomi Long MLA (2016-), Alliance doubled its Assembly seats in 2022. (© NI Assembly)

Times surveys: 33% of the 18-24 age group claimed to have no religion in the 2018 survey compared with 7% of those in the 65+ cohort.[28]

The socio-demographic structure of the Northern Ireland electorate has also militated against the party. Working class voters tend to favour the Democratic Unionist Party or Sinn Féin more often than they do more moderate parties. The perception that Alliance is a middle-class phenomenon seeking to capture the middle ground seems largely correct and limits its appeal.

Ideology

Alliance projects itself as a radical centrist organisation, although only around one-third of members surveyed agreed that Alliance actually is a radical party. While it claims to be 'not doctrinaire' on the economy, its economic policies are mainly centrist and similar to many centre or left of centre parties elsewhere.[29]

The Farry and Neeson description of 'fundamentally a liberal, pluralist, non-ethnic party, rather than a collection of soft unionists and soft nationalists co-habitating together in an uneasy coalition'[30] appeared to be broadly true.

It is certainly in the liberal tradition, inherited many of its founding members from the Ulster Liberal Party, and is linked with the Liberal International, the Alliance of Liberals and Democrats for Europe (ALDE), and the Liberal Democrats in Great Britain (but does not take the latter's party whip in the UK Parliament).

---

28   www.ark.ac.uk/nilt/2018
29   www.allianceparty.org/economy
30   S. Farry and S. Neeson, 'Beyond the Band-Aid Approach: op.cit., p.1224

Its strongest trait has been its anti-sectarian stance, which its recent literature interprets as a vision of 'a shared society, free from intimidation, discrimination and fear, where everyone is safe, can play their part and is treated fairly and with respect' - an ambitious aim even now in Northern Ireland.

From minor to major?

That Northern Ireland continued to be a politically fragile society, a fact of which the centrality to the campaign of loyalist opposition to the NI Protocol to the UK Withdrawal Agreement from the EU was a sharp reminder, suggested that Alliance success in achieving its founding aims was at best partial.

Dr Stephen Farry MP won the North Down seat in the 2019 UK general election, a result attributed in part to his opposition to Brexit; he was elected unopposed as his party's deputy leader in 2016, and was MLA for North Down 2007-19. (© UK Parliament)

While the Alliance Party succeeded in showing that there was a non-sectarian alternative to unionism and nationalism, for the first half century of its existence voters showed limited appreciation of what it offered. With social and demographic change in Northern Ireland, however, and a concurrent increase in voters identifying as neither unionist nor nationalist, the appeal of a non-sectarian party has grown.

In 2019, the year in which it won seats at all levels, from local to European, the annual Northern Ireland Life and Times survey recorded an upsurge in support for Alliance to 15%, higher than any other party that year. Many dismissed this as an unsustainable glitch, but they were proved wrong in 2022 when Alliance became the third party in the Assembly, having taken seats from the DUP, SDLP and Greens.

The party's 13.5% of first preference votes plus transfers (mainly, but not solely, from soft unionists and soft nationalists) gave them 17 seats in the 90-seat Assembly, and made them the dominant party by far in the 20-strong non-aligned bloc. Despite the Alliance surge – probably the most historic takeaway from the 2022 election – the non-aligned bloc still lagged significantly behind nationalists and unionists. It was hard to see how that gap could be bridged anytime soon.

The radically moderate party was in a more influential position after the 2022 election, but still limited by the power-sharing rules for the Stormont Executive, rules that the Alliance Party has consistently criticised but accepted as necessary for peace and devolution. While provision exists for a review of the rules in the interests of efficiency and fairness, that would be of little benefit given that the party can be said to be over-represented in the Assembly if its first preference votes (13.5%) are compared with its seats (18.8%). It would still face the hard slog of convincing a sufficient proportion of Northern Ireland's growing bloc of non-voters, doubters and 'others' to support it at the polls.

Alliance Party of Northern Ireland	
Founded:	1970
Leaders:	Oliver Napier and Bob Cooper 1970-1972; Phelim O'Neill 1972-73; Oliver Napier 1973-84; John Cushnahan 1984–87; John Alderdice 1989-98; Seán Neeson 1998-2001; David Ford 2001-16; Naomi Long 2016-
In office:	NI Executive: 2007-11; 2011-16; 2020-
Affiliations:	Liberal International; Alliance of Liberals and Democrats for Europe
Elected representatives:	2022: 17 MLAs (9M, 8F); 1 MP (M)

9

The Social Democratic and Labour Party

Successful peacemakers in electoral doldrums still seeking shared island

Overview

The Social Democratic and Labour Party (SDLP) was launched on 21 August 1970 in the heat of agitation for civil rights and amid predictions of a descent into chaos.[1] It brought together politicians from several parties with individuals who had come to prominence in the Northern Ireland civil rights movement during the preceding few years.

This convergence of several strands of Northern Ireland's political life – nationalist, republican, labour and civil rights – created a party that became a far more effective constitutional movement than the old Nationalist Party.[2]

The SDLP played a leading role in the process that led to inter-governmental agreements and eventually to peace after three decades of violence. This achievement was internationally recognised, including with the award of a Nobel Peace Prize to the SDLP leader, John Hume, alongside Ulster Unionist Party (UUP) leader David Trimble.

However, the SDLP would become one of the political casualties of the peace. Its time at the helm of the Northern Ireland Executive alongside the UUP was short: the hard-line Democratic Unionist Party (DUP) and Sinn Féin displaced the UUP and SDLP as the largest parties and, in 2007, Ian Paisley and Martin McGuinness took office as the first and deputy first ministers.

---

1   See e.g. CAIN (Conflict Archive on the Internet)
2   J.J. Lee, *Ireland* 1912-1985: *Politics and Society*, op.cit., p.431

The party that brought together nationalists and socialists on a progressive and anti-sectarian platform, that played a major role in achieving historic agreements between the UK and Irish governments, that withstood political and physical attacks because of its policies, that was key to the achievement of the 1998 Belfast Agreement, lost momentum in peacetime politics.

An alternative to chaos

From different parties or none, the SDLP's founding members were united by their belief that Northern Ireland needed a strong political alternative to the Ulster Unionist Party, which had held power since the state's foundation in 1921.

Gerry Fitt MP was the first leader of the SDLP and former leader of the Republican Labour Party, itself founded in 1964 by members of the Socialist Republican Party and the Irish Labour Party. Senator Paddy Wilson, also from the Republican Labour Party, and Paddy Devlin of the Irish Labour Party completed the socialist side of the top table. Joining them were John Hume and Paddy O'Hanlon, Independent nationalist members of the Northern Ireland Parliament, and Austin Currie and Ivan Cooper, both independent members of the Parliament. All were civil rights activists.

Four of the SDLP's founders: (left to right) Austin Currie, Gerry Fitt, John Hulme and Paddy Devlin. (© PA Images)

The fusion amounted to an admission that, singly, their parties and movements could not stop what the SDLP founders described as the very real possibility of 'an extreme right-wing takeover of the government of Northern Ireland with consequent interference in the reforms which have been recently placed on the Statute Book'.[3]

The reforms in question, which had been passed by the Stormont parliament in November and December 1969 in response to the civil rights movement and under pressure from the UK Government, aimed to improve democratic accountability in local government and reform the police. This unleashed a unionist backlash, in particular against the proposal to disband the 'B' Specials, an armed part-time police force that Catholics distrusted and feared.

Crucially, the SDLP's younger leaders coming from the civil rights movement brought a level of campaigning experience to the new party that helped it build a functioning organisation. This was in sharp contrast to the old Nationalist Party (1918-77) that, according to Lee, 'was merely a coalition of individuals controlling their personal fiefdoms'.[4]

The consent principle

The SDLP's constitutional position was based on a belief that there could not be a united Ireland without the consent of a majority within Northern Ireland – at a time when the region had a clear Protestant majority that was presumed, with reason, to favour union with Britain. This consent principle underpinned SDLP proposals for achieving peace and building democracy. Like the Alliance Party launched earlier in 1970, it set its face against sectarianism and sought to eliminate violence from Northern Ireland politics.

Emphasising its opposition to the use of violence by the then renascent IRA or any other grouping, the new party's founders made clear that they did not believe a united Ireland could be achieved by force. Its first leader, Gerry Fitt MP, stressed that violence was destructive irrespective of religion or politics: 'Every single stone that is thrown in the riots that have taken place has meant distress

---

3   G. Fitt quoted in *The Irish Times*, 22 August 1970, www.irishtimes.ie
4   J.J. Lee, *Ireland 1912-1985: Politics and Society*, op.cit., p.431

and despair to one or other section of the community in Northern Ireland.'[5]

Additionally, Fitt's declaration that the new party would have no connection 'with any secret or sectarian organisation'[6] laid down a clear demarcation line and a challenge to groups such as Provisional Sinn Féin and its secretive partner the Provisional IRA.[7]

Pledged to socialism

'New party in North is pledged to socialism' ran the headline in *The Irish Times* above a report of the SDLP launch. That was a fair summary based on the principles and policies announced at the launch.

Each of the founding strands brought its own, sometimes radical, traditions to the table. Where the old Nationalist Party had been socially conservative, the SDLP 'propounded a set of social and economic policies which left it somewhat left of centre in the conventional ideological spectrum'.[8]

Many policies reflected the influence of the Labour movement, from which the SDLP drew its first leader and other key figures. These included 'just and adequate distribution of wealth'; a minimum living wage; equal pay for equal work; establishing State industries in areas of high unemployment; promoting financial, industrial, consumer and agricultural co-operatives; and upholding the principles of organised labour. Civil rights for all citizens, also on the list, reflected the founders' involvement with the Northern Ireland civil rights movement.

The promotion of co-operation between the north and south of Ireland was not necessarily a key concern for the founding members from the Labour tradition, but they agreed that it was essential to find cooperative mechanisms that would promote better relations, if not necessarily unity, between north and south. Unification would soon move centre stage, however, and would prove divisive.

---

5   G. Fitt, *The Irish Times*, 22 August 1970, www.irishtimes.ie
6   G. Fitt, Ibid.
7   The split in the IRA and Sinn Féin was fresh at that time and both sides claimed the historic titles; the breakaway faction was known as Provisionals or, colloquially, the Provos.
8   J.J. Lee, *Ireland 1912-1985: Politics and Society*, op.cit., p.431

Towards a New Ireland

In 1972 the SDLP launched a manifesto, *Towards a New Ireland*, which began by calling on Britain to declare that 'it would be in the best interest of all sections of the communities in both islands, if Ireland were to become united on terms which would be acceptable to all the people of Ireland'.[9] Britain and the Republic of Ireland, it suggested, should sign a treaty under which both would accept joint interim responsibility for the administration of Northern Ireland.

The paper proposed a new political structure, including an Assembly and an Executive, but also – more controversially – a National Senate drawn equally from the Belfast and Dublin parliaments, whose purpose would be to plan how to integrate the two jurisdictions and harmonise structures, laws and services.

The SDLP's 1972 idea of a National Senate involving both states on the island of Ireland may have looked like a fantasy at the time, but versions of it would emerge later, under other names, and be met with varying degrees of unionist rejection. A Council of Ireland formed part of the December 1973 Sunningdale Agreement, and the 1985 Anglo-Irish Agreement and 1998 Belfast Agreement included a lesser but still significant role for Dublin in Northern Ireland affairs.

Breakthrough at Sunningdale

In May 1973 the Westminster parliament passed the Northern Ireland Assembly Bill, legislating for a devolved parliament at Stormont. This was based on proposals outlined in a White Paper[10] published in March. Elections were held on 28 June 1973, three years after the SDLP was launched.

The SDLP emerged as the second largest party with 19 of the 78 seats.[11] Formation of a new government would take months of

---

9   SDLP, *Towards a New Ireland – Proposals by the Social Democratic and Labour Party* (1972)

10   Northern Ireland Constitutional Proposals, cain.ulster.ac.uk

11   The 1973 Assembly was elected on the basis, set out in the British government White Paper on the future of Northern Ireland, that the government could 'no longer be solely based upon any single party, if that party draws its support and its elected representation virtually entirely from only one section of a divided community.'

talks, however, culminating in a conference held in Sunningdale (in Berkshire, England) in December 1973.

Sunningdale was the first occasion since 1925 on which the UK prime minister, the taoiseach, and the Northern Ireland government – the latter in the form of the Northern Ireland Executive (designate) – had all attended the same talks on the future of Northern Ireland. Representatives of the SDLP, the Ulster Unionist Party and the Alliance Party of Northern Ireland also participated.[12]

One of the SDLP's central policy planks, a role for Dublin in any future government of Northern Ireland, was the main source of discord at the talks, but agreement was eventually reached that there should be a Council of Ireland consisting of a Council of Ministers and a Consultative Assembly with advisory and review functions.[13] The Consultative Assembly was to be made up of 30 members each from the Northern Ireland Assembly and the Dáil – the SDLP'S 'National Senate' by another name, it could be argued.

The Sunningdale Agreement[14] was as good as it would get for the SDLP for many years, however, until the 1998 peace agreement and election of a new Northern Ireland Assembly.

Birth and short life of a new Stormont

A power-sharing Northern Ireland Executive took office on 1 January 1974, led by Brian Faulkner of the Ulster Unionist Party as Chief Executive, and SDLP leader Gerry Fitt as Deputy Chief Executive. The SDLP held three other ministries.

The Executive was short-lived, however, collapsing just months later due to unionist opposition. The Ulster Unionist Council, which controlled Ulster Unionist Party policy, rejected the Council of Ireland proposal in the Sunningdale Agreement, but a more dramatic form of opposition would prove more decisive.

While the outlook for success for Sunningdale had never been strong, the deciding factor in the fall of the new Stormont administration was the strike called by the Ulster Workers' Council

---

12 https://cain.ulster.ac.uk/events/sunningdale/chron.htm
13 The Government of Ireland Act 1920 included provision for a Council of Ireland
14 1974 chronology: https://cain.ulster.ac.uk/othelem/chron/ch74.htm

(UWC). This 'modern rebellion'[15] lasted for 14 days (15-28 May 1974) and paralysed the region.

The strike harnessed the 'deep sense of alienation that had grown in the Protestant community during the previous five years'[16] and won support from workers in key industries such as power generation and gas and petrol distribution, sectors that were also in turmoil in Britain. The response by the British Government and the Northern Ireland Office has been described as 'shambolic' and a major reason for the strike's success in sabotaging the Sunningdale Agreement.[17]

In the corridors of a new power: Front (left to right) Séamus Mallon, deputy first minister of Northern Ireland and deputy leader of the SDLP; US President Bill Clinton; David Trimble, first minister of Northern Ireland and leader of the UUP; second row: UK Prime Minister Tony Blair.

On 28 May 1974 Brian Faulkner resigned as chief executive, the Assembly collapsed, and responsibility for Northern Ireland reverted to the UK Government in London under arrangements for direct rule.

The SDLP's John Hume had called for an end to the Government of Ireland Act 1920 (the 'partition' Act, which legislated for two jurisdictions on the island) and for the British government to create a new system in which religious sectarianism would be neutralised. Hume could hardly have foreseen that almost a quarter century would pass before the journey towards those aims would begin in earnest – nor perhaps the role he himself would play.

The SDLP would not hold government office again for 25 years, when a new devolved administration was established under the 1998 peace agreement.[18] While SDLP representatives were elected

15 M. Dillon, in the foreword to D. Anderson, *Fourteen May Days: The Inside Story of the Loyalist Strike of 1974*, Dublin, Gill & Macmillan, 1994

16 M. Melaugh, in https://cain.ulster.ac.uk/events/uwc/sum.htm

17 https://cain.ulster.ac.uk/events/uwc/sum.htm

18 www.ark.ac.uk/elections/fa73.htm

to a 1975 Constitutional Convention, established to consider what provisions for the governance of Northern Ireland would be likely to command the widest acceptance, the convention's conclusions mainly impacted the internal dynamics of the unionist parties.

The darkest years

Following the collapse of the power-sharing Executive in 1974, the feared descent into chaos gathered pace. Sectarian divides deepened alongside a soaring toll of death, intimidation and destruction. Political killings accelerated: more than 3,500 individuals were murdered in the name of politics between 1969 and the end of 2001, the majority of them by republican (2,000+) or loyalist (1,000+) paramilitaries.[19]

The victims included SDLP members. Senator Paddy Wilson was stabbed to death in a sectarian killing in 1973; and in one of Northern Ireland's many incongruities, his killer was one of the loyalist representatives in the negotiations that led to the 1998 peace agreement.[20] SDLP leaders and activists came under attack from both sides. Radical republicans and loyalists regularly attacked Gerry Fitt's home in Belfast and eventually he moved his family to safety in England.

In his memoir, Séamus Mallon evokes some of the hostility and attacks he and colleagues endured – shots fired at elected representatives, canvassers assaulted, character assassination – as well as blatant intimidation: openly armed men at polling stations, instilling fear into election officials and voters. Mallon's parliamentary assistant, John Fee, a talented poet and traditional musician, was badly beaten up by a gang that broke into his house after he had spoken out against violence; he never completely recovered and died aged 43 with a brain tumour.

The H-Blocks hunger strikes at the Maze prison during 1980-81, staged by republican prisoners to gain political status and treatment, raised the temperature further, much further. Mallon likened the May 1981 local elections during the hunger strike to a pitched battle during which SDLP canvassers were frequently assaulted.

---

19   'The Sutton Index of Deaths', cain.ulster.ac.uk
20   S. Mallon, *A Shared Home Place*, Dublin, The Lilliput Press, 2019, p.99

Mallon also points out that 69 other people were killed during the seven months of the hunger strike, 37 of them by the IRA. The situation during the 1980-81 hunger strike period could have tipped over into civil war in some areas, he believed.

The SDLP struggled on with 'no resources, no money, no backup', Mallon records. Then another election came along in 1982, this time to a newly created Assembly, one without power sharing or an Irish dimension, and with ministers appointed by the London government.

The SDLP decided to contest this election in order to maintain credibility as a democratic party, but to abstain from taking their seats. In the event it won 14 seats, compared with the UUP's 26, 21 for the DUP, Alliance's 10, and Sinn Féin's five.[21] This Assembly lasted until 1986 but in a very limited form, with the SDLP and Sinn Féin abstaining and the UUP participating intermittently.

Peace comes dropping slow...

Séamus Mallon was deputy leader of the SDLP from 1979 to 2001 but, in effect, he carried most of the burden of leadership in the strife-ridden region while party leader John Hume concentrated on winning the necessary international support to change the political dynamic.

Hume, who succeeded Gerry Fitt as SDLP leader in 1979, played a major role in negotiating the Sunningdale Agreement. He led his party in the New Ireland Forum Talks of 1983, the Brooke Talks in 1992, the Forum for Peace and Reconciliation in 1994 and the All-Party Talks that led to the 1998 Belfast Agreement. However, it was his direct talks with Sinn Féin's Gerry Adams – which in effect meant indirectly talking to the Provisional IRA – that sparked the greatest controversy, drawing accusations that he was abetting violence.

Hume began a series of secret contacts with Adams in 1988. The SDLP leader aimed to persuade Sinn Féin that the problem was less the British presence in Ireland, rather 'the divisions between the people of Ireland, unionist and nationalist.'[22]

Further talks in 1993 became known and unleashed considerable hostility especially from unionists. The SDLP leader reportedly

---

21   www.ark.ac.uk/elections/fa82.htm
22   www.sdlp.ie

John Hume, leader of the SDLP (1979-2001) and Nobel Laureate 1998 for his work in bringing peace to Northern Ireland.

responded defiantly that he did not care 'two balls of roasted snow' about the criticism.[23]

Elsewhere he was more measured in his justification of talks with Adams, saying in a House of Commons speech: 'Unfortunately, there are in our society a substantial number of people who vote for political organisations which support violence and what they call 'armed struggle'. If one happens to be a public representative in that society, does one not have the responsibility to do everything in one's power to try to bring that violence to an end, in particular by talking to people?'

Breakthroughs

Hume continued to meet rival parties across the sectarian divide, negotiating with unionist leaders as well as Adams. The outcome was the 1993 Joint Declaration by Britain and Ireland (known as the Downing Street Declaration), and the 1994 cease-fire by the IRA and unionist paramilitaries.

The risk Hume took with the Adams talks, and his unstinting pursuit of other means of breaking the deadlock, eventually and tortuously led to the process that culminated in a peace accord. Along the way he brokered key initiatives. Michael Lillis, a senior Irish official who was closely involved with the process, credits Hume with achieving two breakthroughs in particular.[24]

The first was breaching the British veto on any US government involvement in Northern Ireland, a convention that had been 'impermeable since partition'. This amounted to new ground

23   S. Mallon, *A Shared Home Place*, op.cit., p.94
24   M. Lillis, 'John Hume's Legacy', *Dublin Review of Books*, 1 May 2018

rules for US engagement in affairs relating to Northern Ireland. In August 1977 US President Carter made a historically unprecedented statement in which he called for a human-rights-based solution to the Northern Irish problem, one that would be acceptable to Dublin and London as well as to the divided communities in Northern Ireland. He also called on Irish-Americans not to support violence in Ireland.

Under these new rules of engagement President Reagan would persuade Margaret Thatcher to commit to the Anglo-Irish Agreement of 1985, and President Clinton would intervene decisively in the process that culminated in the 1998 peace accord.[25]

Hume's other major achievement, according to Lillis, was redefining the constitutional nationalist consensus and ensuring that a new set of principles became central to the policy of all succeeding Dublin governments. Hume drafted these principles – partnership, human rights, equality of esteem, acknowledgement of the British rights and identity of unionists, and consent – in his own home in Lillis' presence.[26]

The SDLP aimed to achieve not just an end to violence but also an inclusive solution that tackled its causes, with the principle of consent as the basis for change. This and other goals – including institutional structures for co-operation and development between north and south, plus a decision-making partnership between Ireland and the UK within the EU framework – were all achieved and embedded in the Belfast Agreement.

The Agreement was approved in simultaneous referendums north and south on 22 May 1998, passed into law by the UK and Irish parliaments, and deposited with the United Nations as an international treaty.[27]

Hume and Ulster Unionist Party leader David Trimble were awarded the Nobel Peace Prize in 1998. In his Nobel lecture Hume declared that he wanted Ireland to be 'an example to men and women everywhere of what can be achieved by living for ideals, rather than fighting for them'.[28]

---

25   Ibid., September 2020
26   Ibid.
27   www.peacemaker.un.org/uk-ireland-good-friday98
28   J. Hume, 10 December 1998, www.nobelprize.org/prizes/peace/1998/hume/
     lecture/

Matthew O'Toole MLA, a former UK Government civil servant, became Leader of the Opposition in the Northern Ireland Assembly in 2022 when the SDLP decided to form a 'constructive opposition'. (© NI Assembly)

A new democracy

In the June 1998 elections to the Legislative Assembly established under the peace accord the SDLP topped the poll with 22% of first preference votes, slightly ahead of the UUP's 21.3%. After transfers, however, the UUP had 28 seats, while the SDLP's 24 made it the second-largest party. SDLP deputy leader Séamus Mallon became deputy first minister alongside the UUP's David Trimble as first minister. The Democratic Unionist Party and Sinn Féin also joined the Executive. Upon Mallon's retirement in 2001, to care for his seriously ill wife, Mark Durkan succeeded him as deputy first minister.

The balance between political parties soon changed, however. In November 2003 the DUP and Sinn Féin became the largest parties in the Assembly. This rise to dominance by the more extreme parties owed much to their having put down deep roots in their respective core communities during the Troubles. There may also have been other reasons, including failings by the SDLP and UUP as well as the British government's positioning.

The price of success

Despite its major contribution to peace, the SDLP did not enjoy an electoral 'peace dividend' in the longer term. A few scant years after the 1998 peace accord it looked as if the party could become redundant, a victim of its own success. Tonge suggested in 2003 that the future of Northern Ireland's 'moderate constitutional nationalist party' appeared to be in doubt and argued that the Hume-Adams dialogue may have been the 'ultimate piece of altruism' by the former SDLP leader.[29]

Certainly the start of a downward electoral trend was clear by then. The SDLP's seat tally fell from 24 in 1998 to 18 in 2003. Worse was to come. Its Assembly presence dropped steadily until it halved to just 12 seats in 2017. That was the year in which it also lost its three Westminster seats.

Left without any MPs, and relegated to the role of a minor party in the Assembly (by then suspended again), predictions of wipe-out for the party were understandable. However, it won two Westminster seats in 2019, albeit aided by an electoral pact between anti-Brexit parties. The 2022 Assembly election, however, was a bruising experience for the party, with the loss of four more seats.

'You have no guns'

It was perhaps inevitable that the SDLP would lose voters to Sinn Féin, once that party had decided to participate in the management of Northern Ireland despite continuation of the British rule against which it had fought bitterly for decades.[30]

The SDLP had long been aware of this danger. As early as 1976, Mallon recalled, leading party figures were warning that 'good people' in their areas were joining the Provisionals. Sinn Féin, Séamus Mallon claimed with reason, had subjected his party to relentless, totally focused attacks for decades – but there were also other factors at work.

How the UK Government handled its relationships with the Northern Ireland parties may have played a part in the electoral drift from the SDLP to Sinn Féin. The SDLP felt that there had been a shift in the UK attitude towards them during the later stages of the peace talks. The Blair Government, they sensed, was marginalising the party in favour of Sinn Féin.

When he challenged Tony Blair on why his party had been left out of key discussions, Mallon found Blair's reply 'breathtaking': 'The trouble with you fellows, Seamus, is that you have no guns.'[31]

---

29   J. Tonge, *Victims of Their Own Success?*, op.cit., pp.39-59

30   Ibid.

31   S. Mallon, *A Shared Home Place*, op.cit., p.96

The election of party leader Colum Eastwood MP (left) and Claire Hanna MP (right) to Westminster in 2019 raised hopes of a SDLP revival, but those hopes were dashed in the 2022 elections to the NI Legislative Assembly.
(left © B. O'Neill; right © D. Woolfall)

Generational challenge

In its extensive coverage of the SDLP launch in 1970, *The Irish Times* (Ireland's 'paper of record') showed a row of men at a top table. Their varied backgrounds - Republican Labour, Irish Labour, independent nationalists, civil rights activists – hinted at the compromises this political symbiosis entailed, and the challenge of keeping the disparate elements united.

Séamus Mallon frankly admitted that there were 'plenty of divisions within the ranks of the SDLP' in the 1970s, and these continued into the 1980s, but personality clashes were also present from the start, crucially between Gerry Fitt and John Hume.

Early on it became clear that Fitt was leader in name only and Hume was the driving force. 'John Hume's intellectual dominance always irked Fitt, though he preferred to characterise it as conservative and nationalist Catholicism' was one description of that conflict.[32] Fitt opposed Hume's push to include a role for the Dublin government in

---

32   www.irishtimes.com/news/sdlp-founder-and-foe-ofsectarianism-1.485010

constitutional talks and he resigned as leader in 1979, to be replaced by Hume.[33]

Hume, Fitt and Mallon – these three independent spirits embodied the potential strength of the alliance that was the original SDLP concept. Their tenacity, dedication and personal sacrifices in the face of enormous odds are the stuff of legend, but, a generation after the peace accord, what relevance did they have for the 21st century voters the SDLP needed to attract in order to survive and thrive?

Future prospects

The SDLP has always been able to take a long view, but shorter-term practical considerations matter too, if only to maintain credibility for the long haul. The new generation leadership appeared to see the need for long-term strategies. In July 2020 the party launched a *Commission for a New Ireland*, through which it sought 'to engage with every community, sector and generation on this island to build new proposals that can generate a consensus on our future constitutional arrangements'.

Could such engagement, combined with strong representation on everyday issues, spark a resurgence for the party of peace and reconciliation? Could it persuade a society still divided by political, religious and possibly murkier loyalties to vote for the SDLP'S vision of the future? Not, it transpired, in the short term.

The election of Claire Hanna and party leader Colum Eastwood to Westminster in 2019 had suggested that electoral recovery might have begun. In May 2022, however, the party lost four Assembly seats, leaving them with eight in the 90-seat chamber. A sharp contrast with 1998, when it won the highest percentage of first preference votes in elections to the newly established NI Assembly, at a time when war-weary voters appreciated the SDLP's role in achieving peace.

In the 2022 Assembly election campaign the SDLP vote was squeezed by the battle for the first minister post between the big beasts of NI politics, Sinn Féin and the DUP. While the first and deputy first minister posts are equal, perception matters in politics, or can be made to matter. In this case, the symbolism of a nationalist first

---

33 www.theguardian.com/politics/2005/aug/26/obituaries.uk

minister for the first time gave Sinn Féin an edge and they emerged on top, ready to claim the first minister position and nationalist leadership of Northern Ireland. That symbolic victory was at least partly due to voters switching from the SDLP to Sinn Féin, though whether temporarily or not was unclear.

After the SDLP's disappointing showing party leader Colum Eastwood told RTÉ News: 'The pull of the flag and the pull of the first minister issue just was too strong for people and we have to think about that'. Eastwood nevertheless put a confident spin on the party's dilemma: 'We've been counted out before and we've always come back, so we just have to regroup and reorganise and get stuck in to try and continue to represent people, because that's what we're about.' Worthy, admirable even, but sufficiently inspiring? Probably not, and certainly not without major change in public perception of his party.

Why a party that was highly instrumental in ending decades of violence began to fade away in peacetime is one of the great mysteries of Irish politics. Or is it? Did the overriding focus on ending violence and starting the long walk towards what Séamus Mallon called a 'shared home place' make it particularly difficult for the SDLP to find its place in peacetime politics?

The SDLP's achievements are historic but may appear precisely that, something in history, to a post-Troubles generation. Improving its contemporary credibility may require a mission comparable to that of those who founded the party in 1970. Leading the long walk towards genuine reconciliation on a shared island – living amicably in what Séamus Mallon called a 'shared home place' – would be a challenge to equal the SDLP's founding aims.

Meanwhile, something more immediate appeared to be essential, something to boost belief in the SDLP as a party with serious political prospects. A cross-border merger, for example, but with whom? Opting for either Fianna Fáil or Labour could split the northern party – but a merger with Fianna Fáil would be unlikely to win over many Sinn Féin voters, which the SDLP needed to do. Besides, Irish Labour hit rock bottom in 2020, returning a mere six TDs to Dáil Éireann, while Fianna Fáil, though in government, was also experiencing challenging times.

In the event, the SDLP appeared to prefer independence. Having already toughened its stance by going into opposition in the NI Executive, Eastwood declared that the SDLP needed to move forward by 'standing on its own two feet'. Seen as signalling an end to the policy partnership with Fianna Fáil, both partners downplayed that interpretation. Retaining influence in Dublin could enhance SDLP prestige and, eventually, its electability when the tide turns, as it normally does in politics, even in Northern Ireland.

Social Democratic and Labour Party (SDLP)	
Founded:	1970
Leaders:	Gerry Fitt 1970-79; John Hume 1979-2001; Mark Durkan 2001-10; Margaret Ritchie 2010-11; Alastair McDonnell 2011-15; Colum Eastwood 2015-
In office:	NI Executive 1998-2002; 2007-11; 2011-16; 2016-17; 2020-22
Affiliations:	Party of European Socialists (PES); Socialist International. Sister party: UK Labour Party.
Elected representatives:	2022: 8 MLAs (6M, 2F); 2 MPs (1M, 1F)

10

The Democratic Unionist Party

Sectarian provocation, power sharing and Brexit battle lines

Overview

Strong leaders – almost always men – have played starring roles in most political parties, but few more strikingly in modern Ireland than Ian Paisley. The Democratic Unionist Party (DUP) was his creation, founded in 1971 after he had made his name as a rabble-rousing preacher, established his own Free Presbyterian Church and dabbled in extreme loyalist political ventures. The DUP was the vehicle that took Paisley to the highest political office in Northern Ireland, as first minister in a legislature he and his party had vehemently opposed.

Paisley engineered the DUP's political ascent using shock tactics, often anti-Catholic in words and impact, adopted an 'Ulster Says No' response to most political initiatives and associated with paramilitaries until it became politically inconvenient. *En route* to the top Paisley and the DUP won a turf war with the previously hegemonic Ulster Unionist Party as well as a long war for the support of members of the Orange Order, a politically influential organisation founded to promote Protestant interests.

Provisions of the 1998 peace accord that the DUP had condemned enabled it to enter government in 2007, in a partnership of political convenience with Sinn Féin. Paisley became first minister of Northern Ireland alongside Sinn Féin's Martin McGuinness as deputy first minister and the two appeared to have an amicable relationship.

Intentionally or not, the DUP made a significant contribution to equality when Arlene Foster became party leader and Northern Ireland's first female first minister.

In the 2016 referendum on UK membership of the European Union, Northern Ireland voted to remain but the DUP backed Brexit. The Northern Ireland Protocol that gave the region access to the EU Single Market, but with customs checks on trade with Great Britain – a 'border in the Irish sea' – gave the DUP a new *cause célèbre*, which it pursued in its traditional confrontational style. The party's fall to second place in the 2022 Assembly election, behind Sinn Féin, raised questions about that approach in the longer term, despite its seeming utility at the time.

In the beginning ...

The DUP's origins were personal and religious as much as political. The party was the creation of Ian Paisley, a fundamentalist preacher. Religious affiliation had been a core consideration in Northern Ireland's formation and divided much of society. When mixed with politics, the two were at times a dangerous combination.

The boundaries of the recently created Northern Ireland into which Ian Paisley was born in 1926 were the result of a careful calculation of the proportion of Protestants to Catholics. The aim was to ensure a substantial Protestant majority that would elect a unionist government – a successful strategy that gave the Ulster Unionist Party control of the sub-state for 50 years (see chapter 2).

By the time Paisley founded the Democratic Unionist Party in 1971, he had carved out a career as a radical fundamentalist preacher and established his own Free Presbyterian Church. He experimented with other political activities, sometimes alongside quasi-paramilitary groups, before founding the DUP, the vehicle that took him to the pinnacle of Northern Ireland politics.

Paisley was the son of a hot gospel preacher but, says Moloney, he got most of his religious fire and fury from his Scottish mother.[1] He became a preacher in his teens, training in Wales at what was then the Barry School of Evangelism, and later developing a close relationship with a fundamentalist Christian US institution, the Bob Jones University in South Carolina, from which he received an Honorary Doctorate.

---

1   E. Moloney, *Paisley: From Demagogue to Democrat?*, Dublin, Poolbeg Press, 2008, p.7

Beyond religious dogma, however, Paisley's career was, in Kaufman's view, 'defined by his desire to carve out a niche for himself to the right of the traditional institutions of unionism: the mainstream churches, the Orange Order and the UUP'.[2]

One of his biographers, Ed Moloney, wonders if the most pertinent question to ask about Paisley might be: 'Was Ian Paisley possibly the only member of his flock who never really or fully believed his own gospel?'[3] A more irreverent question might be: Did Ian Paisley simply spot a gap in the market for a party that could exploit the deeply embedded fears and insecurities of a section of Northern Ireland's Protestants?

Whatever the truth, Paisley, his son and other DUP members took up ministerial posts in a devolved administration they had fiercely opposed, on terms that conflicted with the beliefs of the Church he founded and continued to lead.[4] The tactics used to get there also raise fundamental questions.

Preaching, politics and provocation

Paisley's early ventures into politics, like his religious career, suggested a readiness to use risky tactics, including rekindling old fears of Catholicism. In June 1959, for example, a Paisley speech provoked an outbreak of 'some of the worst anti-Catholic violence' Belfast had seen for years.[5]

Addressing a rally organised by Ulster Protestant Action (UPA) in Belfast's Lower Shankill area, Paisley called out the addresses of 'Pope's men' and 'Papishers' – plus an Italian ice-cream shop. Stirred by the rhetoric and Orange band music, the crowd attacked suspected Catholic homes, breaking windows and painting slogans on doors, and looted a shop selling Catholic religious items. Paisley drove away, and disclaimed any responsibility for what he had inspired.

Paisley continued to work with the UPA, a small loyalist party founded in 1956, to provoke further conflicts involving a classic

---

2   E.P. Kaufman, *The Orange Order: A Contemporary Northern Irish History*, Oxford University Press, 2007, p.230

3   E. Moloney, *Paisley: From Demagogue to Democrat?*, op.cit., p.xiii

4   Ibid., pp.497-500

5   Ibid., pp.84-5

unionist mix of flags, marches and shipyard workers,[6] in a populist style that harked back to earlier Ulster unionism and Belfast's reputation as a city that resorted readily to sectarian rioting.

His activities took place against the background of a control system constructed by the Ulster Unionist Party (UUP), which ruled from 1921 to 1972. That system had held together a broad spectrum of unionists, from landed gentry to labourers, by means that were often far from fair (see chapter 2). After decades in power the UUP was not used to serious challenge, and responded ineffectually when the Northern Ireland civil rights movement began demonstrating for an end to sectarian bias against Catholics.

Paisley and his associates were already old hands at confrontation when the first civil rights march took place in August 1968. Reaching its destination, Dungannon, it was met by counter-demonstrators under the banner of the Protestant Volunteers, a group 'politically inspired by Ian Paisley and para-militarily groomed by Major Ronald Bunting'.[7] On that occasion a police cordon separated marchers, and injuries were few.

On 4 January 1969 at Burntollet Bridge the police largely failed to protect the People's Democracy students who had marched from Belfast.[8] Some 200 loyalists, described as followers of Paisley and Bunting, attacked the marchers with sticks, iron bars, bottles and stones.

The Cameron Commission, appointed by the Northern Ireland prime minister to investigate the disturbances, singled out 'the deliberate and organised interventions by followers of Major Bunting and the Rev. Dr. Paisley, especially in Armagh, Burntollet and Londonderry, [that] substantially increased the risk of violent disorder on occasions when Civil Rights demonstrations or marches were to take place'.[9]

Historian Paul Bew, who was a member of People's Democracy and later an adviser to UUP leader David Trimble, concluded: 'No one

---

6   Ibid., pp.86-7
7   Northern Ireland Civil Rights Association (NICRA), *We shall overcome: The History of the Struggle for Civil Rights in Northern Ireland 1968-1978*, Belfast, NICRA, 1978.
8   Cameron Report, *Disturbances in Northern Ireland*, September 1969. (Cmd 532), Summary of Conclusions (paragraph 15)
9   Ibid., Chapter 16 (paragraph 913)

did as much damage to the unionist cause as the people who attacked the marchers at Burntollet.'[10]

While they damaged unionism's image and the UUP's future, the opposite may have been true for Paisley's ambitions and the fortunes of the party he would soon establish. The future founder of the DUP was amongst those on the right of unionism putting pressure on the UUP government to resist calls for reform – but doing it his way. He would soon get his breakthrough into parliamentary politics.

A winning streak

In a by-election on 16 April 1970, Paisley won Bannside, the Stormont parliament seat vacated by former prime minister Terence O'Neill. William Beattie, also a Free Presbyterian Church minister, won another by-election on the same day. Both stood as candidates for the Protestant Unionist Party (1966-71), forerunner of the DUP.

In September 1971, Paisley and Beattie founded the Democratic Unionist Party, and a month later two Stormont MPs who had resigned from the UUP joined them.

Paisley was on a roll, accumulating political positions. He became a Westminster MP, winning the North Antrim seat in June 1970, held it for 40 years, and was succeeded by his son. He topped the Northern Ireland poll in the first elections to the European Parliament in 1979, and remained an MEP for nearly a quarter of a century.

The DUP contested its first election as a party in June 1973, taking eight seats in a new Northern Ireland Assembly. That Assembly fell as a result of unionist opposition to the Sunningdale Agreement between the British and Irish governments, which sought a democratic solution to the violence that was engulfing Northern Ireland.

The agreement would have given the Dublin government a say in Northern Ireland affairs, through a Council of Ireland with a Council of Ministers and a Consultative Assembly with 30 members each from the NI Assembly and Dáil Éireann, the Republic's parliament. The Ulster Workers' Council strike (15-28 May 1974) defeated Sunningdale, toppled the Assembly and triggered a return to direct rule from London.[11]

---

10   S. O'Hagan, 'Northern Ireland's lost moment', op.cit.
11   https://cain.ulster.ac.uk/events/uwc/sum.htm

There had been previous attempts to mobilise the power of Protestant workers for political ends, but new circumstances gave the 1974 strike greater clout. The strike leaders were able to harness a deep sense of alienation that had been growing amongst Protestants over the previous five years as conflict escalated and security deteriorated. There was also an extra element: the support from workers in key industries such as power generation, gas and petrol distribution paralysed the economy.

Opposition to Sunningdale also united a large swathe of unionism, if temporarily. The DUP, the Vanguard Unionist Progressive Party and much of the UUP (led by Harry West since January 1974) joined together under the banner of the United Ulster Unionist Council (UUUC). This was also when the DUP openly sat around a table with leading paramilitaries 'at a time when there were no illusions about who was responsible for the many sectarian murders of Catholics and bomb attacks on bars in nationalist areas', as Steve Bruce notes.[12]

The DUP and UUP found common ground again in 1985 when they opposed the Anglo-Irish Agreement signed by Prime Minister Margaret Thatcher and Taoiseach Garret FitzGerald. The two parties teamed-up again, in 1991–92, when Paisley and UUP leader James Molyneaux cooperated during talks between Northern Ireland's major parties and the British and Irish governments. However, the two parties took increasingly divergent stances in multiparty peace talks in the mid-1990s, and the DUP left when Sinn Féin was admitted to the negotiations in 1997.

Meanwhile, the party had been on a winning streak: 12 seats in a Constitutional Convention in 1975; three MPs elected to Westminster in 1979; 21 members elected to a new NI Assembly in 1982; and 24 members in the 1996 Northern Ireland Forum.

Joining the mainstream

The DUP rejected the 1998 Belfast Agreement that ended the 30-year conflict, known as the Troubles. Denouncing the Agreement's main provisions, it campaigned for a 'no' vote in the confirmatory referendum, but contested the June 1998 elections and won 20 seats in the new Legislative Assembly. As the third largest party the

---

12 S. Bruce, *Religion and Violence: The Case of Paisley and Ulster Evangelicals*, The Irish Association for Cultural, Economic and Social Relations, October 2003

Ian Paisley Snr (left), founder of the DUP, and his son Ian Paisley Jnr (right), who succeeded him as MP for North Antrim in 2010. While Paisley Snr was famed for his provocative politics Paisley Jnr has been associated with controversies of a different kind, including accepting hospitality from the Sri Lankan government without declaring it to the House of Commons. (left © Scottish Govt.; right © UK Parliament)

DUP was given two ministerial positions on the Executive, which it accepted while declining to participate fully in Executive affairs.

In the 2003 elections, the DUP surpassed the UUP as Northern Ireland's largest unionist party with a tally of 30 MLAs (Members of the Legislative Assembly), but Ian Paisley's elevation to first minister didn't happen immediately, or even soon, as the Assembly had been suspended since 14 October 2002.

The party pulled off another coup in January 2004 when three MLAs (including future DUP leaders Arlene Foster and Jeffrey Donaldson) defected from the UUP, taking the DUP Assembly group to 33. In 2005 its Westminster presence soared to nine MPs, leaving the UUP with just one.

The IRA's failure to decommission its arms, a condition of the 1998 peace agreement, was the major cause of the Assembly's continued suspension. In July 2005 the IRA ordered its members to end hostilities and dump arms, but distrust lingered and the Assembly remained suspended.

The St. Andrews Agreement between the UK and Irish governments and main NI parties, signed in October 2006, broke the deadlock. Fresh elections took place in March 2007, the DUP returned twice as many MLAs as the UUP (36 to 18), and Sinn Féin took second place with 28 seats, giving it the right to nominate the deputy first minister.

The St. Andrews Agreement rocked the DUP, especially in the context of Paisley's declaration in July 2006 that the party would enter into power-sharing with Sinn Féin 'over our dead bodies'.[13] A party dissident captured the fiery atmosphere at one ratification meeting, where members heckled Paisley and accused him of hypocrisy and blackmail. Paisley's response:

Having succeeded Ian Paisley as DUP leader in 2008, Peter Robinson MLA served as NI first minister from 2008 to 2016, and was also a Westminster MP 1979-2010. (© NI Office)

you can say anything you like in opposition but things are different in a position of power.[14]

Power was devolved from London on 8 May 2007 and, when the Assembly met, Ian Paisley took office as first minister with Sinn Féin's Martin McGuinness as deputy first minister – an unlikely partnership that would have been hard to predict on the basis of either man's career, but one that appeared amicable.

Scandals and deals

Paisley stepped down as leader and first minister in June 2008. His deputy, Peter Robinson, who took over, then stepped aside briefly in 2010 following allegations that his wife made improper use of a £50,000 loan. In May 2010 he lost his seat at Westminster, reducing the DUP to eight MPs, but continued his role as first minister at Stormont until 11 January 2016, with one further interregnum in 2015 when, as previously, Arlene Foster deputised for him.

---

13   E. Moloney, *Paisley: From Demagogue to Democrat?*, op.cit., p.447
14   Ibid., p.527

Arlene Foster replaced Robinson as leader in December 2015 and, in January 2016, became NI's first female first minister. Elected as an MLA on the UUP ticket, she defected to the DUP in 2004. She was a rarity in the DUP, not just a high flying woman but also a practising Anglican in a party where Paisley's Free Presbyterian Church was the favourite religious affiliation. Her politics had a deep personal element: the childhood memory of a Provisional IRA assassination attempt on her father.[15]

Foster refused to step down while alleged mismanagement of sustainable energy funding, the Renewable Heat Incentive (RHI), was investigated,[16] but Deputy First Minister McGuinness resigned in protest and the Executive collapsed.

In an election in March 2017 the DUP retained top place but by a slim margin, only one seat ahead of Sinn Féin (after a reduction in the number of Assembly seats from 108 to 90). Crucially, on first preference votes the DUP lead over Sinn Féin was barely 1,200 votes.

In the London limelight

When UK Prime Minister Theresa May lost her parliamentary majority in June 2017, the DUP's Westminster MPs found themselves in demand. A confidence and supply agreement gave May's government its majority and the DUP got an extra £1 billion funding over two years for Northern Ireland. The moment of influence ended when the next UK Prime Minister, Boris Johnson, won a large majority in a December 2019 snap election. Attention shifted back to Northern Ireland as post-Brexit border arrangements moved centre stage.

The DUP had backed Brexit in the 2016 referendum on UK membership of the European Union, but Northern Ireland voted to remain. The Northern Ireland Protocol, which Johnson's government negotiated and signed, was designed to prevent a hard border on the island of Ireland by giving Northern Ireland customs-free access to the EU Single Market in goods. This also gave the DUP a new mission, to oppose what it called a border in the Irish Sea between Northern Ireland and Britain.

---

15 www.rte.ie/news/analysis-and-comment/2021/0501/1213138-tommie-gorman/

16 www.bbc.co.uk/news/uk-northern-ireland-38301428

NI First Minister Arlene Foster (DUP), UK Prime Minister Theresa May and NI Deputy First Minister Martin McGuinness (Sinn Féin), at Stormont Castle, Belfast, 25 July 2016. (© UK Govt.)

New decade, new issues

A three-year shutdown of the Assembly ended in January 2020 when the UK and Irish Governments and the main NI parties reached a deal. The 'New Decade, New Approach' agreement included commitments on health, language, legacy and the environment. None was more controversial than the Irish language aspect.

The agreement mandated support for the Irish and Ulster Scots languages, and the recognition and celebration of Northern Ireland's 'diversity of identities and culture', including 'ethnic and newcomer communities'[17] but the Irish language provisions were contentious. In the words of one DUP MLA: 'unionists ... are about as enthusiastic about the Irish language as nationalists are about

---

17   *New Decade, New Approach*, www.dfa.ie , January 2020, p.15 and pp.31-7 (Annex E):

Jeffrey Donaldson MP became fifth leader of the DUP in June 2021, the party's third leader within two months. (© UK Parliament)

the Orange Order'.[18] This issue would play a part in the DUP's 2021 leadership saga.

First, there was the overthrow of Arlene Foster soon after she abstained on an Assembly motion calling for the banning of conversion therapy, rather than joining most of her socially conservative DUP party colleagues in opposing it.

Edwin Poots succeeded Foster, and soon afterwards affirmed his commitment to implementing the 'New Decade, New Approach' deal in full, including its Irish language provisions. Poots' leadership lasted a mere three weeks, though the reasons were wider than his language comment, and included his decision to propose another MLA, his former constituency assistant Paul Givan, for the first minister position.

Next up was Jeffrey Donaldson MP, who broke with convention by deciding to lead from Westminster rather than seek a seat in the Assembly and become first minister. He took on the job in what, despite previous scandals and internal discord, looked like being possibly the DUP's most challenging period.

Reflecting concern about the predicted tight contest in Assembly elections scheduled for 2022, Donaldson made an early pitch for a pan-unionist electoral pact. The Traditional Unionist Voice (TUV) response was lukewarm, the UUP's an outright 'no' – both fancied their chances as polling suggested the DUP was in trouble. All three feared that Sinn Féin could become the largest party, giving it the right to the first minister title, even though the first and deputy first ministers are equal.

Retaining the pre-eminent place in Northern Ireland politics carved out under Paisley's long leadership looked like a daunting task for Donaldson. In a very different society to that into which

---

18   www.rte.ie/news/2021/0618/1228897-irish-language-actexplainer/

the DUP was born, demographically and in terms of electoral politics, would he run with the old DUP practice of provocation and confrontation? Or would he pursue something more politically astute, more in tune with the times and the needs of some of the party's core constituents?

The Paisley way

Paisley had spent decades building up a following, firstly through fundamentalist evangelism, then by re-igniting old fears and anti-Catholic prejudice for political effect. The nature of the state in its early decades also provided a congenial ecosystem in which to operate. The centrality of religion to identity and politics in Northern Ireland, which its first prime minister called a 'Protestant state',[19] was a key factor for the Paisley *modus operandi*.

The perpetuation of a 'Protestant state' was inextricably linked with the Orange Order, or Loyal Orange Institution (LOI), founded in 1796 to further the aims of Protestantism. Kaufman argues that the Order's *raison d'etre* makes it 'an ethnic Association representing the Ulster Protestant people'.[20] The Order was deeply influential in Protestant communities and, through the Ulster Unionist Council, had a virtual veto over the policies of the ruling UUP. The Order did not welcome Ian Paisley's intrusion.

In 1951 the Order barred clergymen from Paisley's Free Presbyterian Church from serving as Orange Lodge chaplains. By the time it lifted the ban in late 1998, the peace agreement was the central dividing line in unionism and the DUP was an established protagonist.

'The DUP sensed a thaw in its 50-year cold war with the Order, and the Order sensed the rising power and ideological compatibility of the DUP.'[21] Those members Kaufman categorises as 'rebels' – Scots-Irish Presbyterians and Methodists – favoured the DUP, whereas the Anglo-Irish and Church of Ireland 'traditionalists' preferred the UUP.[22] This worked to the DUP's benefit at the ballot box.

---

19 Parliamentary Debates, Northern Ireland House of Commons, Vol. XVI, Cols 1091-95
20 E.P. Kaufman, *The Orange Order*, op.cit., p.2 & 316-7
21 Ibid., p.233
22 Ibid., pp.11-12

Playing with fire

Why was it the DUP that took off as the party of discontented Protestants rather than, for example, a UUP breakaway such as William Craig's Vanguard? Both Paisley and Craig played with fire but Paisley was more calculating and was quick to distance himself if danger loomed, as happened with Ulster Resistance (UR).

When the UR was launched in 1986 to oppose the Anglo-Irish Agreement, Paisley and his DUP deputy Peter Robinson appeared at its rallies and marches wearing the group's trademark red berets. Paisley urged resistance 'by whatever means the situation demands [against] those who would drive us against our wills into an all-Ireland republic'.[23] However, he could not disown UR quickly enough when it emerged that weapons from an arsenal it had smuggled into Northern Ireland, jointly with the paramilitary UVF and UDA, had been used to murder innocent civilians. Such as in one notorious case in rural Loughinisland, where gunmen burst into a tiny bar and shot dead six people who were watching the Republic's football team playing a World Cup match on television.[24]

While there is no convincing evidence that Paisley was directly involved in paramilitary activities, Bruce concludes that the most compelling charge is that Paisley and his supporters created a political environment in which others found it easy to see terrorism as acceptable.[25]

Despite his high octane rhetoric, by 1998 Paisley knew that times had changed. Like the Provisional IRA and Sinn Féin, he judged that people wanted peace and the institutions established by the Belfast Agreement offered a new road to power and influence.

Easter rioting

In late March 2021, while DUP politicians were gearing up for a leadership coup, rioting broke out in several towns and cities, heralded by posters and graffiti declaring: 'Protocol Equals War' and 'RIP Good Friday Agreement'. There were reports of men teaching

---

23   www.theguardian.com/politics/2017/jun/27/troubled-pastthe-paramilitary-connection-that-still-haunts-the-dup

24   www.rte.ie/culture/2019/1001/1079485-no-stone-unturnedinside-the-loughinisland-massacre-documentary/

25   S. Bruce, *Religion and Violence*, op.cit.

teenagers to make petrol bombs[26] and suggestions that the riots were an attempt to radicalise a new generation and draw them into sectarian violence.

There were also barely veiled charges of DUP encouragement of the riots, although party leaders condemned them. Could the modern power-sharing DUP have lost its self-preservation instinct to the extent of playing with sectarian fire again? One Orange Order member, blogging anonymously, claimed that the DUP's problems included 'loose links with loyalist paramilitaries'.[27] Politically, that could be a turn-off for some voters but perhaps not for all, in the way that its links with the IRA appeared not to be a major problem for Sinn Féin's supporters.

Credible evidence that loyalist paramilitary groups still existed emerged in late 2020. The Independent Reporting Commission (which monitors progress on tackling their activity) warned that they remained a 'clear and present danger' and estimated that the UVF had about 7,500 and the UDA 5,000 card-carrying members.[28]

Back to basics?

The Easter 2021 rioters were unlikely to be members of the UVF or UDA, yet. Mainly teenagers from poorer Protestant working class communities, some said boredom drew them to the action. Whatever their personal motivations, the young rioters became cannon fodder in a new round of northern clashes.

Prioritising a better future for areas suffering from entrenched deprivation, like those in which the young rioters lived, might have strengthened support for the DUP in the 2022 Assembly election and beyond. Instead, they campaigned in constitutional rhetoric against an 'Irish Sea border' (with a sideline in warnings that a nationalist could become first minister of Northern Ireland) – although this approach was not illogical in the political context of the time.

26 www.irishtimes.com/life-and-style/people/the-north-riotsstopped-because-prince-andrew-or-philip-or-something-he-sdead-1.4538444

27 Choyaa, 'Fragmented Unionism and Broad Churches', sluggerotoole.com, 29 May 2021

28 Independent Reporting Commission, Third Report, Belfast, November 2020

The Easter 2021 clashes appeared to be designed, in large part, to stiffen unionist resistance to the NI Protocol of the agreement on UK withdrawal from the EU.[29] To avoid a hard border on the island of Ireland, a key point in the 1998 peace agreement, the Protocol gave Northern Ireland special status: free movement of goods within the EU Single Market, but with customs checks on goods entering the NI market from Britain. The latter gave rise to some bureaucratic challenges for business but also trade opportunities. Significantly in political terms, however, it created a difference in trade-related regulations within the United Kingdom of Great Britain and Northern Ireland, or what unionists called a border in the Irish Sea between NI and GB.

The DUP manifesto[30] for the 2022 Assembly elections promised to 'make Northern Ireland a place of peace, stability and prosperity' with investments in health, schools, jobs, childcare and measures to ease cost of living pressures. There was much more, including opposition to abortion in Northern Ireland (which had been legalised by the Westminster parliament) – but all were peripheral to the party's main campaign. As it turned out, however, the decision to woo their core supporters may have been the right one electorally, by helping them to mop up loyalist transfers.

On 5 May 2022 a nationalist first minister became a potential reality when the DUP dropped to second place behind Sinn Féin in both first preference votes and Assembly seats. At 21.3% the party's share of first preferences was significantly lower than in 2017 (28.1%), but transfers limited their losses, giving them 25 seats (27.8%) in the Assembly, two fewer than Sinn Féin. Considering the forecasts of severe losses this was a strong outcome for the DUP, which retained its clear lead as the largest party within the 37-strong block of unionist MLAs.

Significantly, however, the main source of the transferred votes that saved the DUP from a harder fall was the ultra loyalist Traditional Unionist Voice (TUV), which had campaigned forcefully against the NI Protocol and appeared on ballot papers as 'TUV - No Sea Border'. The TUV's strong showing – winning 7.6% of the

---

29 Full official titles: Protocol on Ireland and Northern Ireland; Agreement on the withdrawal of the United Kingdom of Great Britain and Northern Ireland from the European Union and the European Atomic Energy Community

30 https://s3.eu-west-1.amazonaws.com/my-dup/029311-DUP-Manifesto.pdf

popular vote (though only one seat) – made it harder for the DUP to compromise on its anti-Protocol position and it proceeded to block the creation of a new Executive (Northern Ireland's government). Without cross-community (i.e. unionist + nationalist) support it was impossible to take the first essential steps towards approving a new Executive.

Blocking government formation was hardly a novel move for the party founded by Ian Paisley. Confrontation was the hallmark of the early DUP, its precursors and associates, although Paisley later used the opportunities presented by devolution to pursue his aims, alongside tough bargaining and strategic disruption of democracy. (Sinn Féin has also in its time been responsible for collapsing the Assembly.) Paisley's political descendants appeared to be reverting to type.

The Democratic Unionist Party's decision to block the formation of an Executive in 2022 was within the rules of Northern Ireland power sharing, however anti-democratic that may have appeared. Besides, the party clearly represented a substantial section of NI opinion, whether measured in first preference votes or Assembly seats.

That strand of opinion wanted no sea border, no Brexit Protocol, but changing the Protocol was not within the competence of the NI Assembly (although it was due to have the right to vote on it in 2024). Nor could the UK change it unilaterally, at least not under international law, but the Johnson government introduced a Bill[31] that could do so in effect. DUP leader Jeffrey Donaldson welcomed that Bill, but the stalemate looked set to continue.

There were suggestions that the DUP were pawns in a Tory power play, evoking Edward Carson's declaration a century earlier that he, Ulster and Ireland had been puppets 'in the political game that was to get the Conservative party into office' – but what if the political dynamic in 21st century London were to change? Would NI benefit from a different, more serious involvement by London, similar to that of the Blair-led Labour government in 1998? That would need reciprocal seriousness by the major NI parties, at least, and certainly a serious re-think by the DUP.

Assuming no dramatic change, no shifting of constitutional parameters in Ireland or Britain, could the DUP continue to be a

---

31   https://bills.parliament.uk/bills/3182

major player in a Northern Ireland characterised by an evolving and increasingly agnostic electorate? The 2022 election confirmed that there was still a large constituency for the DUP's brand of politics, and that looked likely to be the case for some considerable time. The DUP weren't going away, were mostly not for changing and would be a serious force to be reckoned with in any Northern Ireland future, even one in which the island's two jurisdictions agreed to unite.

Democratic Unionist Party (DUP)	
Founded:	1971
Leaders:	Ian Paisley 1971-2008; Peter Robinson 2008-15; Arlene Foster 2015-May 2021; Edwin Poots May-June 2021; Jeffrey Donaldson 2021-
In office:	First Ministers 2007-22; in Executive: 1998-2002; 2007-11; 2011-16; 2016-17; 2020-2022
Affiliations:	n/a
Elected representatives:	2022: 25 MLAs (19M, 6F); 8 MPs (7M, 1F)

11

The Progressive Democrats / An Páirtí Daonlathach

Steering Ireland 'Closer to Boston than Berlin'

Overview

The Progressive Democrats (PDs) – launched in December 1985 and dissolved in 2009 – influenced the direction of Irish government policy at a time of rapid change. In line with the then prevalent economic orthodoxy, the PDs urged the adoption of neo-liberal policies in Ireland, but mainly took a liberal approach to social issues.

This was a new kind of party in the Republic of Ireland, one that self-classified as a liberal democratic party but, based on its policy priorities, could more accurately be described as right-wing: it placed a heavier emphasis than most European liberal parties on economic and fiscal policies, and on law and order rather than individual liberties. Nevertheless it can be argued that it was not a party of the European 'new right'.

The founders of the Progressive Democrats were mostly dissident Fianna Fáil politicians, joined by some defectors from Fine Gael. Having split from Fianna Fáil they then entered into coalition with that party, not once but four times between 1989 and 2009.

The party achieved its best result in the first election it contested and was mainly on a downward slope in popularity afterwards, but it left a lasting mark on the policies of successive Dublin governments, influencing decisions during the so-called Celtic Tiger era when the economy strengthened at a dramatic pace. In this boom period Ireland moved ideologically 'closer to Boston than Berlin', as the shift was described by Mary Harney (PD leader 1993-2006 and 2007-

Des O'Malley TD, first leader of the Progressive Democrats, left Fianna Fáil to found the new party following clashes with Charles Haughey but later served in a Haughey-led government. (© Glucksman Library)

08), who was the first woman to lead a political party in Ireland and the first to become tánaiste.

The end of the party was decisive if not necessarily inevitable: reduced to two Dáil seats, they decided to call it a day – a decision that could be considered the epitome of realism in light of the 2008 financial collapse.

Formed in frustration at perceived economic ineptitude and corruption, the Progressive Democrats' impact on the policies of other parties and of the State reduced their relevance as a political alternative. Despite their original concern about corruption, their very success in achieving a rightward shift in economic policy may have made it easier for corruption to flourish during the boom years, contributing to the conditions that bred the banking and construction crash that threatened the State's very sovereignty.

A family row

Des O'Malley, main architect of the Progressive Democrats and the party's first leader, attributed his discontent with his previous party, Fianna Fáil, to two main factors: the economic state of the country and its fiscal position by the mid-1980s, and Fianna Fáil's attitude to Northern Ireland and to unionists.

A senior Fianna Fáil TD and three times a cabinet minister, O'Malley had long been on a collision course with his party leader, Charles Haughey. He saw in Haughey an opportunist who ignored the merits of any policy position 'if there was some political advantage to be gained'. Haughey's rule, he claimed, was autocratic, with 'little or no ideology involved.'[1]

By 1985 O'Malley also feared the 'imminent possibility' of International Monetary Fund (IMF) intervention in Ireland, a prospect he considered 'truly horrendous' because it would constitute a loss of national sovereignty 'which is, by definition, among the greatest losses an independent state can suffer.'[2] That intervention eventually came, but not until after the PDs had made their imprint on state policy.

'Conduct unbecoming'

Two of the foremost political issues of the 1980s – one an attempt to find a path to peace and reconciliation in Northern Ireland, the other a *cause celebre* of the women's rights movement – led to Des O'Malley's expulsion from Fianna Fáil.

All parties in the Dáil had signed the report of the New Ireland Forum,[3] which Garrett FitzGerald's government had set up to identify how a lasting peace in Northern Ireland and stability across the island could be achieved by democratic means. Yet, according to O'Malley, 'half an hour after signing it, Haughey repudiated the kernel of it'. When O'Malley objected, the parliamentary party whip was withdrawn from him. Later that year, he was expelled from Fianna Fáil for 'conduct unbecoming' when he refused to vote against a Bill to liberalise the availability of contraception.

O'Malley claims that Garrett Fitzgerald, the then taoiseach and Fine Gael leader, offered him a place in his government, but he considered Fine Gael as well as Fianna Fáil to be 'slightly vague conservative parties' with little or no ideology,[4] and ideology was an important part of what motivated O'Malley to take the next step of founding a new kind of Irish party.

On 21 December 1985, he launched the Progressive Democrats, alongside Fianna Fáil TDs Mary Harney, Bobby Molloy and Pearse Wyse, Fine Gael TD Michael Keating and former Fine Gael activist

---

1   D. O'Malley, in L. Weeks and A. Clarke, *Radical or Redundant*, op.cit., p.80
2   Ibid., p.79
3   cain.ulster.ac.uk/issues/politics
4   D. O'Malley, in L. Weeks and A. Clarke, *Radical or Redundant*, op.cit., p.80

Bobby Molloy TD left Fianna Fáil for the Progressive Democrats at the PDs' foundation and retained his Dáil seat until he retired in 2002; Molloy served as a minister in both Fianna Fáil governments and Fianna Fáil-led coalitions. (© Connacht Tribune)

Michael McDowell. With several TDs on board, the new party had a ready-made parliamentary presence and a base in some constituencies, giving them an organisational head start.

A voice for middle Ireland

The launch of the new party caught the public imagination, or at least that of a section of middle Ireland who feared their country was incapable of consistent good governance or sustained economic development, never mind prosperity.

Within weeks of its launch, polls showed the PDs on 20% to 25% support. Crowds flocked to 'town hall' meetings, some of which attracted 3,000 to 4,000 attendees each. O'Malley described these as 'possibly the last of what might be regarded as mass political meetings'.[5]

Those early signs reflected a growing appetite for modernisation, for which the PDs offered an economic recipe: let the private sector take over from a State often seen as inefficient and increasingly as corrupt. This appealed to segments of the support base of both Fianna Fáil and Fine Gael. Or as Pat Rabbitte – Labour leader 2002-07 – described it: 'A significant section of middle Ireland was eager

---

5   Ibid., p.81

to embrace the low-tax, deregulation and small government model' advocated by the PDs.[6]

Initially the party polled quite well across all social groups and across all age groups, some of that possibly because of its liberalism on social issues. Support contracted, however, to a voter base that was mainly middle-class (ABC1). There was also a period in the late 1990s when women were more likely to vote PD than men.[7] This coincided with the election of Mary Harney as party leader, the first woman to head a political party in Ireland and the first to hold the office of tánaiste.

However, the first flush of voters' faith in the new political saviour was not sustained. The best election result came in 1987, when the PDs won 14 Dáil seats, but after that the trend was mainly downwards, possibly because the party lost its distinctive edge.

Ó Muineacháin argues that it did better in elections when its distinctiveness was clear,[8] Possibly, however, its appeal also narrowed as the detailed basis for its distinctiveness became clearer.

In government

In the first general election they contested, in February 1987, the Progressive Democrats won 12% of first preference votes and, with 14 seats, became the third largest party in the Dáil. This didn't offer them an *entrée* to government, however. Rather, alongside Fine Gael, they supported a Fianna Fáil minority government that lasted for two years.

They then fought the 1989 election on the basis of a coalition pact with Fine Gael. PD leader Des O'Malley described the two as 'like-minded parties' with 'broad compatibility between policy priorities'.[9]

However, the proposed 'like-minded' coalition was not sufficiently to the liking of the electorate. The PDs won just six of the Dáil's 166 seats, to Fine Gael's 55 and Fianna Fáil's 77. Coalition was the only option on the table, other than a fresh election, and the Progressive Democrats obliged, but not with the expected party: they entered government with Fianna Fáil, the party most of the PDs' founders had left. The symbiosis between the two would continue, translating

---

6   P. Rabbitte, 'Holding the Balance', *Dublin Review of Books*, February 2015
7   L. Weeks and A. Clarke, *Radical or Redundant*, op.cit., p. 134
8   S. Ó Muineacháin, L. Weeks and A. Clarke, *Radical or Redundant*, op.cit., p.130
9   Ibid., pp.127-8

into government partnerships not once but four times, in 1989, 1997, 2002 and 2007.[10]

In February 1992, following allegations that he had been involved with the tapping of journalists' telephones, Haughey resigned as Fianna Fáil leader and taoiseach and was succeeded by Albert Reynolds. Despite his long-time distrust of Haughey, O'Malley was more scathing about his successor who, he claimed, lacked Haughey's intellectual capacity to deal with policy issues.

The relationship between O'Malley and Reynolds deteriorated and in November 1992 the Progressive Democrats left government. The breaking point was a serious row between the two over the evidence each had given to a tribunal inquiring into malpractice in the beef processing industry. That tribunal would eventually uncover what Fintan O'Toole summarised as 'a shocking set of overlapping scandals', including 'a huge tax scam ... fraud ... [and] large-scale theft'.[11]

The PDs' fortunes picked up in the 1992 election but its 10 seats in the Dáil didn't translate into seats around the Cabinet table. The Labour Party enjoyed a bigger boost, from 15 to 33 seats, and went into coalition with Fianna Fáil. O'Malley resigned as party leader in October 1993 and was replaced by Mary Harney, who made history by becoming the first woman to lead a parliamentary party in Ireland.

In Harney's first general election as leader, in June 1997, the party slumped to four seats following a campaign in which they presented themselves as ready to govern alongside Fianna Fáil. As in 1989, the electorate did not warm to this prior declaration of intent to rule collaboratively, but the PDs entered government anyway, as part of a minority administration. Harney became tánaiste and, as the first women to hold that position, made yet more political history.

The PD approach to national policy was by then clearer. Pat Leahy summarised it in an *Irish Times* editorial as 'outdated neo-Thatcherism, clothed in the political vocabulary of the 1980s, (which) has little relevance in the Ireland of the millennium'.[12]

The party again entered government with Fianna Fáil in 2002 and, as health minister, Harney was in a position to advance the PDs' health agenda. Their 2002 election manifesto had promised a 'new model' that would make the public sector 'a buyer of services for its

---

10   1989-92, 1997-2002, 2002-07 and 2007-11
11   www.irishtimes.com/opinion
12   P. Leahy, *Showtime: The Inside Story of Fianna Fáil in Power*, op.cit., p.103

Mary Harney, the first woman to hold the position of tánaiste or to lead a party in the Oireachtas, was also minister for health; here she is seen meeting Alex Azar, a US government health official and a pharmaceuticals company lobbyist.

clients' rather than 'a buyer and provider of services'.[13] They sought to bring the 'positive dynamic of incentives and competition' into 'the relationship between the public health buyer and the health service provider'. They also claimed that healthcare needed 'a multiplicity of competing insurers, not one dominant player in the market owned by the State'.

In other words, no socialisation of the already fragmented and costly health service, no tampering with the existing system of 'mixed funding of health services'. Instead Harney aimed to 'make the market more evenly balanced and more attractive to potential entrants'.

Harney resigned as party leader in September 2006 and was succeeded by Michael McDowell. Within weeks, the government was embroiled in controversy over Taoiseach Bertie Ahern's finances, but McDowell decided to remain in government. The following May just two PD deputies were returned in the general election which resulted in McDowell losing his seat and Harney becoming interim party leader. She also retained the health portfolio in a new, three-

---

13   'Funding Health Services', Progressive Democrats, Manifesto 2002, p.65

party coalition led by Fianna Fáil, and with the Green Party joining government for the first time.

Senator Ciarán Cannon was elected PD leader in April 2008, but later that year the party decided it lacked a viable future and formally wound itself up in 2009.

Ideological shift?

When the Progressive Democrats burst on to the political scene in time for Christmas 1985, some saw them as a sign that Irish politics was about to break with the civil war rivalry model that had dominated for decades. Others hoped the newcomer's policies, seemingly fresh from wealthier countries, would put the Irish economy on track to prosperity.

That was exactly what the Progressive Democrats wanted voters to believe. At the launch, Des O'Malley committed the new party to 'breaking the moulds of Irish politics' and giving voters 'a new and real alternative' to the parties then dominating politics in the Republic. There was, he claimed, 'a great consensus' in Ireland in favour of 'fundamental tax reform' and 'enterprise'.[14]

The PDs also described themselves as a party 'in the European liberal democratic political tradition'[15] but not everyone agreed.

Séin Ó Muineacháin summarises them as 'economically pro-market, fiscally conservative and socially open'[16] but he challenges their claim to be a liberal party in the European sense.[17] Progressive Democrat manifestoes were primarily concerned with the economy – with the opening up of markets, reform of taxation, fiscal rectitude and infrastructure investment – rather than individual rights and freedoms. They also emphasised law and order, which Ó Muineacháin notes 'is not a common feature of an average liberal manifesto'.[18]

Overall, Lucy Mansergh concluded, an analysis of manifestoes and of government programmes they influenced placed the PDs towards the right of the ideological spectrum, especially on economic policy.[19]

---

14   www.progressivedemocrats.ie
15   Ibid.
16   S. Ó Muineacháin, L. Weeks and A. Clarke, *Radical or Redundant*, op.cit.,
17   Ibid., p.126
18   Ibid., p.136
19   L. Mansergh, *Do Parties make a Difference? A Comparison of Party and Coalition Policy in Ireland using Expert Coding and Computerised Content Analysis*, Paper

Legacy

Des O'Malley claimed that the party he founded was 'relevant, influential and effective' out of all proportion to its size.[20] While some commentators dispute O'Malley's claim that the Progressive Democrats broke the mould in Irish politics, few would question their impact on the direction of travel for Irish economic policy.

Fianna Fáil embraced much of the PDs' policy slate and Fine Gael and Labour veered towards the same direction. The downside of this for the PDs was erosion of their distinct electoral appeal. The early support began to evaporate quite quickly, though that could equally have had other causes: its support base was quite volatile and was often a protest against the two main parties.

Dermot McAleese argues that Ireland's 'low-tax, pro-business economy' is based in large part on PD policies and that they 'proved that there was a constituency for this, and they gave the intellectual power to it.'[21]

One significant legacy was the shift in public spending away from social projects, accompanied by a deepening of the private sector's role in areas widely seen as government responsibilities. One such area was social and affordable housing, which, by leaving delivery largely to the private sector, also left subsequent governments with a major problem. It also left parties with the political hot potato of ever-rising housing prices and scarcity, of which Sinn Féin in particular would later take political advantage.

Influence, crash, blame

Ó Muineacháin argues that, while the PDs did exercise 'massive influence' on the governments in which they participated, this was because their partners adopted the PDs' agenda. Likewise, the fact that other parties did so affirms that 'the emergence of the PDs did bring about a change in policy.'[22]

An independent review of Dublin's Department of Finance singled out policies in the 2002 election manifestoes of Fianna Fáil

to workshop 'Estimating the Policy Positions of Political Actors', Mannheim, March 1999

20   D. O'Malley, in L. Weeks and A. Clarke, *Radical or Redundant*, op.cit., p.84

21   *The Irish Times*, 31 December 2004

22   S. Ó Muineacháin, L. Weeks and A. Clarke, *Radical or Redundant*, op.cit.,p.141

and the PDs as having contributed significantly to the 2008 property market crash. It laid the blame for most of the damage suffered by the Irish economy on the 2007-11 government.[23] That Fianna Fáil-led coalition was the last in which the PDs participated, admittedly as the smallest party.

Between 1999 and 2008, according to the review, the government introduced tax and spending packages that were €6 billion more generous than those recommended by finance officials. It found that the department of finance had warned about the overheating of the construction sector, but the warnings were ignored and the cabinet 'did not strategise a response to the situation'. It also noted that the highest expenditure occurred during general election campaigns.

If the Progressive Democrats were as influential as O'Malley claimed, and analysts largely confirm, should they not also have accepted blame for what the country and the citizenry suffered when the economy crashed in 2008? Did they bring the party to an end when they did because they recognised their negative impact? Unfortunately, political parties are seldom so honest in their self-analysis – that requires a different kind of realism that could damage the reputations of those who survive a defunct party.

Progressive Democrats	
Founded:	1985
Dissolved:	2009
Leaders:	Desmond O'Malley 1985–93; Mary Harney 1993–2006; Michael McDowell 2006–07; Mary Harney (in caretaker capacity) 2007–08; Ciarán Cannon 2008–09; Noel Grealish 2009
In office:	In coalition with Fianna Fáil: 1989-92; 1997-2002; 2002-07; 2007-08; 2008-09
Affiliations:	Liberal International; European Liberal Democrat and Reform Party Group; ALDE (Alliance of Liberals and Democrats for Europe)

---

23 'Strengthening the Capacity of the Department of Finance: Report of the Independent Review Panel', Dublin, 2010, www.gov.ie

12

The Green Party /
Comhaontas Glas

Greening Ireland to save the planet, one law at a time

Overview

If most parties in Ireland originated in the clash of constitutional aims for the island, the Green Party is out on a limb. Not mired in traditional domestic divisions, it's internationalist in a modern way. Part of a global environmentalist movement, it's also an all-Ireland party since a hook-up between northern and southern Greens in 2006.

It's still a fairly young political movement, having emerged in the 1980s to protect the environment: an insurgent party trying to cajole and regulate Ireland into taking responsibility for its impact on the planet.

The Green Party hasn't done badly for what was seen as a 'hippy-dippy' curiosity when it emerged in 1981 as the Ecology Party of Ireland, part of an international upsurge in political action to protect the environment. A couple of name changes later – to Green Alliance in 1983 and Green Party in 1987 – the focus had broadened to embrace a strong emphasis on social justice. It also became electable, at least as a 'nice to have' choice under the proportional representation system.

The timing of the party's first coalition experience was unfortunate, however. The worst crisis in the Republic's modern economic history broke during the Greens' first spell in office (2007-11). Another crisis, the Covid-19 pandemic, was the dominant issue on the agenda when it entered government again, in mid-2020.

Their history confirms the Greens' self-description of 'a collaborative political party, willing to work with all other parties to effect positive change'. Cabinet politics taught the inexperienced idealists some serious lessons about political realities, however. In 2011 the party lost all its Dáil seats, punished by voters for the austerity measures the coalition government had implemented to prevent Ireland becoming a global bankrupt following the 2008 financial crash.

In 2020 they got a second shot at high office after a dead heat general election. The Greens provided the extra numbers that enabled traditional adversaries Fianna Fáil and Fine Gael to form a once unlikely alliance.

In government again, they faced the challenge of ensuring delivery of the Green New Deal and Just Transition that featured in the tortuously negotiated programme for government.[1] They made progress with legislation designed to move an often-reluctant country towards environmental sustainability. The lessons learned from their first stint in government helped, but so did the global climate *zeitgeist*.

Taste of success

The Greens first tasted electoral success in the Dublin and Belfast legislatures in 1989 and 2007 respectively. By 2020 the party had 12 Green TDs in Dáil Éireann, four senators in Seanad Éireann, two MEPs representing constituencies in the Republic, and two Members of the Legislative Assembly (MLAs) in Northern Ireland. Despite their effectiveness, the two Green MLAs lost their seats in May 2022, part of the fallout from a polarised Assembly election.

In the Republic, the party has tended to punch above its weight in elections to the European Parliament, having scored a breakthrough in 1994 when it won two seats with a morale-boosting 15% of the vote in Dublin. That was a big leap forward from its 1984 debut, when Ecology Party founder Christopher Fettes won 5,200 first preferences in Dublin.[2]

The comparatively poor Green performance in local elections – less than 5% of seats in the Republic and 2% in the North – reflects the lack

---

1   'Programme for Government: Our Shared Future', Dublin, www.gov.ie, June 2020

2   www.irishtimes.com/culture/heritage/the-little-known-storyof-the-origins-of-the-green-party-1.3909472

of a strong and geographically diverse base, a weakness that disadvantages the party in all elections. However, the system of proportional representation used in both jurisdictions (other than for NI elections to the UK Parliament) can work to the party's advantage.

Topping the poll, as deputy party leader Catherine Martin did in Dublin Rathdown in 2020, is unusual. Most seats have been won thanks to transfers of lower preferences from eliminated candidates or from the surpluses of those elected on the first count.

Initial successes came in Dublin – Roger Garland in 1987, Trevor Sargent 1992, John Gormley 1997 – a Dublin-centric trend that left them open to the charge of being out of touch with rural Ireland when they introduced animal welfare legislation as part of the 2007-11 coalition programme.

A significant leap from two to six Teachtaí Dála (TDs) in 2002, on 4% of the state-wide vote, brought extra resources and voluntary contributions from TDs' salaries, helping to compensate for the party's rejection of corporate donations and its modest revenue from membership fees.

Disappointed not to make further gains in 2007, their six seats nevertheless caught the eye of Bertie Ahern, then leader of Fianna Fáil, who brought them into coalition. This delivered the Greens their first experience of ministerial roles, but also joint responsibility for dealing with the financial crash, the blame for its impact and their subsequent wipe-out in the 2011 election.

Success has been more elusive in the North, where the first three Green councillors were elected in 2005 and the party won its first Assembly seat in 2007. They made little impact when they first contested European elections in 2009 and Westminster elections

> **ECOLOGY PARTY OF IRELAND**
>
> **Th. 3rd DECEMBER:**
> Inaugural Gathering
> – presenting a radical
> alternative to both
> Capitalism and Socialism
>
> For those who favour a storehouse economy, non-exploitive approach to nature, land reform, human scale institutions, alternative technology, a basic unearned income for all, and the de-centralisation of political power.
>
> **CENTRAL HOTEL at 8p.m.**
>
> Epicentre
> Contact address: E.P.I., Washington Lodge
> Grange Road
> Rathfarnham Dublin 14

A call to Green action: announcing the inaugural meeting of the Ecology Party of Ireland, forerunner of the Green Party.

in 2010 but fared better in the 2016 and 2017 Assembly elections, winning two of the Assembly's 90 seats.

Northern Ireland's political and sectarian divides appeared to present particular challenges for the all-Ireland, globally focused Greens, despite the STV proportional representation system used in most elections. A notable breakthrough by the non-sectarian Alliance Party in the 2022 election suggested a waning of traditional divisions, but this was partly at the expense of the Green Party's two Assembly seats.

Negotiating with the devil

When the Greens got their chance to enter government in the Republic in 2007, it was due to the shrewdness of then Taoiseach Bertie Ahern, who wanted them as an insurance policy to give him a comfortable working majority. Fianna Fáil could have scraped together a majority by doing a deal with some independent TDs and the Progressive Democrats, who had exercised considerable policy influence during three previous coalitions from a position considerably to the right of the Greens. Instead, Ahern opted to invite the Green Party into government.

Negotiations yielded two senior ministries for the party – environment and energy – plus a junior ministry and two Seanad seats. In return they made painful compromises, such as allowing the use of Shannon Airport by US troops, which they had previously opposed.[3] Despite this, a clear majority (84%) of delegates to the party's mandatory special conference gave the green light to a coalition with Fianna Fáil, and the inexperienced Greens stepped into territory that would turn out to be tougher than anyone anticipated.

The odds were heavily stacked against them in the talks, according to Dan Boyle, one of the Green negotiators.[4] He admitted that major issues were parked initially, including taxation and economic policy, funding for public transport versus roads, carbon emissions targets and levies, planning and housing – all central to a Green agenda.

---

3   N. Bolleyer, 'The Rise and Decline of the Green Party', in L. Weeks and A. Clarke, *Radical or Redundant*, op.cit., p.120

4   D. Boyle, *Without Power or Glory: The Greens in Government in Ireland (2007-11)*, Dublin, New Island, 2012

Fianna Fáil made some concessions but, says Boyle, taxation 'remained a bugbear'. The Greens wanted 'a recasting of the taxation system to reduce and then remove the unhealthy emphasis on property-based forms of tax relief'. They also wanted tax breaks to be directed at those who needed them most, but Fianna Fáil would agree only to setting up a commission on taxation.

In hindsight, given the central role property developers played in creating the conditions that caused the 2008 financial crash, the Green position was prescient. However, in the unlikely event of Fianna Fáil agreeing to any reforms at that time, they would have come far too late to ameliorate the impact of the coming crisis.

Just days before the new government took office, the Greens got a lesson in realpolitik when the outgoing environment minister signed an order allowing work to begin on a motorway in the area of the Hill of Tara, a site of cultural and environmental sensitivity associated with the High Kings of ancient Ireland. During the coalition negotiations Fianna Fáil said this would be a decision for the environment minister, which the Greens assumed meant the incoming minister, John Gormley of the Greens. 'In our naivety, we did not seek a written commitment,' Boyle admitted.

Ordeal by government

'We went into this with our eyes open'[5] commented Dan Boyle – a former TD, Senator and party chairperson – in his account of the Green Party in government. Boyle discusses weaknesses, hazards and errors of judgement, but also claims some hard won successes, such as a new tax relief to encourage the development and purchase of energy-saving equipment.

That progress pales, however, beside the list of issues that damaged the Greens in government. Boyle summed these up in three words: 'Tara, Shannon, Rossport'. Each place name stands for a policy on which they compromised or were outmanoeuvred: a motorway at the culturally and environmentally sensitive Hill of Tara; letting US troops use Shannon airport; failing to halt a pipeline from the Corrib gas field to an onshore processing facility, or even, contrary to party policy, to hold an independent review of the plans.

---

5   Ibid.

Green Party parliamentary group during the party's 2007-11 coalition with Fianna Fáil: (left to right) Ciarán Cuffe TD, Minister Trevor Sargent TD, Mary White TD, Minister John Gormley TD (party leader), Senator Deirdre de Burca, Minister Éamon Ryan TD, Senator Dan Boyle. (© Green Party)

Having been wrong-footed on the Tara motorway before taking office, environment minister John Gormley swiftly issued a ministerial order restricting future building development along the motorway route in an attempt to block profiteering land deals. He soon discovered that other deals had already been struck: Dublin City Council entered into a pre-contract arrangement with a US company to develop a waste incinerator two days before he became minister for the environment – to the dismay of green activists.

Waste also proved toxic at the Irish Steel plant on the south coast. In this case the Greens accused Labour of having done a 'tawdry deal' to sell off the state-sponsored company, thus unnecessarily prolonging the life of the plant and increasing toxic dumping, according to Boyle.

Gormley also believed that officials in his ministerial office were less than co-operative in the drafting of key legislation on planning and climate change. If so, that reluctance had waned or been tamed by the time they joined another coalition in 2020.

Even in the best of times, the inexperienced Greens would have struggled to implement their agenda in what Minihan called a 'deal with the devil'.[6] They expected a tough time in government with

---

6   M. Minehan, *A Deal with the Devil*, op.cit.

Fianna Fáil and the Progressive Democrats, but none of the parties could have imagined just how tough the next few years would be, not simply for the government but for the entire country.

Things could only get worse

The global financial crisis of 2008 hit during the coalition's second year in office. Due largely to the additional impact of an indigenous banking and construction crash, the crisis hit the State's finances so hard it almost went bankrupt. While Ireland had been swept up in the global financial crisis, its problems were home-grown.[7]

The Green Party spokesperson on finance, Dan Boyle, claims there were many warning signs from the start of 2008. Tax receipts were falling dramatically, mainly because of a slowdown in new construction; this, he notes, was felt in vastly reduced income from stamp duty and value added tax, and a slowdown in corporation tax payments.

On 30 September 2008, 'a panicked Irish government' guaranteed the liabilities of the country's six major banks. Over the next two years it pumped €46 billion into the banks and nationalised two of them, but these measures just delayed the day of reckoning. 'The country's banks were being kept alive with emergency loans from the European Central Bank.'[8]

By the end of 2010 one in every seven workers – some 300,000 people – had lost their jobs. Public sector workers' pay was cut by 14%, but such savings, though amounting to over 6% of GDP from 2008 to 2010, were insufficient to make up for plummeting tax revenues (down 20%), a soaring budget deficit and higher spending on social services.

In November 2010 the government requested help from the EU and IMF. It came at a very high price in public expenditure cuts.

News of the bailout broke on the morning of 18 November 2010 when the governor of Ireland's central bank announced on national radio that the state would be receiving a loan package worth tens of billions of euros from the IMF.[9] The loans eventually totalled €67.5 billion over the three years. A Troika of technical experts from the

---

7   www.imf.org/en/Countries/IRL/ireland-from-tiger-to-phoenix
8   Ibid.
9   M. Minehan, *A Deal with the Devil*, op.cit., p.193

IMF, the European Central Bank, and the European Commission would help Ireland put its house in order.

Green Party ministers were kept in the dark about the arrival of the Troika, but so too were most other Cabinet members and TDs, as well as the Irish public at large. The Greens announced they were leaving government and demanded an early general election, but stayed on to see through the 2010 budget and Finance Bill, in the hope of passing Green legislation.[10]

As the 2011 general election approached, they were resigned to their fate. Party leader John Gormley told journalist Pat Leahy: 'It didn't matter what we did. We were going to be faced with an immovable object: the narrative of propping up Fianna Fáil and everything that went with that.'[11]

Losing all their Dáil seats was not totally surprising following the collapse of the Green vote in the 2009 local and European elections – all a reaction against stringent austerity measures introduced when the state was on the brink of global bankruptcy.

Could the Green Party, very much the junior partner in the 2007-11 government, have done anything to avert the crisis? No, because the roots of the crisis lay in the permissive policies of earlier governments. Eoin O'Malley suggests that the Greens knew how to analyse the economy and should have known better than most that the property market had grown unsustainable, accounting for a fifth of the economy on some measures. While the Greens may have been the authors of their own downfall, he suggests, they were also unlucky to have been in office 'when one of the largest housing and banking bubbles in economic history burst'.[12]

New Green deal

As the extent of Green Party losses in the 2011 general election became clear, the historian John Bowman forecast that the Greens had a future 'because they're out to save the planet, not their seats.'[13]

---

10 As political reporter Mary Minihan notes, the timing of animal welfare legislation was 'pitifully bad' when people were losing their jobs. Ibid., p.163
11 P. Leahy, *The Price of Power*, op.cit., p.57
12 E. O'Malley, 'Wipeout! Does Governing Kill Small Parties in Ireland?', in L. Weeks and A. Clarke, *Radical or Redundant*, op.cit., p.94
13 M. Minehan, *A Deal with the Devil*, op.cit., p.265

Political recovery began in 2016 with two Dáil seats, surging to 12 in the February 2020 general election. This made them the fourth largest party in the Dáil for the first time, and well placed to make up the numbers for a new coalition – which turned out to be with the unlikely alliance of traditional adversaries Fianna Fáil and Fine Gael.

The Greens seemed to have learned lessons from their earlier experience in government, both in how to strike a deal and how to get their policies implemented. Three months of negotiations yielded three ministries plus three secretaries of state (junior ministries) and gave them control of some sectors crucial to their agenda. The programme for government contained a lengthy mission statement on a Green New Deal, including a 'moral duty to put social justice at the heart of our commitment to decarbonise', and detailed lists of climate actions.[14]

Two years into the tripartite government, they were making good progress, despite the Covid-19 pandemic dominating government business and public concerns. In June 2021 the Dáil approved the Climate Action and Low Carbon Development (Amendment) Bill 2021 by 129 votes to 10 against.[15]

There was, inevitably, criticism of the Bill, but also calls for greater ambition – a reflection of greater public awareness of climate change, and an indication of why other government parties were open to introducing environmental measures. The relatively easy ride that this and other green legislation got in the Dáil suggested that vested interests looked unlikely to succeed in whipping up a backlash as strong as that during the 2007-11 coalition.

In Northern Ireland the Greens had to resort to introducing their own Climate Change Bill as a Private Member's Bill.[16] This won wide cross-party support but was overtaken by a less ambitious Bill tabled by the agriculture minister, which passed its final stage in March 2022.

Personalities

Green ministers sometimes found themselves in the spotlight for reasons not related to their policy agenda. Negatives make news and

---

14   *Programme for Government: Our Shared Future*, op.cit., pp.31-41

15   www.oireachtas.ie/en/bills/bill/2021/39/

16   www.niassembly.gov.uk/assembly-business/legislation/2017-2022-mandate/
non-executive-bill-proposals/climate-change-bill/

Éamon Ryan TD, Green Party leader (2011-) and minister for the environment, climate and communications (2020-).
(© Shutterstock)

there was little sympathy for party leader Éamon Ryan when an image of him seemingly asleep in the chamber went viral.

Roderic O'Gorman's appointment as equalities minister drew an outpouring of homophobia, followed by accusations of supporting paedophiles when he shared a photograph of himself with well-known gay rights campaigner Peter Tatchell. More relevantly and understandably, O'Gorman was criticised when he signed off the final report of a long-running judicial inquiry into the treatment of unmarried mothers, and the fate of their babies, between 1922 and 1998 in the institutions known as mother and baby homes.

Outside the Oireachtas, others with ambition were also making headlines. Leading voices calling for a greater emphasis on social objectives included Hazel Chu, the party's cathaoirleach (chairperson). The first councillor of Chinese heritage in the Republic, and first person of colour to hold the historic post of Lord Mayor of Dublin, Ms Chu's high profile didn't lead to selection as candidate for the Seanad or Dáil, but it spotlighted a murkier side of Irish society when racists targeted her.[17]

The Greens had no shortage of other interesting figures amongst their elected politicians. Some were leading environmental activists, such as Grace O'Sullivan MEP who spent 20 years working for Greenpeace, including crewing the original 'Rainbow Warrior' that was bombed and sunk by French intelligence agents in New Zealand. However, the party's future leadership and direction looked more likely to come from the young parliamentary team of 2020. This was not exactly a diverse group, however: 12 white TDs, only three of them female.[18] Some performed well and polled well: deputy

17   *Western People*, 22 January 2021, www.westernpeople.ie/2021/01/22/hazel-chu-harassed-at-home-by-far-right-protestors/

18   www.greenparty.ie/our-people/representatives

leader Catherine Martin topped the poll in her constituency in 2020, with a surplus to spare. Should she challenge Éamon Ryan for the leadership again (as she did in 2020), she would offer ministerial experience and personal popularity that could refresh public perception of the party.

How Green is the future?

Catherine Martin TD, deputy leader of the Green Party, became minister for tourism, culture, arts, Gaeltacht, sport and media in 2020, having been her party's lead negotiator in government formation talks with Fine Gael and Fianna Fáil. (© Houses of the Oireachtas)

The loss of their two NI Assembly seats in May 2022 was not just a blow to the Greens in Northern Ireland where, in a complex political environment, vote transfers didn't favour the party. It was also a reminder of the challenges Greens across the island face politically and organisationally – given the scale of the climate crisis, vested interests, opposition politicking and the weakness of the Green base outside major urban areas. Both the policies and the party could face setbacks from several directions.

Climate sustainability requires implementation of the policies promoted by green parties. Greens in the 2020 Dublin government won impressive progress towards Ireland's contribution – getting climate action legislation passed, substantial finance to implement it,[19] a requirement for government departments to produce carbon budgets – but not without negative reaction.

Environmental legislation can provoke public unease at best and have adverse electoral repercussions, as the Greens discovered during their first stint in Cabinet in the Republic. Despite or because of their policy influence since 2020, history could repeat itself.

For a country that has long marketed itself as the ultimate green destination, Ireland's environmental record is far from pristine. Europe

---

19   https://www.irishtimes.com/news/politics/green-party-fingers-evident-all-over-economic-recovery-plan-1.4581407

Dublin-born Hazel Chu made history as the first person of colour to hold the historic post of Lord Mayor of Dublin (2020-21), a year after election to Dublin City Council. (© gov.pl)

has chastised the Republic for a range of environmental failings, referring it to the European Court of Justice in 2020 over persistent failures on conservation measures, for example.[20]

Getting ambitious legislation on the statute books is one thing, and a major achievement for the party in the Republic, but hitting targets is altogether more challenging. Green Party members and core supporters can't have been pleased to hear the Environmental Protection Agency forecast that, even with the additional measures in the 2021 Climate Action Plan, Ireland would fail to hit its 2030 emissions reduction targets.

What distinguishes the Greens from most political parties presents specific challenges. If other parties adopt environmentalist policies – and they are doing so, though not with obvious enthusiasm – the Green Party could go the way of many small parties in Ireland.

Then there's the matter of internal unity. Reports have suggested there was a serious gap between grassroots activists and the party's political elite in 2007-11, although Boyle denies this was a major problem. Grassroots unease also emerged when the party re-entered government in 2020, with resignations and disputes around environmental versus social objectives. If a just transition (party and government policy) were to trump core green policies, the Greens' distinctiveness could be eroded and put them in more direct competition with parties of the left.

The quandary: to what extent should a party founded to save the environment expend its energies on the social challenges other

---

20 https://www.irishtimes.com/news/environment/commission-to-refer-ireland-to-court-of-justice-of-the-eu-over-failure-on-conservation-measures-1.4294916

parties have failed to resolve from one government to the next? The Greens could find themselves facing a classic dilemma for political parties – compromise or split.

The fierce social media attacks on Green policies and personalities, added to mainstream political scapegoating of the party for the impact of climate legislation on everyday life, were likely to have heightened the danger of another shock election outcome. If they avoid another wipeout, Green Party representatives would be likely to base a decision about participating in government again on what they think can be achieved.

Who they find themselves facing in the next round of government formation negotiations could be crucial. Another coalition with their 2020 partners could be comparatively straightforward. Sinn Féin, however, could be a much tougher proposition. Scenting political advantage, they have hounded the Greens in parliament and elsewhere. In government they would be much more focused on the traditional 'green Ireland' issue of territorial re-unification than the state of the Irish or global environment.

It's worth reiterating what John Bowman said after the party was wiped out in the 2011 general election: 'the Greens have a future because they're out to save the planet, not their seats.' If that remains true and the party remains united, they may continue to be a force in the greening of Ireland whether or not they help to make up the numbers in Dublin governments. Survival in some form is likely, at worst as a ginger group on the edge of mainstream politics.

· **Green Party / Comhaontas Glas**	
Founded:	1981 as Ecology Party of Ireland; renamed Green Party/ Comhaontas Glas 1987; Northern Ireland Green Party joined as region 2006
Leaders:	Trevor Sargent 2011-2007; John Gormley 2007-2011; Éamon Ryan 2011-; Northern Ireland region: Steven Agnew 2011-18; Clare Bailey 2018-2022; Malachai O'Hara 2022-
In office:	Coalitions: 2007-11; 2020-
Affiliations:	Greens/European Free Alliance group in European Parliament
Elected representatives:	2022: 12 TDs (9M, 3F), 4 Senators (1M, 3F), 2 MEPs (1M, 1 F)

Epilogue

A century after Ireland was divided into two jurisdictions – one to become an independent state, the other a devolved administration or sub-state – the political arena was highly competitive in both, with no genuinely dominant party on either side of the border. Both jurisdictions had experienced major changes, impacting on political parties as well as society but also, obviously, influenced by the parties' decisions.

The era of single party dominance had long ended in Northern Ireland, replaced by three clear political divisions: similarly sized nationalist and unionist blocks, plus non-aligned parties ('Others') which won 20% of Assembly seats in 2022.[1] Although 'Others' were trending upwards the two traditional sides, enjoying about 40% support each, still dominated NI's political space.

The southern spectrum was more diverse but had also changed notably. Three parties – the two that had led all governments for nearly a century plus their new rival – won 66% of Dáil seats between them in 2022. A plethora of small parties, mostly of the left, plus independent TDs held the rest. To varying degrees all southern parties were republican, but that did not mean that an early end to partition was a priority for all of them.

Survival and shifts

The survival rate amongst the parties considered here was high, but how many of the survivors were likely to thrive much beyond the centenary of partition?

There were casualties amongst the 12, notably the Irish Parliamentary Party, which collapsed just as radical constitutional change was unfolding in the early 20th century. Ireland's first modern political party left a legacy of democratic experience, however, plus a

---

1   See also: J. Garry, B. O'Leary and J. Pow, 'Much more than meh: The 2022 Northern Ireland Assembly Elections', LSE British Politics and Policy, 11 May 2022

belief in the value of a disciplined party that many new entrants to politics embraced.

In the 21ˢᵗ century, the two formerly dominant parties in the Republic, Fianna Fáil and Fine Gael, were clearly struggling, while the latest iteration of Sinn Féin was enjoying an electoral surge.

Having activated the negotiations that ended armed conflict in Northern Ireland, the SDLP lost out in the 21ˢᵗ century to Sinn Féin, the political voice of the Provisional IRA during the decades of violence.

The Ulster Unionist Party (UUP), also a peace broker and the undisputed ruler of NI for half a century, had been dethroned by the Democratic Unionist Party (DUP), which had opposed the peace accord.

The DUP, political *enfant terrible* of the late 20ᵗʰ century, had become the establishment when it decided that sharing office with Sinn Féin was better than not being in power. The two became partners in government in 2007. Or, it can be argued, they were in a relationship of stasis: technically governing side by side, they also took a confrontational approach to issues that were emblematic for their respective 'sides' – which at times meant NI had no government at all.

Under a dynamic new leader from 2016, support for the non-aligned Alliance Party grew until, in 2022, it more than doubled its Assembly representation, making it the third largest NI party.

Other parties entered Stormont too, thanks in large part to the PR-STV voting system. Transfers helped the Green Party and the hard-left People Before Profit alliance into the Assembly while, to the right of the DUP, the Traditional Unionist Voice and other radical loyalists achieved their electoral breakthroughs.

A similar scene was playing out across the border where the political operating environment had shifted markedly away from the decades-long norm of a 'two and a half party' system consisting of Fianna Fáil, Fine Gael and Labour. Seven parties and a four-party left-wing alliance, plus 20 independents, won representation in the 2020 Dáil. A surge by Sinn Féin left only one viable option for Fianna Fáil and Fine Gael: a coalition deal between the two long-time rivals, augmented by the Green Party.

Did this mean that the older southern parties were heading towards terminal decline, about to be done for by demographics over the longer term? They certainly faced a serious challenge from Sinn

Féin, which was ahead of them in opinion polls, but both Fine Gael and Fianna Fáil have a long history as political realists capable of reinventing themselves for changing times, as the once-unimaginable 2020 coalition showed.

Labour's fall from voter favour reduced it to minor party status, competing in a crowded left-of-centre space with other small parties and its big-brother rival, Sinn Féin. An early resurrection looked unlikely and could require a reunion with old comrades in the Social Democrats to even get started, although new leader Ivana Bacik raised Labour hopes in 2022.

The Green Party disappeared from the Dáil in 2011 but, back in greater numbers, joined the 2020 coalition government. Its policy successes and a growing recognition of the threat from climate change suggested the Greens would not fade away again anytime soon. However, effective climate measures ask a lot from the public and this mainly urban party was under attack from vested interests and rivals on the left, especially Sinn Féin.

Meanwhile, having held the deputy first minister post in the NI Executive since 2007, Sinn Féin emerged as the largest NI party in 2022 and was throwing its all at trying to win power in Dublin. Was it moving inexorably towards leading both governments and ending partition? Was the party, in the process, also metamorphosing into the new realists on the block, following in the footsteps of other parties that left their violent pasts behind? Though soaring in opinion polls, getting the numbers to form a government in Dublin continued to look like a tough call for Sinn Féin.

Apart from their own performance – historically very much open to question and criticism – the future of the island's political parties depends on many factors. These include the impact of Brexit on the political environment on either side of the border, as well as the direction of relations with London and potentially with the individual nations of Britain.

Beyond the usual practical challenges for parties and governments, an increasingly fraught global environment looked likely to be a major constraint on policy choices and implementation. Cross-border cooperation could, for example, enhance the island's response to climate change – but in Ireland historic attitudes to the border could make that problematic.

The border question

Speculation about a possible reunification poll intensified around the centenary of partition, propelled by Sinn Féin, especially after their striking results in the Republic's 2020 general election. Feelings were mixed on both sides of the border and of the question, however, as opinion polls showed in late 2021.

Voters in the Republic mostly liked the idea of unity, but not the prospect of paying the associated tax bill or giving up their symbols.[2] In a survey of more than 3,000 people in NI, 54% of those who expressed a view on how they would vote in a border poll favoured remaining in the UK; but a majority also thought the ratio could be reversed within a decade.[3]

In reality, nothing about possible unification was simple, not even getting to the point of holding a referendum. The Belfast Agreement allocated that decision to the secretary of state for Northern Ireland, who should organise a referendum if it appeared likely to 'him' that 'a majority of those voting would express a wish that Northern Ireland should cease to be part of the United Kingdom and form part of a united Ireland'.[4]

The Belfast Agreement doesn't specify how to decide that the decisive moment has arrived. One option would be to treat election results as a perfect reflection of public opinion: 'all systems go' should nationalist parties win more votes than unionists. However, that would amount to excluding the views of the substantial number who vote for non-aligned parties or choose not to vote.

Nor does the Agreement set a threshold for turnout or size of majority. Which means a majority of one vote (50% + 1) in favour of unification would trigger constitutional change. That simple majority would not, though, automatically provide simple solutions to the problems associated with NI's divisions. The nexus between religion and identity that previously dominated political loyalties is of decreasing importance, but still significant, at least in terms of formative cultures.

---

2   *The Irish Times*, Irish Times/Ipsos MRBI Poll, Dec 2021
3   Lord Ashcroft Polls, 'Ulster and the Union: the view from the North', December 2021
4   Belfast Agreement, Schedule 1(ii)

Elements beyond old loyalties have entered the equation too, not least modernisation and the age profile of voters – younger people are more likely to be secular and less likely to align with either side of NI's traditional political divide.

In the 2011 NI census, the most recent available at the time of writing, 40% described themselves as 'British Only', 25% as 'Irish Only', 21% as 'Northern Irish Only' and 14% as 'Other'. In NI elections since then, some 20% of votes have been cast for candidates who were neither unionist nor nationalist, suggesting that a united Ireland might be in the gift of 'Others'. Research also notes, however, that two-thirds of 'Others' are from a culturally Protestant background, which could matter in a constitutional referendum.

Shared island or winner takes all?

A vote in favour of unification would be just the start of a new beginning, and constitutional arrangements that could bring people together in adequate harmony would be central to success.

Could immediate incorporation of Northern Ireland into a single unitary state with Dublin as its capital achieve those outcomes? Not easily. Would a federal state work better and be more inclusive? Could a confederation with both the Republic and Northern Ireland as independent sovereign states gain majority acceptance in both?

Perhaps any referendum should offer multiple options, with a further round of voting in the event of a clear preference failing to emerge from the first. Although such an approach would be more complex than a simple yes or no question, the learning from a well-handled process could achieve a more widely acceptable outcome, whatever that might be.

In the event of unification the Irish state would become the guarantor for those in Northern Ireland identifying as British, a duty arising from the 1998 Belfast Agreement. To fulfil that responsibility Dublin would have to act in a spirit of genuine inclusiveness. The 2020 coalition government's 'Shared Island' initiative – established to promote dialogue about a future in which all traditions are respected, and allocated serious finance for cross-border projects – suggested this was recognised and in hand. How a future government under a more radically republican leadership might proceed is open to question.

Party scenarios

If partition were to end, what might that mean for political parties? Cross-border hook-ups between parties that share ideological common ground might not be off the agenda. Suggestions that Fine Gael and the Alliance Party could become an island-wide liberal party look plausible at first glance, but Fine Gael has been burnishing its republican credentials and Alliance has been attracting liberal unionists.

Might the SDLP merge with Fianna Fáil (with which it agreed a formal, and influential, policy partnership in 2019) or Labour? Would SDLP members like to shape Fianna Fáil into the kind of social-democratic party they think Ireland needs, or prefer to inject some northern vigour into the Irish Labour Party? Either option could split the SDLP into its socialist and nationalist parts, and leave the door wide open to Sinn Féin hegemony in NI at least.

The likelihood of the DUP and UUP forming a single unionist party was negligible; likewise the possibility of either of them linking up with an existing party in the Republic. Tactical associations involving northern and southern parties to bargain on specific issues might not be impossible, however, and could be stimulating for parties that have grown comfortable in their separate cultures.

Such scenarios were unlikely to be of early relevance in real-life politics where parties, in government or not, needed to boost public trust in their ability to solve challenging problems.

Housing was the prime example in the Republic, a problem that some earlier Dublin governments had faced and temporarily resolved since the state inherited some of the worst slums in Europe at independence. Implementing solutions that would satisfy contemporary expectations, and doing so quickly while also dealing with other high demands on state finances, was not only daunting but could change the balance between parties.

Tackling Northern Ireland's challenges – even the NHS, the cherished UK public health service envied by many in the south, was in far from good health – was exacerbated by the stop-start status of the devolved Legislative Assembly.

How might it all go wrong?

The decades after the 1998 NI peace agreement were a time of considerable parliamentary accommodation and political realism.

Protagonists of violence became political leaders, whether as elected representatives or as their backroom boys and girls. Few now subscribe to the use of bombs and bullets, but lingering still are the paramilitary traditions; the authoritarianism, the unresolved traumas, and the matter of weapons decommissioned but not necessarily totally destroyed.

Dissident republican groups have proclaimed their continued commitment to armed action. The main loyalist paramilitary groups, the UVF and UDA, had about 12,500 members between them in 2020, according to estimates by the Independent Reporting Commission (IRC), which monitors progress on tackling their activity.

The IRC has warned of a 'clear and present danger' from paramilitaries and flagged NI's 'continuing levels of poverty' as a factor. It has also noted 'the fractured nature of politics' and the 'turmoil and turbulence in political life' as factors militating against 'the kind of sustained, cross-party policy interventions and approaches' needed to address paramilitarism – a thinly veiled criticism of the NI Executive.

It also warned of 'new complexities' around reactions to the Brexit Protocol, citing the 2021 street rioting, which supposedly flared up in protest against the EU Withdrawal Agreement's NI Protocol. Testimony by young people involved in or observing the riots mentioned adults facilitating the confrontations.[5] Others have described those riots as the old paramilitaries training up a new generation, drawn from unemployed young people in areas suffering from largely unaddressed inequalities.

Brexit and the related NI Protocol offered a warning that negotiations on any future transfer of sovereignty from the UK to the Republic could be fractious and prolonged. Not forgetting a danger that unification could ignite extreme extra-parliamentary reactions. Or, indeed, the radicalising effect of other controversies that at times erupt into violent confrontation, such as protests against Covid-19 regulations.

In harmony and friendship?

Transformations that have occurred over recent decades suggest that most people in Ireland are capable of living with diversity. Though

---

5   Dr C. Walsh, 'Beyond The Spark: Young people's perspectives on the 2021 Northern Ireland Riots', Belfast, Queen's University Belfast and NI Dept. of Justice, 2021

not all: racism is well documented. Would the Irish who voted to liberalise the Republic's Constitution, giving the go-ahead to equal marriage and abortion rights, be open to further changes designed to make northern communities and the 'new' Irish feel more welcome? What would it take for parties to recommend such changes?

Secularising the preamble to the 1937 Constitution might be a good starting point.[6] Or reforming the Seanad (upper house) to guarantee representation for minorities, alongside other democratising and modernising changes such as diversifying its franchise.

If a week is a long time in politics, a century is surely a defining span of time. Long enough for the two jurisdictions sharing the island of Ireland to have consolidated their existence as distinct entities. Also long enough, perhaps, for all the island's political parties – with their distinct though related histories – to re-assess relationships between communities in the interest of mutual respect and cooperation. After all, Ireland has had a lot of practice at political compromise.

In 1998 voters on both sides of the border approved the tortuously negotiated peace agreement and the changes required to implement it. For Northern Ireland that brought hope for a definitive end to political violence, though the road to normal democracy has been far from smooth.

Southern voters agreed to amend their Constitution, removing the territorial claim to Northern Ireland and replacing it with a desire for unity – but a unity to be achieved in 'harmony and friendship' and 'with the consent of a majority of the people', as the 19th Amendment of the Constitution Act states.

Living up to that promise requires political parties to find ways of making the island a 'shared home place' by mutual consent, one in which they can effectively pursue their responsibilities to the planet as well as to the home island and its peoples. While the onus lies more heavily on those parties seeking unity, other parties have an equivalent duty of responsibility. How they respond in an era of growing global shocks will test all of them, but perhaps especially those with a more inward-facing focus.

---

6   Preamble to the 1937 Constitution: 'In the Name of the Most Holy Trinity, from Whom is all authority and to Whom, as our final end, all actions both of men and States must be referred, We, the people of Éire, Humbly acknowledging all our obligations to our Divine Lord, Jesus Christ, Who sustained our fathers through centuries of trial, ...' - irishstatutebook.ie

Chronology

Conquest of Ireland

1169	Invasion of Ireland begins, launched from Wales by Norman lords
1264	First Irish parliament meets [June]
1541	King of England declared to be also King of Ireland
1607	Flight of the Earls begins, marking beginning of the end of Gaelic order and near completion of English conquest
1608	Survey of ownership of six Ulster counties begins, followed by the 'Plantation of Ulster' by English and Scottish settlers
1649	Cromwell's re-conquest of Ireland begins following 1641 Irish rebellion; followed by confiscation of Catholic-owned lands and settlement by colonists
1690	Battle of the Boyne: William of Orange's troops defeat the forces of the Catholic King James
1798	The United Irishmen rebellion begins in May; provides rationale for abolition of Irish parliament
1800	Parallel Acts of Union in Irish and British parliaments create the United Kingdom of Great Britain and Ireland; comes into force 1 January 1801

Home Rule and Unionism

1845	The Great Famine begins with potato blight [autumn]; lasts until 1849
1873	Home Rule League founded; becomes Irish Parliamentary Party 1882
1885	Irish Loyal and Patriotic Union founded; becomes Irish Unionist Alliance 1891 (forerunner of Ulster Unionist Party)
1886	First Home Rule Bill defeated in House of Commons
1893	Second Home Rule Bill defeated in House of Lords
1905	Ulster Unionist Party and Ulster Unionist Council established
1907	Sinn Féin League founded; merges with National Council 1908 becoming Sinn Féin Party
1912	Campaign launched in Ulster against Home Rule

1912	Third Home Rule Bill introduced [11 April], passes final stage 25 May 1914; implementation suspended due to outbreak of war in Europe
1916	A nationalist rebellion, known as the Easter Rising, is defeated in Dublin [24-29 April]
1918	Sinn Féin wins majority of Irish seats in general election [14 December]
1919	First Dáil (Irish parliament) meets in Dublin [21 January]
1919	War of Independence begins [21 January]; ends with truce 9 July 1921
1920	UK parliament passes Government of Ireland Act, providing for partition of the island and the establishment of two parliaments

Partition and new parliaments

1921	House of Commons of Northern Ireland Parliament meets [7 June]
1921	Anglo-Irish Treaty signed [6 December]; approved by Dáil Éireann 7 January 1922; powers formally transferred to provisional government 16 January 1922
1922	Dáil Éireann general election [16 June]; pro-treaty parties win substantial majority
1922	Northern Ireland opts out of Irish Free State, triggering Boundary Commission; commission reports 1925 but does not recommend substantial change to border
1922	Irish Free State formally established as a dominion of the British Empire and a constitutional monarchy [6 December]
1922	Irish Civil War begins [28 June]; ends May 1923
1926	Éamon de Valera and others leave anti-treaty faction of Sinn Féin; form Fianna Fáil; contest the 1927 election and take their seats in Dáil
1931	Statute of Westminster grants legislative independence to six dominions, including the Irish Free State
1933	Fine Gael party formed through amalgamation of Cumann na nGaedheal, the National Centre Party and the National Guard
1937	New Constitution of Ireland comes into effect 29 December; renames Irish Free State as Éire or Ireland
1948	Republic of Ireland Act 1948 ends last links with English Crown and Commonwealth; Irish Free State becomes a republic 18 April 1949

1949   UK enacts Ireland Act 1949 to deal with consequences of declaration of Irish republic; Act strengthens Northern Ireland's status as part of UK

Northern Ireland 1968-98

1968   Northern Ireland Civil Rights Association holds first protest march [24 August]

1969   Rioting and sectarian conflict in Derry [August]; in Belfast families driven from their homes by loyalists; Britain deploys troops to Northern Ireland with peacekeeping remit

1971   Internment without trial introduced [9 August]

1972   UK government suspends NI Parliament [30 March]

1973   Ireland Constitution Act 1973 abolishes NI parliament

1973   Sunningdale Agreement signed [9 December]; aims to establish power-sharing NI Executive and cross-border Council of Ireland

1974   Ulster Workers' Council strike paralyses Northern Ireland, defeats Sunningdale Agreement, topples recently devolved Assembly and triggers direct rule by London

1981   Hunger strikes by republican prisoners, of whom 10 died (7 Provisional IRA, 3 Irish National Liberation Army, 'INLA')

1983   New Ireland Forum convened by Dublin government; Forum report in May 1984 suggests options for new relationship between NI and Republic; leads to Anglo-Irish Agreement

1985   The Anglo-Irish Agreement signed by Prime Minister Margaret Thatcher and Taoiseach Garret FitzGerald aims to end the NI conflict; gives the Irish government advisory role in NI affairs; agrees conditions for a devolved NI government; confirms NI's constitutional position can change only if majority agrees

1992   Official IRA begins ceasefire [30 May]

1993   Downing Street Declaration [15 December]: Prime Minister John Major and Taoiseach Albert Reynolds confirm NI constitutional change requires majority consent and that parts of Irish Constitution would be changed in the context of an overall settlement

1994   Provisional IRA ceasefire begins [31 August]; ends 9 February 1996

1994   Combined Loyalist Military Command announces ceasefire by loyalist paramilitary groups [13 October], bringing them into peace process

1997   Final Provisional IRA ceasefire [19 July]

1998   Belfast/Good Friday Agreement [10 April] signed by UK and Irish governments and main NI political parties (except the DUP), ending NI conflict and establishing a devolved power-sharing Legislative Assembly

Economic landmarks – Irish Free State / Republic of Ireland

1932   'Economic War' with Britain begins; ends 1938 with Anglo-Irish Trade Agreement

1957   Republic of Ireland joins the European Free Trade Association (EFTA), alongside the UK

1958   First Programme for Economic Expansion approved by Houses of the Oireachtas; new economic direction begins officially

1973   Republic of Ireland joins the European Economic Community (EEC), alongside the UK

1978   Introduction of independent currency marks break with UK

1992   Ireland joins Single European Market

1994   Republic dubbed Celtic Tiger economy due to strength of growth

2008   Global financial crisis plus domestic banking and construction crash bring Republic to brink of bankruptcy

2010   Package of 'bailout' loans from the IMF, European Commission and European Central Bank (the Troika) announced [18 November]

2013   Ireland exits the 'bailout' programme, the first eurozone state to do so [15 December]

Appendices

1(a): Governance – Republic of Ireland

Ireland is a parliamentary democracy in which authority is shared between the Oireachtas (the legislature), the Government and the Judiciary.

The Constitution specifies that the name of the State is either Éire (in Irish) or Ireland; its description is the Republic of Ireland.

The Oireachtas consists of an elected president (Uachtarán na hÉireann), a fully elected lower House (Dáil Éireann) and an upper house (Seanad Éireann). The head of Government is called the **Taoiseach** and the **Tánaiste** is the deputy prime minister.

General elections to Dáil Éireann are held at least every five years; a Seanad election takes place up to 90 days after Dáil Éireann has been dissolved; and presidential elections are held at seven-year intervals.

Voting is by the single transferable vote (PR-STV) system, which has been used since 1922 and is enshrined in the Constitution. It is also used for presidential, local authority and European Parliament elections.

Seanad Éireann, the upper house, has 60 members. The Taoiseach nominates eleven members, usually to help ensure a government majority; but Taoisigh have at times nominated individuals from Northern Ireland or from under-represented sectors e.g. a woman of Traveller ethnicity in 2020. Graduates of certain universities elect six. Members of the incoming Dáil, the outgoing Seanad and local government elect 43 members from five 'vocational' panels of candidates.

The President of Ireland, the Head of State, is elected directly every seven years. In accordance with article 12 of the 1937 Constitution, a president can hold office for two seven-year terms. Presidential candidates must be nominated by at least 20 members of the Oireachtas or at least four local authorities; a former or retiring president can nominate themselves.

The Constitution, Bunreacht na hÉireann, was adopted by referendum in 1937 and can only be amended by referendum. Significant amendments have included consent to membership of the European Economic Community (later the European Union) and various EU Treaties; the removal of Articles 2 and 3 that had made a territorial claim to Northern Ireland; and the legalisation of divorce, abortion and gay marriage. https://www.irishstatutebook.ie/eli/cons/en/html

1(b): Governments, 1922-2022 – Republic of Ireland

Period	Government party/parties
1922-23	Sinn Féin (Pro-Treaty) minority government
1923-27	Cumann na nGaedhael minority government
1927	Cumann na nGaedhael minority government, Jun-Sept
1927-32	Cumann na nGaedhael minority government
1932-33	Fianna Fáil minority government
1933-37	Fianna Fáil minority government; confidence & supply with Labour
1937-38	Fianna Fáil minority government; confidence & supply with Labour
1938-43	Fianna Fáil
1943-44	Fianna Fáil minority government
1944-48	Fianna Fáil
1948-51	Inter-Party Government: Fine Gael, Labour, Clann na Poblachta, Clann na Talmhan, National Labour & Independents
1951-54	Fianna Fáil minority government
1954-57	Fine Gael, Labour & Clann na Talmhan
1957-61	Fianna Fáil
1961-65	Fianna Fáil minority government
1965-69	Fianna Fáil
1969-73	Fianna Fáil
1973-77	Fine Gael & Labour
1977-81	Fianna Fáil
1981-82	Fine Gael & Labour minority government
1982	Fianna Fáil minority government, Feb-Nov
1982-87	(1) Fine Gael & Labour; (2) Fine Gael minority government, Jan'87
1987-89	Fianna Fáil minority government
1989-92	Fianna Fáil & Progressive Democrats
1993-94	(1) Fianna Fáil & Labour, Jan'93-Nov'94; (2) Fianna Fáil minority government, Nov-Dec'94
1994-97	Fine Gael, Labour & Democratic Left, Dec'94-June'97
1997-2002	Fianna Fáil & Progressive Democrats minority government
2002-07	Fianna Fáil & Progressive Democrats
2007-11	(1) Fianna Fáil, Green Party & Progressive Democrats; (2) Fianna Fáil, Green Party & Independent, Nov '09; (3) Fianna Fáil minority government, Jan'11
2011-16	Fine Gael & Labour
2016-20	Fine Gael & Independents minority government; confidence & supply with Fianna Fáil
2020-	Fianna Fáil, Fine Gael & Green Party

Note: This refers to the governments of the Irish Free State (established following the 1921 Anglo-Irish Treaty) and of the Republic (established 1949)

1(c): Taoisigh (Prime Ministers), 1922-2022

Taoiseach	Party	Term
1. William T. Cosgrave	Cumann na nGaedheal	1922-32
2. Éamon de Valera	Fianna Fáil	1932-48; 1951-54
3. John A Costello	Fine Gael	1948-51; 1954-57
4. Seán Lemass	Fianna Fáil	1957-61; 1961-66
5. Jack Lynch	Fianna Fáil	1966-73; 1977-79
6. Liam Cosgrave	Fine Gael	1973-77
7. Charles J Haughey	Fianna Fáil	1977-81; Feb-Nov 1982; 1987-92
8. Garret FitzGerald	Fine Gael	1981-82; 1982-87
9. Albert Reynolds	Fianna Fáil	1992-94
10. John Bruton	Fine Gael	1994-97
11. Bertie Ahern	Fianna Fáil	1997-2008
12. Brian Cowen	Fianna Fáil	2008-11
13. Enda Kenny	Fine Gael	2011-17
14. Leo Varadkar	Fine Gael	2017-20
15. Micheál Martin *	Fianna Fáil	2020-

* The June 2020 coalition agreement required Martin to hand over the office of Taoiseach to the leader of Fine Gael after 2.5 years

2(a): Governance – Northern Ireland

Northern Ireland is a region or sub-state of the United Kingdom of Great Britain and Northern Ireland. It was created in 1921 when Ireland was partitioned under the terms of the **1920 Government of Ireland Act**. The House of Commons of the bicameral Northern Ireland Parliament first met on 7 June 1921.

The Ireland Act 1949, enacted by the UK government in response to Dublin's declaration of a republic in 1948, guaranteed Northern Ireland's status as part of the UK unless the parliament of Northern Ireland should decide otherwise. This strengthened NI's de facto constitution, the 1920 Government of Ireland Act.

The Northern Ireland Constitution Act 1973 abolished the 1921 Parliament and brought Northern Ireland under direct rule from London. Initiatives aimed at re-establishing devolved government were unsuccessful until a peace agreement was reached in 1998.

The Northern Ireland Act 1998 gave effect to the peace accord known as the Belfast or Good Friday Agreement. It established a single-chamber devolved Legislative Assembly known as the Northern Ireland Assembly, which first met on 1 July 1998, initially in 'shadow' form until full powers were devolved on 2 December 1999. It was suspended on five occasions up to 2021.

The Northern Ireland Assembly operates on the basis of consociationalism, a form of power sharing between ethnic, religious or other opposing groups. Mandated by the Belfast Agreement 1998, this was intended to promote cross-community consensus by managing the competing aims of unionism and nationalism.

Members of the Legislative Assembly (MLAs) must designate themselves as either unionist, nationalist or 'other'. Certain key decisions require cross-community support.

The NI Executive, or cabinet, must consist of at least two parties, one from each of the two largest designations. The largest party nominates a first minister and the largest party of the next largest designation nominates the deputy first minister. Parties nominate seven ministers to the Executive in accordance with their share of seats in the Assembly, while the Justice Minister is nominated jointly by the first and deputy first ministers and approved by a cross-community resolution of the Assembly.

Elections for 90 Assembly members are held in multi-member constituencies under the system known as PR-STV (proportional representation – single transferable vote).

Northern Ireland is also represented by 18 MPs in the **UK House of Commons**, elected by the 'first past the post' method in single-member constituencies. A **secretary of state** has responsibility for Northern Ireland in the UK cabinet.

2(b): Political Institutions, 1921-2022 – Northern Ireland

Parliament of Northern Ireland, 1921-1972

A bicameral parliament created by the Government of Ireland Act 1920. Duration: 7 June 1921-30 March 1972. Abolished by Northern Ireland Constitution Act 1973. Direct rule from London 1972-1998.

Political initiatives, 1972-1998:

Power-sharing Assembly and Executive	1973-1974
Constitutional Convention	1975
Consultative Assembly	1982-86
Northern Ireland Forum	1996

Legislative Assembly and Executive, established 1998

A single-chamber Assembly created by the 1998 Belfast Agreement. Elected 25 June 1998, it met 1 July 1998 and existed in 'shadow' form until full powers devolved 2 Dec 1999. Suspended: 11 Feb-30 May 2000; 10 Aug 2001 (24-hours); 22 Sept 2001 (24-hours); 14 Oct 2002-7 May 2007; 9 Jan 2017-11 Jan 2020.

2(c): Leaders, 1921-72 – Northern Ireland Parliament

Prime Minister	Party	Term
James Craig	Ulster Unionist Party	1921-40
John Millar Andrews	Ulster Unionist Party	1940-43
Basil Brooke	Ulster Unionist Party	1943-63
Terence O'Neill	Ulster Unionist Party	1963-69
James Chichester-Clark	Ulster Unionist Party	1969-71
Brian Faulkner	Ulster Unionist Party	1971-72

Note: The Northern Ireland (Temporary Provisions) Act suspended the NI parliament on 30 March 1972 and introduced direct rule from London exercised by ministers in the Northern Ireland Office.

2(d): Leaders, 1998-2022 – Northern Ireland Legislative Assembly

First & Deputy First Minister	Party	Terms
David Trimble & Séamus Mallon	UUP / SDLP	1998-2001
David Trimble & Mark Durkan	UUP / SDLP	2001-02
Assembly suspended 2002–2007		
Ian Paisley & Martin McGuinness	DUP / Sinn Féin	2007-08
Peter Robinson & Martin McGuinness	DUP / Sinn Féin	2008-16
Arlene Foster & Martin McGuinness	DUP / Sinn Féin	2016-17
Assembly suspended 2017–2020		
Arlene Foster & Michelle O'Neill	DUP / Sinn Féin	2020-21
Paul Givan & Michelle O'Neill	DUP / Sinn Féin	2021-2022

Notes: Arlene Foster deputised for Robinson Jan-Feb 2010 and Sept-Oct 2015; John O'Dowd deputised for McGuinness Sept-Oct 2011.

3(a): Constitutional Relationship between the Republic of Ireland and Northern Ireland

The 1998 Belfast Agreement is central to the constitutional relationship between Northern Ireland and Ireland. As well as establishing a devolved Assembly and Executive for Northern Ireland (**Strand One**), the Agreement sought to build north-south and east-west relationships. **Strand Two** established an Irish dimension to the governing arrangements for Northern Ireland. **Strand Three** set up east–west institutions to promote cooperation between the Irish and UK governments, Northern Ireland, Scotland, Wales, Guernsey, Jersey and the Isle of Man.

The Nineteenth Amendment of the Irish Constitution Act, 1998, authorised Government to proceed with the Belfast Agreement's provisions. A constitutional referendum on the amendment approved deletion of the divisive Articles 2 and 3 from the Irish Constitution. Article 2 had claimed all of Ireland as the national territory, while Article 3 claimed the right 'to exercise jurisdiction over the whole territory'. New wording included a commitment to a democratic solution to the question of unification: '*It is the firm will of the Irish nation, in harmony and friendship, to unite all the people who share the territory of the island of Ireland, in all the diversity of their identities and traditions, recognising that a united Ireland shall be brought about only by peaceful means with the consent of a majority of the people, democratically expressed, in both jurisdictions in the island. ...*' (Article 3.1)

The North–South Ministerial Council, established 2 December 1999, brings together ministers from the NI Executive and the Irish Government, for consultation, co-operation and action on designated topics within the island of Ireland.

The North–South Implementation Bodies encourage co-operation of benefit to both Northern Ireland and the Republic of Ireland, including waterways, food safety, trade and business development, the Irish and Ulster-Scots languages, and EU programmes.

The North/South Inter-Parliamentary Association provides a forum for formal discussions between parliamentarians. Its 48 members plus two Joint Chairs are drawn in equal numbers from the Northern Ireland Assembly and the Houses of the Oireachtas. It held its first meeting on 12 October 2012, although an inter-parliamentary forum had been envisaged in the Belfast Agreement (1998) and the St Andrew's Agreement (2006).

3(b): Women in Political Office

(i) Heads & Deputy Heads of State or Government, 1990-2022

Mary Robinson	President of Ireland	1990-97	Independent
Mary McAleese	President of Ireland	1997-2011	Fianna Fáil
Mary Harney	Tánaiste (Deputy PM of Ireland)	1997-2006	Progressive Democrats
Mary Coughlan	Tánaiste (Deputy PM of Ireland)	2008-11	Fianna Fáil
Joan Burton	Tánaiste (Deputy PM of Ireland)	2014-16	Labour
Frances FitzGerald	Tánaiste (Deputy PM of Ireland)	2016-17	Fine Gael
Arlene Foster	First Minister of Northern Ireland	2016-17; 2020-21	DUP
Michelle O'Neill	Deputy First Minister of Northern Ireland	2020-22	Sinn Féin

(ii) Ministers, 2022

	Women	Total
Members of the Northern Ireland Executive	5	12
Ireland: Cabinet Ministers	4	14
Ireland: Ministers of State	5	20

(iii) Parliamentarians, 2022

	Women	Total
Northern Ireland Legislative Assembly	32	90
Dáil Éireann	37	160
Seanad Éireann	24	60
European Parliament (Ireland only)	5	13

(iv) Female Party Leaders, 1976-2022

Anne Dickson	1976-81	Unionist Party of Northern Ireland
Mary Harney	1993-2006; & 2007-08	Progressive Democrats
Dawn Purvis	2007-10	Progressive Unionist Party
Margaret Ritchie	2010-11	SDLP
Joan Burton	2014-16	Labour
Catherine Murphy & Róisín Shortall	2015-	Social Democrats
Arlene Foster	2015-21	Democratic Unionist Party
Naomi Long	2016-	Alliance Party of Northern Ireland
Mary Lou McDonald	2018-	Sinn Féin
Claire Bailey	2018-22	Green Party Northern Ireland
Ivana Bacik	2022-	Labour Party

3(c): Descent and Dissent: a 'family tree' of nationalist parties in Ireland, 1900-2022

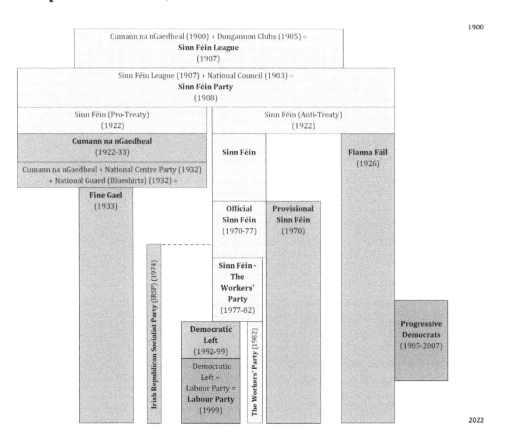

Several political parties in Ireland are descended, via splits and mergers, from groups founded between 1900 (Cumann na nGaedheal) and 1908 (the Sinn Féin Party). The first significant divergence occurred in 1922, when pro- and anti-treaty forces split into two major strands. The pro-treaty side became Fine Gael in 1933, with few defections other than to the Progressive Democrats (which itself was founded mainly by Fianna Fáil dissidents). Two main lines of descent emerged from the anti-treaty side: Fianna Fáil (1926) was politically near-hegemonic for decades, while the more hard-line republican Sinn Féin spawned various splinter groups and iterations, the most dramatic being in 1970 when Provisional Sinn Féin split from the main body and, over time, became the contemporary Sinn Féin party. The Official Sinn Féin side changed its name twice and continued in very diminished form as The Workers' Party. Democratic Left, which split from Official Sinn Féin/Workers' Party, amalgamated with the Labour Party (1999). The IRSP (see 'Minor Parties' appendix) is a rare surviving splinter group from Official Sinn Féin with a tiny support-base.

3(d): Selected minor parties

Aontú (Unite): a conservative nationalist party founded in January 2019, it operates in both jurisdictions. Founded by Peadar Tóibín TD, whose reasons for leaving Sinn Féin included disagreement with its support for liberalisation of abortion, it is broadly anti-immigration and Eurosceptic but takes a left-populist position on some economic issues. *Elected representatives 2022: 1 TD*

Democratic Left: a democratic socialist party founded in 1999 following a split in The Workers' Party, it served in the 'rainbow coalition' government with Fine Gael and the Labour Party (1994-1997) and later merged with the Labour Party. *Dissolved 1999.*

Independents 4 Change (I4C): registered as a political party in the Republic in 2014, its two MEPs, Clare Daly and Mick Wallace, became Russian and Chinese media favourites for positions such as voting in the European Parliament against condemnation of Russia's invasion of Ukraine. *Elected representatives 2022: 2 MEPs*

IRSP (Irish Republican Socialist Party): founded in 1974 by Séamus Costello after he was expelled from Official Sinn Féin, it opposed the Belfast Agreement and supported Brexit. Its paramilitary associate, the Irish National Liberation Army (INLA), engaged in armed conflict during NI's Troubles and three INLA members died in the 1981 'H-Blocks' hunger strike. Former Mid-Ulster MP Bernadette Devlin-McAliskey was a member briefly. *Elected representatives 2022: none*

Northern Ireland Labour Party (NILP): founded in 1924 it was active to varying degrees until 1987. It came out in favour of the union with Britain in 1949, which diminished its appeal to Catholic voters. Its electoral success was limited, never rising above four members of the NI Parliament. After 1970 it lost heavily to the SDLP, Alliance and the DUP. *Dissolved 1987.*

Northern Ireland Women's Coalition (NIWC): founded in 1996 by women's groups in NI, it succeeded in putting equality and social inclusion on the agenda of the peace negotiations and sought mechanisms to enable local communities to participate in peace building. Two of its members, Monica McWilliams and Jane Morrice, were elected to the NI Assembly in 1998, but were not re-elected in 2003. *Dissolved 2006.*

People Before Profit/Solidarity: an electoral alliance formed in 2015 between three left-wing groups, People Before Profit, Solidarity and the Socialist Party. In 2021, RISE (the Revolutionary, Internationalist, Socialist, and Environmentalist party) joined the alliance. *Elected representatives 2022: 5 TDs, 1 MLA*

Progressive Unionist Party (PUP): formed in 1979 by left-leaning loyalists, PUP won two seats in the NI Assembly in 1998, held one in each of the next two elections, but failed to win any afterwards. Dawn Purvis (leader 2007-10) resigned from the party because of its relationship with the paramilitary Ulster Volunteer Force. PUP supported the 1998 Belfast Agreement but said in 1921 that, due to the Brexit NI Protocol, there was no longer a basis for unionists to support the peace accord. *Elected representatives 2022: none*

Social Democrats: founded in 2015 by three independent TDs, Catherine Murphy (ex-Workers Party and Democratic Left), Róisín Shortall (a former Labour Party TD) and Stephen Donnelly (who later joined Fianna Fáil and became health minister in 2020). *Elected representatives 2022: 6 TDs*

Traditional Unionist Voice (TUV): a socially conservative unionist party in Northern Ireland founded in 2007 by Jim Allister, who resigned from the Democratic Unionist Party when it agreed to enter the NI Executive with Sinn Féin. TUV supports devolution but rejects mandatory power sharing. *Elected representatives 2022: 1 MLA*

Unionist Party of Northern Ireland: founded in 1974 by Brian Faulkner after he lost leadership of the UUP to Harry West, who opposed the Sunningdale Agreement. Its electoral performance was mediocre, but good enough to split the centrist unionist vote. *Dissolved 1981.*

Vanguard Unionist Progressive Party: founded in 1972 by William Craig, an NI home affairs minister who was fired by Prime Minister Terence O'Neill, Vanguard opposed the power-sharing Sunningdale Agreement and helped organise the loyalist workers' strike that brought down the NI Executive in 1974. Craig addressed large loyalist rallies and speculated openly about a unilateral declaration of independence. After poor electoral results, Craig merged the remainder of Vanguard into the UUP. Some Vanguard members became prominent in the UUP, including future leaders David Trimble and Reg Empey. *Dissolved 1978.*

Workers' Party: directly descended from the original Sinn Féin, it changed its name to Sinn Féin – The Workers' Party in 1977 and to The Workers' Party in 1982. In 1992 six of its seven TDs formed Democratic Left. *Elected representatives 2022: none*

Note: The term 'elected representatives' above refers to members of the NI Assembly, Dáil Éireann, Seanad Éireann, the UK parliament or the European parliament.

Bibliography

Books

Anderson, Don: *Fourteen May Days: The Inside Story of the Loyalist Strike of 1974*, Dublin, Gill & Macmillan, 1994.

Bale, Tim: *European Politics: A Comparative Introduction*, Basingstoke, Palgrave MacMillan, 2008.

Bell, J. Bowyer: *The Secret Army: A History of the IRA 1916-1970*, London, Sphere Books, 1972.

Bew, Paul and Gibbon, Peter and Patterson, Henry: *Northern Ireland 1921-1994 – Political Forces and Social Classes*, London, Serif, 1995.

Boothroyd, David: *Politico's Guide to the History of British Political Parties*. London, Politico, 2001.

Boyle, Dan: *Without Power or Glory: The Greens in Government in Ireland 2007-11*, Dublin, New Island, Kindle edition, 2012.

Chambers, Anne: *T. K. Whitaker: Portrait of a Patriot*, Dublin, Doubleday Ireland, 2014.

Coakley, John and Gallagher, Michael: *Politics in the Republic of Ireland*, London, Taylor & Francis, 1999.

Collins, Stephen & Meehan, Ciara: *Saving the State: Fine Gael from Collins to Varadkar*, Dublin, Gill Books, 2020.

Daly, Mary E.: *Industrial Development and Irish National Identity, 1922-1939*, Syracuse, Syracuse University Press, 1992.

Dudley Edwards, Ruth: *An Atlas of Irish History*, London, Methuen, 1973.

Eggins, Brian: *History and Hope: The Alliance Party of Northern Ireland*, Dublin, The History Press, 2015.

Farren, Seán: *The SDLP: The Struggle for Agreement in Northern Ireland 1970–2000*, Dublin, Four Courts Press, 2010.

Fearon, Kate: *Women's Work: The Story of the Northern Ireland Women's Coalition*, Belfast, Blackstaff Press, 1999.

Ferriter, Diarmaid: *The Transformation of Ireland 1900-2000*, London, Profile Books, 2005.

Ferriter, Diarmaid: *A Nation and not a Rabble: The Irish Revolution 1913-1923*, London, Profile Books, 2015.

Ferriter, Diarmaid: *Judging Dev: A reassessment of the life and legacy of Éamon de Valera*, Dublin, Royal Irish Academy, 2019.

Ferriter, Diarmaid: *The Border: The Legacy of a Century of Anglo-Irish Politics*, London, Profile Books, 2019.

FitzGerald, Garret: *Towards a New Ireland*, Dublin, Gill & MacMillan, 1972.

FitzGerald, Garret: *All in a Life*, Gill & Macmillan, Dublin, 1992.

Fitzpatrick, David: *The Two Irelands 1912-1939*, New York, Oxford University Press, 1998.

Foster, R.F.: *Modern Ireland 1600-1972*, London, Penguin, 1989.

Foster, R.F. (Ed.): *The Oxford History of Ireland*, Oxford University Press, 1992.

Foster, R.F.: *Luck and the Irish: A Brief History of Change 1970-2000*, London, Penguin, 2008.

Foster, R.F.: *Vivid Faces: The Revolutionary Generation in Ireland 1890-1923*, London, Penguin Random House, 2014.

Gallagher, Michael: *The Irish Labour Party in Transition 1957-82*, Dublin, Gill & MacMillan, 1982.

Gallagher, Michael: *Political Parties in the Republic of Ireland*, Manchester, Manchester University Press, 1985.

Gallagher, Michael and Marsh, Michael: *Days of Blue Loyalty: The politics of membership of the Fine Gael party*, Dublin, PSAI Press, 2002.

Garvin, Tom, *Preventing the Future. Why was Ireland so poor for so long?*, Dublin: Gill and Macmillan, 2004.

Gibbons, Ivan: *Partition: How and Why Ireland was Divided*, London, Haus, 2020.

Gilmore, Éamon: *Inside the Room: The Untold Story of Ireland's Crisis Government*, Dublin, Merrion Press, 2016.

Godson, Dean: *Himself Alone: David Trimble and the Ordeal of Unionism*, Harper Collins E-Books, 2013.

Harbinson, John: *The Ulster Unionist Party, 1882-1973*, Belfast, Blackstaff Press, 1973.

Kaufman, Eric P.: *The Orange Order: A Contemporary Northern Irish History*, Oxford, Oxford University Press, 2007.

Kee, Robert: *The Green Flag: A History of Irish Nationalism*, London, Penguin Books, 2000.

Kelly, Henry: *How Stormont Fell*, Dublin, Gill and MacMillan, 1972.

Kennedy, Kieran A. and Dowling, Brendan R.: *Economic Growth in Ireland: The Experience since 1947*, Dublin, Gill & MacMillan, 1975.

Kennedy, Liam: *Who was responsible for The Troubles? The Northern Ireland Conflict*, Belfast, McGill-Queen's University Press, 2020.

Kiely, Benedict: *Proxopera*, Quartet Books edition, London, 1979.

Leahy, Pat: *Showtime: The Inside Story of Fianna Fáil in Power*, Dublin, Penguin Ireland, 2010.

Leahy, Pat: *The Price of Power: Inside Ireland's Crisis Coalition*, Dublin, Penguin Ireland, 2013.

Lee, J. J.: *Ireland 1912-1985: Politics and Society*, Cambridge, Cambridge University Press, 2010.

Lee, Joseph: *The Modernisation of Irish Society 1848-1918*, Dublin, Gill & Macmillan, 1979.

Lewis, Geoffrey: *Carson: The Man Who Divided Ireland*, London and New York, Hambledon & London, 2005.

Longford, The Earl of, and O'Neill, Thomas P.: *Éamon De Valera*, London, Hutchinson, 1970.

Lyons, F.S.L.: *The Irish Parliamentary Party, 1890-1910*, London, Fontana Press, 1951.

Lyons, F.S.L.: *Charles Stewart Parnell*, London, Fontana Press, 1978.

Lyons, F.S.L.: *Ireland since the Famine*, London, Fontana Press, 1985.

MacDermott, Eithne: *Clann na Poblachta*, Cork, Cork University Press, 1998.

Mallon, Seamus with Pollak, Andy: *A Shared Home Place*, Dublin, Lilliput Press, 2019.

McCullagh, David: *A Makeshift Majority: The First Inter-Party Government, 1948-51*, Dublin, Institute of Public Administration, 1998.

McInerney, Michael: *Peadar O'Donnell, Irish Social Rebel*, Dublin, O'Brien Press, 1974.

McNeill, Ronald: *Ulster's Stand for Union*, London, John Murray, 1922; Project Gutenberg eBook 2004.

Meehan, Ciara: *The Cosgrave Party: A History of Cumann na nGaedheal, 1923-33*, London, Prism, 2010.

Gallagher, Michael: *Political Parties in the Republic of Ireland*, Manchester, Manchester University Press, 1985.

Minehan, Mary: *A Deal with the Devil: The Green Party in Government*, Dunboyne, Maverick House, 2011.

Moloney, Ed: *Paisley: From Demagogue to Democrat?*, Dublin, Poolbeg Press, 2008.

Ó Gráda, Cormac: *A rocky road: The Irish economy since the 1920s.* (Manchester 1997)

O'Hearn, Denis: *Inside the Celtic Tiger: The Irish Economy and the Asian Model*, London, Pluto Press, 1998.

O'Toole, Fintan: *Ship of Fools: How Stupidity and Corruption Sank the Celtic Tiger*, London, Faber & Faber, 2010.

O'Leary, Brendan: *A Treatise on Northern Ireland: Volume 2 | Control: The Second Protestant Ascendancy and the Irish State*, Oxford, Oxford University Press, 2020.

O'Leary, Brendan: *A Treatise on Northern Ireland, Volume 3 | Consociation and Confederation: From Antagonism to Accommodation*, Oxford University Press, 2020.

Puirséil, Niamh: *The Irish Labour Party 1922-73*, Dublin, University College Dublin Press, 2007.

Rafter, Kevin: *Democratic Left: The Life and Death of an Irish Political Party*, Dublin, Irish Academic Press, 2011.

Rafter, Kevin: *Fine Gael: Party at the Crossroads*, Dublin, New Island, 2009.

Rafter, Kevin: *The Road to Power: How Fine Gael Made History*, Dublin, New Island, 2011.

Roche, Patrick J. and Barton, Brian (Eds.): *The Northern Ireland Question: Nationalism, Unionism and Partition*, London, Ashgate Publishing, 1999.

Shirlow, Peter: *The end of Ulster loyalism?*, Manchester, Manchester University Press, 2012.

Sutton, Malcolm: *Bear in Mind These Dead: An Index of Deaths from the Conflict in Northern Ireland*, Belfast, Beyond the Pale Publications, 1994.

Tonge, Jonathan: *Northern Ireland: Conflict and Change*, Routledge, 2013.

Townshend, Charles (Ed.): *Consensus in Ireland: Approaches and Recessions*, Oxford, Clarendon Press, 1988.

Walker, Brian M.: *A Political History of the Two Irelands: From Partition to Peace*, London, Palgrave Macmillan, 2012.

Walker, Graham: *A History of the Ulster Unionist Party: Protest, Pragmatism and Pessimism*, Manchester, Manchester University Press, 2004.

Walsh, Colm: *Beyond The Spark: Young people's perspectives on the 2021 Northern Ireland Riots*, Belfast, Queen's University Belfast and NI Dept. of Justice, 2021.

Walsh, Maurice: *Bitter freedom: Ireland in a Revolutionary World 1918-1923*, Faber & Faber, 2015.

Weeks, Liam and Clark, Alistair (Eds.): *Radical or Redundant? Minor Parties in Irish Politics*, Dublin, The History Press, 2012.

Whelan, Noel: *Fianna Fáil: A Biography of the Party*, Dublin, Gill Books, 2011.

Whitaker, T.K.: *Economic Development*, 1958.

Yeats, William Butler: *Responsibilities and other poems*, Macmillan, New York, 1916.

Articles, Book Chapters and Lectures

Andeweg, Rudy B.: *Consociational Democracy, in Annual Review of Political Science*, Vol. 3:509-536, June 2000.

Bolleyer, Nicole: 'The Rise and Decline of the Green Party', in Weeks and Clark (eds) *Radical or Redundant?: Minor Parties in Irish Politics*, Dublin, The History Press Ireland, 2012.

Bolleyer, Nicole: 'The Rise and Decline of the Green Party', in Weeks and Clark (eds) *Radical or Redundant?: Minor Parties in Irish Politics*, Dublin, The History Press Ireland, 2012.

Bowman, John: 'When Lloyd George met de Valera', in *The Irish Times*, 10 July 2021.

Breathnach, Ciara: 'How the Irish government fought the TB epidemic in the 1940s', rte.ie, 23 March 2020.

Bruce, Steve: 'Religion and Violence: The Case of Paisley and Ulster Evangelicals', The Irish Association for Cultural, Economic and Social Relations, October 2003.

Choyaa, 'Fragmented Unionism and Broad Churches', sluggerotoole.com, 29 May 2021.

Evans, Jocelyn & Tonge, Jonathan: 'The Future of the 'Radical Centre' in Northern Ireland after the Good Friday Agreement', *Political Studies* (Vol. 51, Issue 1 - March 2003), pp.26-50.

Evans, Jocelyn and Tonge, Jonathan: 'From Abstentionism to Enthusiasm: Sinn Féin, Nationalist Electors and Support for Devolved Power-sharing in Northern Ireland', in *Irish Political Studies*, Vol. 28 – Issue 1, 2013.

Farry, S. and Neeson, S.: 'Beyond the Band-Aid Approach: An Alliance Party Perspective upon the Belfast Agreement', in *Fordham Int'l Law Journal* (Vol. 22, No. 4 - 1998) pp. 1221-49.

Fitzpatrick, David: 'Ireland Since 1870', in R.F. Foster (Ed.), *The Oxford History of Ireland*, Oxford, Oxford University Press, 1992.

Foster, R.F.: in *Revolutionary States: Home Rule and Modern Ireland*, Dublin, Dublin City Gallery The Hugh Lane, 2012.

Freeman, David: 'Leading Churchill Myths (19): Churchill was drunk and not being serious when he proposed the unification of Ireland in 1941', *Finest Hour* 147 (Summer 2010), winstonchurchill.org.

Garry, John: 'The EU referendum Vote in Northern Ireland: Implications for our understanding of citizens' political views and behaviour', Knowledge Exchange Seminar Series 2016-17.

Garry, John, O'Leary, Brendan & Pow, James: 'Much more than meh: The 2022 Northern Ireland Assembly Elections', LSE British Politics and Policy, 11 May 2022.

Gudgin, Graham: 'Discrimination in Housing and Employment under the Stormont Administration', in Roche, Patrick J. and Barton, Brian (Eds.): *The Northern Ireland Question: Nationalism, Unionism and Partition*, Farnham, Ashgate Publishing, 1999.

Hearst, David: 'Sinn Féin votes to fight for seats in the Dáil: IRA political wing to take seats in Irish parliament', *The Guardian*, 3 November 1986.

Honohan, Patrick: 'Is Ireland really the most prosperous country in Europe?', *Economic Letter*, Dublin, Central Bank of Ireland, February 2021.

International Monetary Fund: *Ireland from Tiger to Phoenix*, www.imf.org

Lillis, Michael: 'John Hume's Legacy', *Dublin Review of Books*, May 2018.

Lillis, Michael: 'The Good Statesman', *Dublin Review of Books*, July 2020.

Loretto, Denis: 'Alliance, Liberals and the SDP, 1971-1985: a personal memoir', in *Journal of Liberal Democrat History* (33, Winter 2001-02).

Lyons, F.S.L.: 'To The Northern Counties Station: Lord Randolph Churchill and the Prelude to the Orange Card', in F.S.L. Lyons & R.A.J. Hawkins (Eds.), *Ireland Under the Union: Varieties of Tension: Essays in Honour of T. W. Moody*, Oxford, Clarendon Press, 1980.

Mansergh, Lucy: 'Do Parties make a Difference? A Comparison of Party and Coalition Policy in Ireland using Expert Coding and Computerised Content Analysis', Paper to workshop 'Estimating the Policy Positions of Political Actors', Mannheim, March 1999.

McCord, Rhona: Book Review, 'A Just Society for Ireland?', *theirishstory.com*, 16 December 2013.

Meehan, Ciara: 'The Constitutional Crusade', in *A Just Society for Ireland? 1964-1987*, London, Palgrave Macmillan, 2013.

Moriarty, Gerry: 'De Valera, Dillon's 'jaundiced' view of women's suffrage', *The Irish Times*, 27 April 2012.

Moriarty, Gerry: 'Internment explained: When was it introduced and why?', *The Irish Times*, 9 August 2019.

Norris, Michelle: 'Financing the Golden Age of Irish Social Housing, 1932-1956 (and the dark ages which followed)', Working Papers 201901, Geary Institute, University College Dublin, 2018.

Northern Ireland Civil Rights Association (NICRA): *We shall overcome: The History of the Struggle for Civil Rights in Northern Ireland 1968-1978*, Belfast, NICRA, 1978.

Ó Gráda, Cormac: 'Five Crises', Central Bank of Ireland T.K. Whitaker Lecture, Dublin, 29 June 2011.

O'Connor, Emmet: 'A Concise History of the Labour Movement and the Birth of Northern Ireland', sluggerotoole.com, 29 September 2019.

O'Donoghue, Martin: 'Independence and the shadow of Home Rule: the legacy of the Irish Parliamentary Party', *The Irish Times*, 17 February 2020.

O'Donoghue, T.O.M.: *The Legacy of the Irish Parliamentary Party in Independent Ireland, 1922-49*, National University of Ireland Galway, PhD. Thesis, 2016.

O'Hagan, Seán: 'Northern Ireland's lost moment: how the peaceful protests of '68 escalated into years of bloody conflict', *The Observer*, 22 April 2018.

O'Malley, Des: 'Life in a Minor Party', in Weeks and Clarke (Eds.), *Radical or Redundant?: Minor Parties in Irish Politics*, Dublin, The Irish History Press, 2012.

Patterson, Henry: 'Defending the Union', in *Dublin Review of Books*, October 2020.

Puirséil, Niamh: 'Labour and Coalition: The Impact of the First Inter-Party Government 1948-51', in *Saothar* (Vol. 27), Dublin, Irish Labour History Society, 2002.

Rabbitte, Pat: 'Holding the Balance', in *Dublin Review of Books*, February 2015.

Radford, Mark: 'Closely Akin to Actual Warfare', *History Ireland*, (Issue 5, Vol.7), 1999.

Sheridan, Kathy: 'Mary Lou is an enigma with leadership in her sights', *The Irish Times*, 19 June 2021.

Shirlow, Peter: 'Interdependence is the antidote to Northern Irish politics', *The Irish Times*, 1 January 2021.

Tonge, Jonathan: 'Victims of Their Own Success? Post-Agreement Dilemmas of Political Moderates in Northern Ireland', *The Global Review of Ethnopolitics* (Vol. 3, No. 1 - Special Issue: Northern Ireland), September 2003, pp.39-59.

Walsh, Colm: 'Beyond The Spark: Young people's perspectives on the 2021 Northern Ireland Riots', Belfast, Queen's University Belfast and NI Dept. of Justice, 2021.

Yeates, Padraig: 'A Revolutionary Janus', in *Dublin Review of Books*, Dublin, November 2009.

Yeates, Padraig: 'The Dublin 1913 Lockout', in *History Ireland* (Issue 2, Vol. 9), Dublin, 2001.

Party publications

Fine Gael: *Towards a Just Society*, Dublin, 1965.

SDLP: *Towards a New Ireland – Proposals by the Social Democratic and Labour Party*, 1972.

Ulster Unionist Party: *EU Withdrawal Agreement and the Ireland/Northern Ireland Protocol*, Belfast, Sept 2021.

Official publications

Department of Finance and Department of Industry and Commerce: *Programme for economic expansion*, Dublin, The Stationery Office, 11 November 1958.

Department of Finance: *Strengthening the Capacity of the Department of Finance: Report of the Independent Review Panel*, Dublin, 1 March 2011.

Department of Foreign Affairs: *New Decade, New Approach*, Dublin, January 2020.

Department of the Taoiseach: *Programme for Government: Our Shared Future*, Dublin, June 2020.

Beef Tribunal: *Report of the Tribunal of Inquiry into the Beef Processing Industry*, Dublin, The Stationary Office, July 1994.

Independent Reporting Commission: *IRC Third Report*, Belfast, November 2020.

Joint Committee of Inquiry into the Banking Crisis: *REPORT of the Joint Committee of Inquiry into the Banking Crisis*, Report of the Oireachtas, January 2016.

Moriarty Tribunal: *The Final Report of the Tribunal of Inquiry into Certain Planning Matters and Payments*, Dublin, The Stationery Office, 2012.

New Ireland Forum: *Report*, Dublin, The Stationery Office, 2 May 1984.

Northern Ireland Parliament: *Disturbances in Northern Ireland*, (Cmd. 532), (The Cameron Report), Belfast, HMSO, September 1969.

United Nations: *Northern Ireland Peace Agreement (The Good Friday Agreement)*, The Agreement reached in the multi-party negotiations 10 April 1998, peacemaker. un.org/uk-ireland-good-friday98, 1998.

Media

Irish Civic Films: *Our Country,* short documentary (a party political film for Clann na Poblachta), Dublin, 1948

BBC: *Spotlight on the Troubles: A Secret History*, 2019.

Gibney, Alex (director): *No Stone Unturned: Loughinisland*, documentary, 2017

Index

Lightning Source UK Ltd.
Milton Keynes UK
UKHW021142181222
414050UK00003B/7